NURSES, NOMADS, AND WARLORDS

2/12/08

To Francisco
Thanks so much for
all you do —
Good luck in all
your future endeavors

NURSES, NOMADS, AND WARLORDS

Mary Lightfine

With Kathy Craven

LUTHERS
New Smyrna Beach
FLORIDA

Published by
LUTHERS PUBLISHING
1009 NORTH DIXIE FREEWAY
NEW SMYRNA BEACH, FL 32168-6221
www.lutherspublishing.com

Original oil on canvas cover art and
author's portrait on page 244 by Yvonne Peterson
studio-Yvonne@hotmail.com

LIBRARY OF CONGRESS
CATALOGING-IN-PUBLICATION DATA
Lightfine, Mary, 1955–
Nurses, nomads, and warlords / Mary Lightfine;
with Kathy Craven. —1st ed.
p.   cm.
ISBN 1-877633-79-8 (pbk.)
1. Lightfine, Mary, 1955– 2. Nurses—Somalia—Biography.
3. Medical assistance, American—Somalia—Personal narratives.
4. Humanitarian assistance, American—Somalia—
Personal narratives. 5. International Medical Corps.
6. Missions, Medical—Somalia. 7. Somalia—History—1991–
8. Somalia—Social conditions—1960–
I. Craven, Kathy, 1964– II. Title.
R722.32.L54A3 2006
362.17'3096773—dc22
[B]
2006048717

Author's Note

After sixteen years as an Emergency room nurse I packed my bags and moved from New Straitsville, Ohio to Mogadishu, Somalia. Why would any sane woman choose to live in a dangerous war zone voluntarily? *Keep reading.* This book is a story of the most exciting, most frightening and most enlightening thirteen months of my life. I hope that through my words, you will see the humor, feel the tragedy and discover how one person can make a difference in the world. Perhaps you'll even feel inspired.

In order to remain true to the characters and situation it was necessary to include harsh language and graphic descriptions of the wounded. If you are sensitive to strong realities you may not want to read this book.

All events described in this book actually occurred, those in Somalia between February 1992 and April 1993, and are described in the book to the best of my memory. Some of the characters' names and physical appearance are different in the book than in actuality, and some book characters are amalgams of several different actual people. The locations of some events are different in the book than in actuality, and in the interest of story continuity, the times that some events occurred in the book are different than the actual times that these events occurred.

Acknowledgements

It took me only four months to compose the first draft of this book and another six years to edit and fine tune every chapter. I am grateful to the many wonderful folks who assisted in my writing efforts. Thanks to Paul Rooy, my soul mate and husband, for his patience, understanding and support during the many days, weeks and months I spent working on this book. Additional credit is due to Paul for his photographic and contract writing ability, as well as his legal and editing counsel. Paul is working on his third book now, *The Skymaster and the Piranhas*, about our most recent adventure flying the Amazon River basin in a twin-engine Cessna. See www.PaulSRooy.com for information about Paul's books and intellectual property law practice. Much credit is due to Kathy Craven who has helped me in so many ways that her name appears next to mine on the cover. To Manley Clodfelter, M.D., I am grateful for his medical opinions and for introducing me to Kathy Craven. Manley is one of the kindest ER doctors with whom I've had the pleasure of working. Thanks to Lynn Matthews, my IMC Somalia colleague, and her husband Mark, for their editing assistance and suggestions. Lynn and I shared so many Somalia memories together that we will forever be bonded as friends. To my friend Penny Roberts, who after Paul Rooy, was able to locate more mistakes in my manuscript than anyone else, and for her great suggestions, I am indebted. Penny is currently working on her third book so I'll soon be marking up her pages! Thanks to my African Friends, Ken Sheldrick and Robin Bairstow, who made sure my memory of Africa was clear and concise. Ken's late father, David Sheldrick founded Tsavo National Park in Kenya, and his stepmother, Dr. Dame Daphne, runs an elephant orphanage in Nairobi in addition to many other East African wildlife charities. With such an exceptional family Ken has turned into a virtual expert on Kenyan plants, animals and life in the bush. His editing, suggestions and support are greatly valued. To Ken's American wife Marty Sheldrick, who shares my passion for Africa and nursing, I appreciate her assistance and advice. With their teaching and artistic background, Barbara and Jon Sandberg were valuable members of the editing team and made many vital suggestions—thanks, Barb and Jon! No book has been completely edited until my friend, Richard Uschold has a look at it. Richard, also known as "Gilligan," has a passion for sailing, biking and computers, but his engineering background and attention to fine detail contribute to his exceptional ability to find errors in any printed document. Gilligan, I appreciate your diligent efforts. Thanks to my parents and siblings who contributed to my adventuresome nature and helped me become the person I am today, and to the Ike Chapman family who taught me the wonders of farming, horses and country life. I'm grateful to Bill Fry and Carol Studer who encouraged me to write this book and got me started as a speaker so that I could share my experiences with public audiences, and to the folks at Wolfman Productions who coordinate my lectures today. To book one of my lectures, please visit: www.marylightfine.com

— Mary Lightfine, Author

From Kathy's Desk

I would like to thank the following for their unyielding faith and support. Thank you to Kate and Shannie, my beautiful daughters, who inspire me everyday with their strength and compassion; to Manley, who will always be my friend; to my parents, who encourage me to explore; to Jeff, who showers me with love and laughter; to Kim, who always has faith; to Barbara and Karen, who give me courage; to Sally, who guided me to my voice; and to Sweetheart, who always knows the way.

— Kathy Craven

Africa

Mediterranean Sea

Red Sea

SOMALIA

KENYA

Atlantic Ocean

Indian Ocean

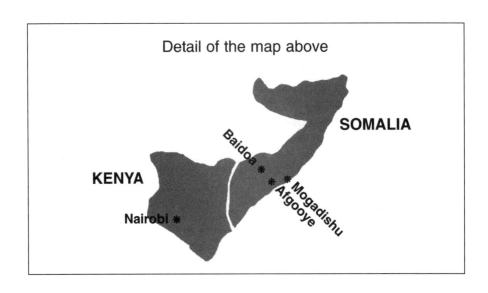

Detail of the map above

SOMALIA

Baidoa

KENYA

Mogadishu
Afgooye

Nairobi

Contents

PROLOGUE

The Dream

Mogadishu, Somalia, 1992

The oppressive night air smothers my body, rousing streams of sweat that bond my breasts to the gauzy fabric of my now translucent nightgown. Tiny pebbles dig into my naked feet as I creep through the dark courtyard. The dim light of a crescent moon guides me through the unfamiliar stillness. My steps are soundless. Iron gates and towering concrete walls surround me like the body of a mythical god, jealous of my burning desire for freedom. Quietly I approach the iron portal and stand in perfect silence, fearful of waking my jealous captor. Just beyond the gate, Freedom lures with dozens of minute flashing lights. The imprisoning metal ribs and resolute walls seem to tighten with every call from freedom's seductive flares.

My fingers grip the cold, iron bars as I press against them with desperate thrusting motions, leaning and pulling in fervent response to freedom's wooing lights. The lights respond with increased frequency until suddenly the gates give way and I am propelled onto a bed of fine sand.

I turn to lie on my back as warm water rhythmically washes over my body. The tiny lights assemble into one glowing sun. My eyes strain to focus and finally reveal miles of perfect coastline. Rays of light dance on gently rolling waves that like a tender lover, soothe my body in the surf.

A small object washes against me but my eyes remain

closed, wanting only to savor the supposed serenity. The surf intensifies and begins to thrash the fleshy object against my body. Finally, I grasp and lift the cool, doughy item towards my line of vision. I am clutching a detached, rotting human foot; putrefied in the salty surf. Abruptly the gently rocking waves become violent torrents of horror filled with hundreds of human appendages.

I wake suddenly with sheets twisted around my sweat-soaked body. Although my eyes are wide open I am unsure of my surroundings until I hear the mournful yelping of a dog out-side my window. My mind connects with the white stucco walls of my room in the International Medical Corps compound. It is Friday the 13th. Mogadishu, Somalia 1992.

The man who shared my bed last night is gone. A note sits on a table just out of reach. Sweet scents of baking bread and fry-ing eggs entice my conscience to embrace the day. Reaching up I move the sheer sheet draped over my window and see a home-less dog barking incessantly in the street below my room. The dog is likely one of the many pets abandoned when diplomats fled the country. A machine gun-clad Somali guard leans against the outside wall near my window. He guards the building that was once a lavish Italian villa but has transformed into the walled International Medical Corps compound. Annoyed by the beast's steady pleas, he casually lifts his weapon and fires sev-eral rounds into the helpless animal. The barking stops. I replace the sheet over the window and my feet find the cold, marble floor. I walk a few steps to the table where the note is leaning against my backpack. My finger follows the rising and falling of the letters that form two words scrawled across the page.

Je t'aime.

I embed the note inside the pages of my journal then hold the book against my chest letting last night's passion pass through me once more. But this moment of departure is brief.

Since I arrived, violence and devastation provide twelve-hour days in Digfer Hospital where my colleagues and I swim in a sea of illness, starvation, and trauma, sometimes at gun-point. Friday is our only day of respite. However, today marks the fifth consecutive Friday my colleagues and I were forbid-den outside the twelve-foot concrete walls of our compound, making it more like a security-imposed prison. The only place of real escape is an ocean paradise where azure waters stroke the shore just eighteen kilometers from the compound. Gezira Beach, once a playground for wealthy European tourists, is now a diversion for war-weary expatriates. Rumors of imminent fighting along the only road to our ocean retreat will keep us sequestered another Friday. A month of captive Fridays meant to ensure the safety of me and my fellow humanitarians provokes a desperate need for freedom.

I am reminded of my nightmare. Even in its gruesome outcome I can still see the lights of freedom beckoning beyond the gripping commands of security. Sitting back down on the edge of my twin mattress that lies on the floor of my room I rub the edges of a small shell between my fingers and thumb, weighing the risk of freedom with the certainty of danger beyond my walls.

Then reality speaks. It whispers nagging images of erratic violence waiting beyond this concrete tomb. My mind hosts images of fellow expatriates and Somalis unpredictably gunned down in the streets of Mogadishu. On her way to a feeding center near Baidoa, mobile gunmen riddle an Irish nurse's body with bullets in order to expedite commandeering her 4x4 vehicle. A Somali girl is raped, drenched in gasoline and set ablaze for being from the wrong clan. The images send a chill across my arms on this hot Somali morning.

But visions of the of the Indian Ocean's azure water lures me like an oasis able to soothe war-torn souls.

Today I want what all living beings want: freedom with the promise of security. A recipe for hope, something the Somali people have not tasted for so long. In my relatively short time working with these people, I have just begun to touch the edges of their experience.

I grab an extra large towel and snuggle into my terry cloth robe before emerging from my room, hoping for a relatively short wait for a shower in the bathroom I share with fifteen others. Three hired Somali guards stand with two expatriates a few steps from my door. Determined to find freedom even on war zone terms, I assist my colleagues to push for the desired answer.

"Is the road to Gezira safe to travel?" we plead.

"Ha," a Somali yes, is our desired answer.

Ignoring the warning of my night visions, I am ready to face the outside of these walls—ready to risk my life for one afternoon of pleasure and escape from war's kaleidoscope of horrors. I can begin to understand the risks so many take for freedom's sweet embrace. Will the warm waters of the Indian Ocean dancing over my toes renew strength only to require the ultimate price? I choose to find out.

-1-

Escape

Marlton, New Jersey, 1965

In the dimming light of the pine barren, a flash signals just ahead. Then another. And another.

The delicate glow of tiny fireflies float on the lead-laced air of summer as crickets begin warming their instruments for the evening performance. Their music lulls the sun to rest and gently marks the end of the day in this forest haven. I turn toward home leading my little sister, who quietly calls the crickets by the name we gave them, "God's dinner bells." The over-sized pockets of her dress bulge like chipmunk cheeks with the afternoon teaberry harvest. Colorless juice from the wild berry runs along the corners of Cindy's mouth.

I pick two more teaberries. On my way back I savor the tingling flavor of one berry while I subconsciously roll the second between my thumb and index finger. Inside it becomes a smooth reminder of the forest's freedom. I know I will need it.

"MARY BETH! CYNTHIA ANN!"

Our mother's voice pierces the crickets' honest melodies. Cindy takes a deep breath. I grab her hand. Twigs crack under our feet as we turn toward our house at the forest's edge. Mosquitoes quickly gather as the sun goes down, their bites might serve as a warning. "Go back," they would say. "Stay among the gentle, harboring pines free from the sting of harsh words and the cold bite of anger."

"Goddamn it, Mary Beth! Cynthia! You look like a couple of ragamuffins. Get yourselves in this house!"

Mother stands outside the back door taking the last desperate drag from her cigarette.

Her agitated call is our welcome as we step inside the walls of our colonial suburban home positioned at the edge of our pine barren. Just before she reaches behind us to slam the sliding glass door I signal Cindy to wipe teaberry juice from her face. Cindy's hand shoots up to cover the spot just in time.

Screams explode from the kitchen where we find my brother Artie, wildly waves his bloody hands, whirling his seven-year-old body in a crazed, maniacal dance. A canned ham lay on the kitchen floor, its metal casing unraveled in a nonsensical spiral formation. Currents of ham drippings and blood mix into a pool of human and animal liquid.

Instead of reaching for his mother or sisters for comfort his rage-fueled strength kicks the bloody ham with such force that it becomes slightly airborne. It grazes past my knees and lands on Cindy's feet at which she releases only a muffled wail of pain. She flees the scene for the refuge of her bedroom where she cocoons herself for the night.

Slowly I back away from the kitchen saying, "monster baby" quietly, almost in a whisper, because I too fear the wrath of my violently capricious baby brother. My mother moves toward Artie whose arms flail and feet pummel anything that gets in their erratic path.

Artie's foot makes contact with a cabinet door, creating a splintered foot-sized hole. I notice the appearance of an enlarging scarlet stain on his white cotton socks. He races past my mother and me, slugging us both on his way to his bedroom. Within seconds we hear a powerful slam followed by the menacing sound of items being thrown against the wall. The hole in the cabinet door is added to the list of his many casualties, both material and human.

By the time he started walking, Artie was already deemed "monster baby." He challenged every babysitter, sending each one fleeing the house and cursing the day they accepted the impossible task of caring for such a defiant and powerful child. My sister and I never considered our superior age to be an advantage when coming to blows with "monster baby." His strength, almost freakish for a child his age, finds its energy in his bottomless rage. He will bite, choke and hit at whim, and on many occasions even causes damage to himself requiring varying degrees of emergency medical care.

After Artie escaped his destruction of the kitchen, I creep away quietly hoping my crisis-driven mother will be occupied with the clean up. Maybe she will overlook the demoralizing evening math drill. Maybe she won't. There is little more futile than predicting my mother's sharp turns of behavior. Because of this I am an astute student of surviving the unpredictable.

Outside pelts of rain precede a powerful summer storm. Flashes of light herald a commanding crash that shakes the house. The storm mimics my mother's arbitrary behavior. The crashes of thunder invariably chase the explosion of light, yet their timing remains indefinable. Certain uncertainty.

"Mary! Sit down."

Even before I have a chance to find a seat the math drill begins.

My hand reaches for the comfort of the teaberry waiting inside my pocket.

"13 times 3," she demands.

My mind races. My fingers and thumb dance over the hidden treasure in my pocket.

"28," springs from a place of fear rather than knowledge.

My head snaps back when my mother pulls my hair in her usual rebuke of my answer. Will I ever get it right? Surely I will lose all of my hair by the sixth grade. I wonder about the possibility of wigs in children's sizes.

"12 times 5," Mother demands.

"50?"

Yank. Maybe I'll be a blonde.

"8 times 12."

"92?"

Yank. Maybe a redhead. Teaberry red.

And as abruptly as it began the math drill ends when my mother glances at the hands on the clock above the oven.

"Oh my God! Look at the time," Mother says, suddenly distracted from the drill. She begins dancing a flurry of activity in an effort to make her bridge game. We are forever in between babysitters, so she leaves us unsupervised, knowing my father will soon be home. Crushing her cigarette she checks and rechecks the iron's off position before flying out the door.

"She'll be back," I say to myself.

As if on cue, the door flies open and nervous energy fills the house once more.

"I left the iron on! I know I did!" She finds it still in the off position and is out the door again.

With the air clear of cigarette smoke and tension I am safe to travel. My transport is the thirteen-inch glowing box facing me. I sit cross-legged on the braided rug that covers the family room's imitation brick linoleum and afford myself the luxury of escape. Each week Tarzan scoops me out of my unpredictable, crisis-filled world into a place of adventure and purpose. Black and white images flash lush jungles filled with animals that revere him and lost travelers whose lives depend on his survival skills. The layers of possibility peel back each time I travel to his African home.

As Tarzan bellows his last jungle call, my father's strong hand gently tickles my ear. In my Tarzan-induced trance, I have not noticed his homecoming nor his kitchen restoration efforts. The familiar smell of oil and grease he brings home each day from his auto repair shop fill me with a sense of promise and connection. A respite from my mother's frightening twists and turns.

"Time for bed, Mare," he gently chides.

I swing down the hall toward the bathroom skillfully avoiding quicksand and a large elephant stampede. As I glide the toothpaste onto the toothbrush I hear the screeching of chimpanzees behind the shower curtain. One jumps from the curtain's rod onto my shoulders and playfully pulls my ears straight out from the side of my head. In the mirror a girl thoughtfully gazes back at me, her neck is adorned with a string of multicolored beads. Exotic dots and stripes enhance the clear green of her eyes and she grasps her feather-topped spear with dignity. When I look down my spear once more becomes a florescent yellow toothbrush.

When I crawl into bed I know what to do to prolong time with my father.

"Tell me a firefighter story. Tell me about saving someone," I plead, always feeling at home with his colorful stories.

My father and a handful of local men comprise the Volunteer Fire Department.

He sits on the edge of my bed and his weight causes me to roll a little closer to him. My cupped hand rocks the teaberry lightly back and forth. His stories bring me to who I am in a way I cannot completely comprehend at ten years old.

"Two days ago," he begins, "the phone rang just when Mrs. Wheeler drove her car into the shop. The car was overheating and…"

"There was lots of steam coming from the hood. Even more when you opened the hood, right Daddy?" I asked, very sure of myself.

"That's right Mare."

"Were you careful not to take the radiator cap off?" I interrupted again.

"You remember about hot radiator caps?"

Time is suspended as he gazes at me, proud to have a "sponge" for an oldest child. Inside I sing the truth of my significance.

"Maybe you should just come down to the station and teach me a few things," he says.

My eyes shine like headlights.

"As I was saying, two days ago, when I was careful not to remove the radiator cap from the Mrs. Wheeler's steaming car, the phone rang," he finally begins.

"It was Bill Henry," he said. "Mrs. McKay had called needing help. Apparently her husband was trimming the branches off an old oak tree when a baby blue jay fell right on his shoe. She rang us because she didn't know of anyone else to call. I wrapped up a hamburger patty and went right over. Of course I knew the mother jay would never accept her baby after being touched by humans, so we tucked the little bird inside a cozy nest of pine needles and leaves."

I hang on every word and long to be just like him.

"Do you know what the hamburger was for?" my father queries.

"You were going to make it into little balls and feed the baby bird, right Dad?"

"That's right, Mare, you remember well. Remember what a job you did raising that baby robin last season? I told Mrs.

McKay that you would be happy to do it all over again if this one got to be too much work for her. She just called a little while ago and, guess what?"

My gasp gives way to unencumbered giggles.

"Yep, we'll pick up the little jay first thing in the morning."

"Oh, Dad, thank you! I will take good care of him."

"I know you will, Mare, now time for sleep. Tomorrow will be here soon enough."

My tender father blows me a kiss and I wrap it around my crimson treasure.

Sleep flirts with me as I hold visions of my neck encircled with dozens of African beads. Gracefully, I swing my way through the jungle canopy. The beads clink together lightly pounding my throat and I slip into a dreamy African adventure. The whining hinge of the kitchen door interrupts my sleep. It closes with a thud. Mother is home. Teaberry juice oozes in my fingers.

-2-

End of Innocence

Marlton, New Jersey, 1967

Artie's black boots splash the melted ice around the shore of the lake that borders the pine barren behind our house. The holidays have passed and the dead gray of winter temporarily gives way to a string of temperate days. Even in this warming period he does not remove his muddy-colored ski cap perpetually perched on his head. It mats his hair beneath and gives off a putrid smell noticeable within several feet.

His Christmas golf clubs, a gift from his grandfather, dangle over his left shoulder. As he walks across the dock the golf bag makes a *thud* sound with every step as it swings forward to meet his left foot.

"Guess what, Jimmy," Artie taunts, with a confidence well beyond his years. "I can hit farther than you, 'cause I'm gonna be nine in three and a half weeks."

The older neighbor boy accompanies him hurriedly saying, "I'm already nine, you baby; I'm already nine and I'm bigger than you. Just watch me. I can hit it farther and can whip you at the same time."

With that Jimmy sends the ball sailing over the ice landing on a distant point barely visible against the frozen lake. Jimmy's successful swing ignites a fiery determination that mixes with Artie's chronic rage. With controlled fury, Artie raises the club. As if appealing to a divine force the club pauses, head facing the heavens. In that frozen moment Artie considers the small round challenge waiting on the ice.

"Hey Artie." A young female voice calls from the end of the dock. An air of smugness sails with it.

Artie's club reacts, making a scraping sound across the aging wooden dock and missing the ball entirely. Living in the same neighborhood as Artie for most of her eleven years, Wendy is alert to her neighbor's indiscriminate and invariably frenzied outbursts. She stands at the other end of the dock, a safe distance between her and the golf club planted firmly in his fists.

Wendy reminds Artie, "Your mother said you are not supposed to be hitting out on the ice."

She says only lightly veiling her self-satisfaction with concern.

"I'm going to tell," she reports and abruptly turns toward his house. She walks away with a slight bounce in her self-congratulatory steps.

Muffled swearing comes from the end of the dock as the boys throw their clubs down. Artie and Jimmy make their way to the house kicking the thawing ground along the way. Just as Wendy mounts the back steps of Artie's house he shoves her out of the way. She stumbles down the steps and is too startled to notice that the boys have returned without their clubs.

Sitting with knees bent Indian style in front of the family room coffee table, Cindy explains to me how the game of solitaire is played. She places an ace of spades on a two of hearts as I watch with mild interest. When Artie and Jimmy bolt past our table the force of their charge disrupts several cards from their carefully placed positions. An airborne golf tee lands in my lap.

"Hey," I yell at the boys, "watch it," as I slip the tiny white object into my pocket. Cindy jumps slightly when Artie's bedroom door slams behind them. With slow intentional movements she begins restoring order to her game.

"Cindy, Mary Beth. Get in the car. We're going to town," our mother dictates.

Without warning, Mother announces an immediate need to shop for a wedding gift and we must both accompany her.

"Mom," I plead, "can you drop me at Dad's station? I can help pump gas or make a bike with the other kids."

"Absolutely not," Mom replies. "The station is no place for

children." There is no questioning Mother.

Defeated, Cindy and I rise from our positions on the braided rug and head for the coat rack by back door.

"Artie, you stay inside until we get back," Mother calls on our way out the door. There is no response from behind Artie's closed bedroom door. She waves a hand in exasperation and slams the front door behind her.

There will never be a response.

Artie and Jimmy hear the car's engine start and scramble to peer out of his bedroom window sending several baseball cards flying. Their eyes follow the car until it is out of sight. The boys bolt for the door. Their feet anxiously take them toward the freedom of the lake. This time no one will stop Artie's chance to prove himself.

Artie is the first one back on the dock. This time he will not relinquish his new club until the ball redeems him from Jimmy's taunts. Each time he swings the ball betrays him. He glares at the balls on the ice and jumps off the dock. Water drips steadily from the ice melting on the sunny side of the dock. With heavy, purposeful strides Artie marches toward the distant golf balls.

Jimmy, not wanting to be outdone by such an act of bravery says, "Do it. I dare you. You're nothing but a big chic-chic, chicken."

Jimmy does not realize these words birth a burden he will carry for many years. The scowling freckled face boy's goading only solidifies Artie's resolve. Artie stops abruptly several yards from the dock and turns toward Jimmy. The clubs; he cannot risk Jimmy molesting his prized clubs while he is on the ice. When he reaches the dock, Artie swings the golf bag over his shoulder. Christmas newness still glistens off the heads. His first step on the ice makes him slip a little. Jimmy watches. The wet, slick ice demands small deliberate steps. Looking back causes him to make a weaving motion with his upper body while his feet and legs are still and steady like the trunk of an oak. He rights his upper body and takes another step just as the bag slips off his shoulder and crashes to the ice. Within seconds he hears what sounds like a slow motion gunshot. The balls are just beyond. Just a few more steps. He leans to pick up the bag and uses his weight to sling it over his shoulder once more. With that motion everything gives way. At first he does not register what has happened. Then his body feels unbearable cold followed by a burning sensation. Disoriented, he wildly spins in the dark, frozen world below the ice. The struggle to free himself from the bag slows when his motions become sluggish. He cannot think. There is a burning in his chest. He can no longer tell his body to move. The tiny white ball drops off the broken ice into the water and sinks slowly past his face.

Minutes pass but Jimmy ages several years. The sudden silence slices through him and he knows he cannot stay. He starts running and does not stop for almost an hour. He tells no one.

Wendy and Darleen are watching the boys from their living room, especially mesmerized when they see Artie begin to climb off the dock. At first they think Artie is hiding, trying to scare Jimmy. When the splashing stops they are out the door, running in the direction of the now deserted dock. They see Jimmy whimpering and running toward the pine barren. Still in the living room, Darleen's mother struggles to keep her hands steady as she dials the fire department.

It is Saturday which means Dad is holding a "bicycle workshop" for a half a dozen neighborhood kids in his service station. Long before the movement to recycle, these workshops were funded with used parts some might consider useless trash. These parts bring discarded bikes new life. The attendees must build two bikes, one to keep and one to give away. Several of those present could not otherwise own their own bike. When the classes are over each child is empowered with a skill, transportation, and a bike to give away. The phone sits unevenly on the desk in my father's auto repair shop. Its ring makes a rattling sound. My father does not pick it up right away.

"Sheila, show Bruce how to attach the chain to the chain ring," Dad says with complete confidence in Sheila's ability. My father teaches, motivates and inspires while still maintaining control of the group. The kids feel comfortable around my dad, whom they call "Bob."

Mom sternly objects to me hanging out at the station with the other kids. However, bicycle class for me is at home. He regularly lifts "treasures" out of the trash and teaches me how to create new and useful objects. Once he brought home an old lawn chair and taught me how to re-strap the webbing.

Bruce watches as Sheila gently teaches him the mechanics of bicycle chains. She wipes her brow and smudges her forehead with grease. My father gets to his feet to answer the phone's persistent plea for attention. His blue eyes gaze over his little group of students with contentment.

"Bob's Mobil Station," my father answers.

The kids look up in unison. My father's expression changes.

It does not indicate a customer with a leaking fuel line. This look springs from humanitarian compassion. Someone needs his help.

"Sorry to cut it short, but I am going to have to go. Someone fell through the ice. Kids, it sounds like it is near my house. I've got to lock up the station now, but we will have another class next week. Who wants a ride in the jeep to the fire station?"

Sheila races Bruce to Dad's 1946 Willies Jeep that doubles as a neighborhood snowplow.

As the Volunteer fire truck turns towards the beach recreation area near our house, my father finds the emergency is at our own dock. Wendy's upper body is hanging over the side of the wooden platform. Feet held by her mother and a neighborhood girl, only the bottoms of Wendy's snow boots are visible. Her two little feet flutter with quick jerky movements. She is reaching for something beyond the dock.

My father and the other firefighters rush to the wafer thin ice. They seem to know what to do but still they struggle for twenty minutes with grappling hooks and poles.

We return from our shopping mission in time to see a crowd forming at the dock. Suddenly my mother cries out, "Oh my God, it's Artie; oh my God, it's Artie. I know it's Artie."

She squeals to an abrupt stop near the commotion and jumps out. Cindy and I remain in the back seat unsure what is expected of us.

Moments later my brother's blue, lifeless body emerges from its icy tomb five yards from the beach where we played ice hockey only five days before.

I stand helplessly watching the tragic scene, turning a golf tee round in my pocket. My father sits on the ground sobbing; his shoulders move up and down as he cradles my brother's lifeless body in his arms.

-3-

Christmas Time

Tampa, Florida, 1989

Paramedics rush through the double doors of the emergency department with the body of a small child strapped to their stretcher. The force of their hurried pace startles the decorative holiday tinsel lining the walls of the ER entrance. A young man and woman, dressed in their holiday finest, follow close behind. The woman weeps uncontrollably, pleading to some unseen power. The man's dress shoes make squishing sounds with every quick step and water drips from the point at the base of his Santa Claus tie.

Pastor Ben, the soft-spoken hospital chaplain, gently ushers the couple into the "quiet room." He waits with the couple while the ER team tries to stir life back into their five-year-old son.

As they release their child into the depths of the trauma room I hear the father saying, to no one in particular, "We could not find him...then I saw him...I jumped in the pool...he was blue...he was so blue..."

I close all emotional doors to memories of my brother and to the anguish embodied in the young parents waiting with Father Ben. Tonight I am trauma nurse two, I must remain focused on the critical tasks at the child's bedside while Susan, who is trauma nurse one, records the procedures and Jon, the ER physician, prepare to intubate the child. This little boy's dark brown curls are still damp as I insert a small needle into his tiny vein and attach the IV. Jon inserts a flexible plastic intubation tube into the tiny circumference of the boy's trachea as I steady his little head. We work as a team to stimulate life into his tiny body.

"Stop," Jon finally says.

All eyes go directly to the cardiac monitor, which confirms the absence of any rhythm indicative of life.

I lift the child's eyelids. His lashes are thick and curl delicately over his lids.

His fully dilated pupils make his eyes black.

Jon places his hand on the child's face and confirms the state of his eyes.

"Fixed and dilated," he reports.

"How long have we been at it?" Jon asks.

Susan looks at her chart and then at her watch.

"We've been coding for 45 minutes now," Susan says.

The doctor looks once more into the child's absent expression.

"Okay, let's call it. Mark time of death at 15:15."

Susan documents the time. Four simple numbers etched on a page that will change the lives of the couple in our hospital quiet room.

Susan finishes her notes and looks at Jon.

"Ready?" he asks.

He and Susan leave the trauma room to deliver the news to the child's mother and father who are huddled together in the cold, windowless quiet room.

I am left behind to disconnect unnecessary equipment from the child's lifeless body and ready him for viewing. My movements are methodical and precise. Emotions are barred from the fortress of my mind. Only now can I move about the confines of my duties without fear of being bombarded by the angelic face of the dead child or the wails of his anguished mother.

I replace the soiled sheets with clean ones and dab a bit of bloody saliva away from the small, colorless lips. An image flashes across my mind as I gently close both eyelids. The image is of the body of a seventeen-year-old victim of a misfiring handgun. He lies in a trauma room like this one with most of his face missing. The sight of his young lifeless body triggered such sadness in me that I was unable to continue working for the remainder of my shift. That was sixteen years ago.

Over the past several years I have trained my mind to serve as an armed guard to my emotions. A towering wall surrounds me now like a fortress, securing me from the palpable pain that enters the emergency department's swinging doors day and night. My emotions live outside the security of my stronghold, allowing me to continue nursing in this environment. And yet I still can't completely bar something calling from outside the fortress.

The boy's parents enter the room to hold the body of their little son one last time. The child's mother slips her arms around his tiny torso and lays her head on his chest. As I leave, the father sits on the edge of the bed and caresses his son's moist brown curls and weeps openly. I leave them, moving easily to the next case.

The memories fade but never completely disappear.

Outside the trauma room an intoxicated man attempts to sit up when I approach his bed. He is only slightly injured, with minor abrasions on his left shoulder and a deep cut above his left eyebrow. I tell him to be still while I prepare the wound for suturing.

A thin privacy curtain separates him from the victim of his drunken driving. A pregnant woman, softly crying, clutches her dying husband's hand.

"I don't give a fuck if he dies," the intoxicated patient yells to the next bed.

As I lean in to clean the gash on his head he spits directly into my face. I am the Iron Nurse standing guard outside the towering gates of my fortress, barring my anger. However, a quiet stirring breeze blows through the portals of my emotional fort. I tighten my focus and calmly leave the man without a word, in the direction of the nearest sink. The mirror reflects slimy, saliva sprayed like angry graffiti over my hard expression.

Humanity exposes its ugly underbelly inside an emergency department. I've seen a patient get out of bed and attempt to choke an ailing man to death. I have treated three-year-olds with gonorrhea and seven-year-olds with vaginal tears; infants with crushed skulls; and a child electrocuted by high-tension wires.

Some patients become their own victims. I have seen men

with objects lodged inside their penises and rectums, and even some who repeatedly ingest corrosive substances in the form of sandwiches. I have seen x-rays of the stomach revealing outlines of pins, needles, batteries and leaded glass. Some tortured souls resort to carving and mutilating their own flesh. And too often people become patients after overdosing to get attention or other forms of attempted suicide.

Sometimes the medical personnel are no better than the patients who abuse themselves and others. I have known doctors who intubate verbally obnoxious patients to keep them from yelling, and others who stole drugs intended for patients. In Columbus, Ohio, I worked alongside a doctor who noted the address of his patient's next of kin so he could slip into their homes and rape them after his shift. Another man, wrongly accused of this crime, was sent to prison until five years later when the rapist doctor was finally caught and convicted.

In emergency departments throughout the United States patients have kicked me, spat in my face, soaked my scrubs with their urine, bit me like a mad dog, and hurled every imaginable obscenity at me and my colleagues.

Although this constant beating fortifies the Iron Nurse's resolve, a soft tapping sounds against the outside walls.

Cold water, antiseptic soap and a dry towel snap me back to my duties for this shift and silences the tapping for now.

After finishing my work on the inebriated spitter I stand at the nurses' station to complete my paper work.

A gentle tug on my scrubs, followed by an angelic voice brings me back to the present.

"Señora, por favor."

When I turn around I see the round face of a six-year-old Hispanic boy holding the edge of my scrub top with one tiny, dimpled hand. His fingers grasp a plastic toy sword in the other. He waves his treasure in the air toward me. His mother stands beside him beaming with humble, generous eyes.

"Rodrigo," I say remembering my brave patient brought in two days ago after being hit by a car.

He and his mother speak very little English. Rodrigo had only minor injuries including a gash on his chin that required suturing. He quietly allowed the doctor and me to clean, anesthetize and suture his gaping chin while his mother's brown, calloused hands soothed his trembling arms. The irises of his amber eyes reflected my face as the needle drove in from one side of torn flesh to the other, gently closing his wound with the tugging of fine blue suture. Rodrigo was one of the bravest patients I had seen in years and he owned my heart.

When he was ready to go I gave his mother a wound care hand-out from our selection of discharge instructions. In broken Spanish I explained they needed to return in five days, and did not expect to see them before then.

Rodrigo's stitches look like unshaven whiskers against his baby smooth face.

"Para usted señora," he says, offering his treasured plastic sword.

His mother smiles proudly and takes a deep breath to begin her rehearsed English.

"Eets for jou. Eets hees favorite juguete. Take eet," she says waving her hand in my direction, as I hold the generous gift.

Rodrigo says, "Feliz Navidad, señora."

It is hard to see his face now as my eyes fill with tears. I cannot remember the last time a patient shared a kind word or gesture of appreciation.

My heart responds faster than my mind can stage a protest in favor of professional distance between health care provider and patient. With revived vigor I lift Rodrigo's small frame easily and kiss him on his dimpled face. We release spontaneous laughter.

In his excited Spanish Rodrigo begins to point out all of the sword's most amazing features.

Silver and gold garlands adorn street lights along the empty boulevard as I travel away from the hospital at the end of this long evening shift. By now most travelers have reached their holiday destinations, and the lights seem to illuminate the way just for me. Bing Crosby croons "Silent Night" through my car radio. Rodrigo's gift lies across my lap. My fingers caress the grip of the plastic sword as I drive. A child's plastic sword skillfully challenges Iron Nurse and her towering fortress. I feel a longing to connect with patients like Rodrigo and his mother. The poor from foreign lands often seem to possess an innate wisdom I rarely see in my own culture. The display of gratitude even for carrying out what I would consider an expected part of my duties is a rare find among the American patients in my line of work.

I sense a journey is about to begin.

-4-

Straitsville

New Straitsville, Ohio, January 1992

The swing just outside the front door of my mother's weather-beaten farmhouse still emits its familiar creaking. With every swing my feet scuff the porch floorboards worn from harsh winters and thousands of steps across its wide planks. The sun is out for the first time in weeks. I wrap the afghan I crocheted for Mom last Christmas around my shoulders and brave the crisp air for as long as I can stand it. Steam curls from the surface of my coffee and the cup balances nicely on the space next to me as I scan the pages of the *Columbus Dispatch*.

My mother lives in a blue, vinyl sided house in the rolling foothills of Appalachia. After Artie drowned she and my father divorced. Soon after the divorce she fell for an unemployed alcoholic named Norm who spent his summers as a "carnie." Norm, aka Aardvark Enterprises, dragged around a blue plywood mini trailer, hitched to his car. This trailer transported a random card sorter Norm called "The Handwriting Analyzer" to state fairs and carnivals across the Midwestern states. For the next few years Mom dragged my sisters and me around the country with the carnival until she finally left him and settled in this Ohio hill country farmhouse.

The dilapidated property's constant need for attention offered a kind of refuge, and the bonus of a practical education gleaned from the absence of expensive conveniences. By the time I was sixteen I could cook, sew my own clothes and raise my own crops. I could milk a cow, train a horse and give myself a haircut. I could pitch a tent, hunt and fish. Self-sufficiency was a way of life.

This independent spirit fortified me through the two years of daily eighteen-mile commutes to Hocking Technical Nursing School. While in school I maintained a small business selling milk, eggs, and cattle, and got my first taste of emergency medicine working as a part-time Emergency Medical Technician (EMT).

Two years have passed since that pivotal holiday shift at Tampa General. That night Rodrigo opened my eyes. Emergency room nursing in several states had threatened to pilfer the compassion from my spirit until that night when I began to listen to the quiet tapping outside my fortress walls. I revived my long lost passion for travel and cultures foreign to me. Soon afterwards I left emergency room nursing. I took a job as a cruise ship nurse, traveled to 36 countries and learned enough Spanish to hold my own. My life was on hold. While waiting to hear about a possible nursing assignment in Saudi Arabia, I decide to spend some time on my mother's farm.

I balance the inner pages of the *Columbus Dispatch* on my lap, retrieve my coffee mug and wrap my hands around its warmth. My whole body seems to thaw as I turn to the local news in the B section. The headline on 1B immediately grabs my attention.

Local surgeon helped hundreds in Somalia

There it is. Africa. The old familiar stomping ground where the valiant Tarzan and I swung on sturdy vines through lush jungles on fast-paced quests to rescue those lost and in need.

The article focuses on an interview with local orthopedic surgeon Dr. Henry Hood. He outlines the work of expatriates volunteering their medical skills in a war-ravaged and starving nation through the Los Angeles-based International Medical Corps. He describes a six-year-old boy, a patient who had his toe blown off during "...automatic weapons fire in a clan war the United Nations estimates already has killed 20,000. As many as 500,000 Somali refugees are thought to have crossed the border into food-poor Ethiopia to escape the fighting."

My eyes race back and forth across the newsprint.

Dr. Hood explains the challenges of working in a 700-bed hospital, struggling to care for 1,300 patients without enough staff, proper sanitary conditions or adequate medical supplies.

Finally, one quote takes me by the hand and sets me down in front of the intensifying call. Dr. Hood says, "No matter how badly someone was wounded, we started medication, because the family wanted something done. For the most part, the (Somali) patient never blames you, and the family never blames you if you make an effort."

After devouring the story I close the paper and lurch forward, barreling into the house in search of the atlas. The cooling coffee sloshes with the movement of the abandoned swing.

In the living room a homemade bookshelf houses the 1981 *World Book Encyclopedia and World Atlas* set mother bought from a convincing door-to-door salesman eleven years ago. The atlas sticks to its neighbors and comes away from the shelf after some prodding. Evidently the book's fundamental usefulness has fallen short of the handsome salesman's pitch.

The pages stick to each other so I must slowly peel forward to Africa. Finally they stop on Somalia—the Horn of Africa. The country juts out to a point like the horn of a rhinoceros. The point of the horn divides the Gulf of Aden along the northern coastline and the Indian Ocean along the southern. The political interior of the horn borders Kenya to the south and Ethiopia to the north. Terrain is mostly flat arid savannah scrub land in the south, turning hilly towards the north. The climate is described as hot and dry inland and somewhat more humid along the coast.

The atlas sits open on the avocado green Formica counter in the kitchen. I place page 1B of the January 13, 1992 *Dispatch* next the Horn of Africa and position the Columbus yellow pages a few inches away, near the phone. My fingers dance through the H's.

Finally, *Hood, Henry M.D.*

My hand shakes a little as I dial numbers on the telephone rotary. An older woman with a lilting southern accent answers the phone.

"Dr. Hood's office."

"Yes, uh, I'd like to speak with Dr. Hood please," I say with adrenaline-driven confidence.

Three weeks later I am on a plane bound for war and famine in the great Horn of Africa, 8,000 miles from the little blue farmhouse in rural Ohio, and decades back in time.

The Journey Begins

Nairobi, Kenya, February 1992

My plane descends over the savanna as it approaches Jomo Kenyata International Airport outside Nairobi, Kenya. In the distance five giraffe stand browsing the umbrella of an acacia tree. The tallest curl their long tongues around clusters of bright green leaves for an afternoon feast. A baby nuzzles under its mother, hungry for closeness and a warm meal. Just as I am about to tuck my binoculars into my backpack, the city skyline comes into view beyond the retreating giraffe herd.

Tray tables and seat backs go into their upright position and passengers jostle their bags in anticipation of landing on African soil. I am simultaneously thrilled and terrified at the prospect of coming into contact with a passion known only to my imagination and longing.

A cosmopolitan city, strewn with modern skyscrapers, looms in far distance through the windows as I walk through the airport corridor. I pass an orderly, well-lit gift shop offering multilingual novels, magazines, newspapers, carved African figurines, and impractical, safari-style accessories. This is not the Africa I expected.

Just ahead a large arrow points to the left. Above the arrow a sign reads "customs" in English and Swahili. I turn the corner and find Africa. Immense waves of people shift irritably in a roped area, shouting and pushing in disorderly groupings.

Customs agents have abandoned all but two counters where papers spill to the floor from disorganized piles. I retrieve two blank forms from the floor and fill one out, saving the second for a future use.

They accept American dollars at the customs counter and permit me entry to the next level. Beyond customs, twenty steps below, a maroon colored sign reads "Something to Declare Here" and an adjacent sign indicates "Nothing to Declare Here." Not a single person in this sea of people even hints of being the greeting party promised by International Medical Corps. I drop my bags containing a year's worth of essentials and scan the crowd feeling increasingly exhausted and overwhelmed. A few feet away a sign indicates a restroom. I wrestle my bags back into my arms and head for the refuge of the facility.

Inside, the commode is cracked and I find out—too late—that there is no toilet paper anywhere in sight. Thank goodness for a British Airways serviette stuffed in my pocket.

After regaining my focus, I walk more confidently in the directions of the customs funnel. People in assorted styles of dress from countless ethnic and cultural backgrounds push their belongings toward a lone declaration desk. Bags of all sizes, shapes and configurations are inspected at random. One is wrapped in brown paper and string. I shove my things forward with one foot closely following a Dutch businessman and a charcoal black woman in a loose-fitting traditional African gown. The regal woman casually balances a hard sided suitcase on her head like a crown. After the Kenyan customs agent has rummaged through every undergarment in my valise, I retrieve my gear and come face to face with a stocky white man wearing a freshly ironed, white button-down shirt and jeans. He holds a small sign that reads "Mary Lightfine."

"Mary?" he says recognizing my obvious confused state.

"Yes, that's me."

Chuckling a little he says, "Yeah. I thought so. I'm Simon from IMC."

Finally.

Simon directs me through the masses while casually giving me vital information about my next steps. I attempt to process this new information while navigating my bags and the waves of bustling humanity around me.

We reach his 70's Toyota Corolla. Taxi drivers solicit passengers to ride in their World War II era rounded-top sedans. American and European made cars from the 1960's and 70's honk and race around us, oblivious to pedestrians and other drivers.

Simon's muscular arms easily throw my bags into the trunk while I walk to the right side and sit down in front of the steering wheel. After three days of travel my exhausted mind sits blank before it registers the error. Simon's laughter embarrasses me, but also lightens the air.

Standing outside the window he asks, "Want to drive, Mary?"

"No worries. Common mistake," he adds graciously as I slide to the left.

Pulling away from the airport I feel slightly nauseous from the unregulated exhaust fumes billowing out of cars all around us.

Simon tells me there will be a three-day layover in Nairobi before a transport plane is available to take me to Mogadishu. My host appears to be a few years younger than me, but self-consciously covers his prematurely balding head with a New York Yankees baseball cap. Tufts of curly gray hair escape and fall past his ears. Confidently, he rapidly offers detailed information about Somalia and International Medical Corps. It is increasingly difficult to listen as he rambles on about Somalia and clans and technicals and NGOs. I have no idea what he is talking about and he cannot entice my mind to focus when there is so much to take in.

On our way past downtown Nairobi the streets are dotted with studies in the surreal. Modern nightclubs, shopping malls and fifteen-story office buildings are the backdrop to dark-skinned men stoking small fires along the roadside. One man in ragged clothes moves toward the car selling soap and trinkets. Casually I roll up my window, trapping the oppressive heat inside the car. The jeans and long sleeve shirt IMC instructed me to wear molds to my body on this summer day in February. Nairobi, although five thousand feet above sea level, is below the equator and I have arrived in the hottest part of the year.

The road unexpectedly becomes surrounded by savanna grassland where zebras graze 15 meters (50 feet) from my window. One looks up casually, then goes back to eating.

Wood-framed doors, shaded with green awnings, welcome guests to the grand Jacaranda Hotel. The open-air atrium invites breezes that lower the temperature in the lobby by fifteen degrees Fahrenheit.

After an attractive Kenyan woman in Western-style professional dress checks me into room 226, I am courteously greeted by a Kenyan hotel employee in crisp dress shirt and black bow tie.

"Madame, may I take your bags to your room?" he asks in well-spoken English.

"Yes, thank you," I say.

"Mary, you'll be here for a couple of days so you might want to play tourist. Another expatriate, a Physician's Assistant from California, is on his way today. Maybe you could hook up and do a wild game park together," Simon suggests.

"Any questions before I take off?"

Of course I have dozens but choose to put them off until a time when exhaustion is not robbing me of the ability to put coherent thoughts together.

"No," I reply a bit reluctantly.

"Get some rest then. You look like hell," Simon says and leaves abruptly.

"Thanks," I mutter as he moves away.

Hardwood floors and lofty natural wood ceilings give an old world estate feel. Guests mill about the lobby; their accents and manner suggest they are well-to-do European travelers. Some wear casual business attire and others ridiculous safari ensembles. There are no dark-skinned guests in sight.

The Kenyan porter closes the door behind him and leaves me alone. I sit on the end of an immaculately made bed and remove both Reeboks so that I may introduce my tired feet to the cool tile floor. An enchanting bronze Sunbird with a delicately curved bill rests in the branches of a jacaranda tree outside the open picture window. The scene below the window is a tropical paradise. A hotel waiter serves a drink complete with a pineapple wedge and tiny umbrella to a woman sunning next to a pristine sapphire blue pool surrounded by tropical plants and birds. She takes the drink and lies back in her chair without acknowledging the server.

One thought haunts me until I speak it out loud.

"What am I doing here?"

My thoughts are a maze of confusion. How can IMC justify my luxurious accommodations, while thousands die violently and starve to death daily? This is not what I signed up for. In spite of feeling a little guilty, I welcome the soothing support the bed gives my aching body and allow soft breezes to lull me to sleep.

I wake suddenly and fumble in the dark to find the alarm clock on the nightstand. Its bold backlit hands indicate 3:13 a.m., but my body is convinced it is six o'clock in the evening. I turn on the lamp knowing that even attempting to sleep will be a frustrating waste of time. For a moment I sit on the edge of the bed trying to register my location.

A picture of Simon dispensing an endless stream of information came to my mind's eye. I reach for my backpack in need of a distraction from the irrational panic often lurking in the wee hours of the morning. Rummaging among books, pens, underwire bras, shampoo, and a copy of *A Manual of Emergency Medicine* I eventually come across the IMC Travel Information Packet. Finally, I am lulled to sleep while reviewing Mogadishu's average monthly temperatures.

Tropical African birds draw the morning out of hiding with their eager songs. My beeping travel alarm calls me into the new day and I hurriedly dress for breakfast. Just as I find the stairway I hear someone shout, "What the fuck?"

In the hallway a young man with close-cropped light brown hair and American clothing straightens the cleaning bucket he tripped over and shakes his soaking left shoe. Dirty water runs down the tiled floor onto the stairway. I hand him the sarong draped over my shoulder to use as a towel and he takes it without a word of grateful acknowledgement. Finally he returns the partially soaked sarong. His sharp blue eyes look directly at me and he gives me a "thank you" nod. This must be the Physician Assistant Simon mentioned.

"I'm Mary Lightfine with IMC. Do you happen to be on your way to Somalia?" I ask, anxious to find someone as confused and out of place as I feel.

"Yeah, I'm Brian," he says.

"How did you get to the hotel? I didn't see you at the airport," I ask.

"IMC didn't send shit to meet me at the airport. I snagged a ride and made it myself. Do you know why the fuck we're here and not on a fucking cargo plane to Mogadishu?" he asks, tensing his square jaw. He is cocky but something vulnerable lingers around his hard edges.

Outwardly Brian is Caucasian but if I close my eyes I could swear he is a black gang member from South Central Los Angeles. His mannerisms and speech do not match his light skinned face, blue eyes and short straight hair.

When the elevator doors open again I stop at the restaurant but Brian but keeps walking, a little strut in his steps. The smell of freshly brewed coffee makes me hesitate before going after him but curiosity overpowers hunger.

"Brian, wait," I call.

He does not turn around or break his strut but calls behind him.

"I'm not hungry."

He stops at the concierge in the lobby and I hear him ask where he can make a phone call.

"I want to get the fuck to Mogadishu. I'm calling IMC to get me out of here. I didn't come here to sit on my ass in this country club," he says determinedly.

In spite of his harsh tone and angry words he actually comforts me, and I feel a sense of kinship with him. Although Simon said there is no transport out of Nairobi for a couple of days, everything in me agrees with Brian.

"The IMC rep told me yesterday there is no way we can get out for two days. Why not see something while we're stuck here? Come with me to a game park," I suggest, trying not to sound desperate for company.

"I'm not here to play fuckin' tourist on some candy-assed safari," he says looking directly at me. "I'll find my own goddamned ride to Mogadishu."

"Okay. You win. See if you can get out of here today," I reply, finally growing weary of his ranting.

"I'm hungry," I declare and head for the restaurant without looking back.

The courteous Kenyan waiter has just poured another cup of coffee in my fine porcelain coffee cup when a muscular frame throws himself into the chair across from me.

"This place is rat-fucked," says my new friend through his grinding teeth.

"No go, huh?" I say with a slightly smug smile.

"Listen, I found out we can get on an overnight safari leaving at noon. All meals and accommodations are included for only 125 US dollars. We can get out of this place and maybe have some fun," I reason calmly. "Somalia will be there when we get back," I continue my sensible rhetoric.

"Fuck it," he says in his now familiar mantra.

Finally he adds, "I'll meet you at noon."

Our open air safari bus rolls across a game reserve in the Masai Mara region approximately 220 kilometers from Nairobi. My eyes scan the horizon as I peer through the open top of the vehicle. We slow as we approach a pair of Acacia trees shading a pride of lions like oversize umbrellas. The ginger-hewed trunks provide an exotic contrast to tall savanna grasses. Finally the bus rolls to a stop and Brian, sitting next to the door, starts to open it.

"Please sir. No, no, no, sir!" insists our Kenyan guide.

"First a teaching of the ways of the beasts of Africa," he says as Brian reluctantly removes his hand from the door.

"You must stay in the Safari bus to take your pictures," begins our guide.

"Last week a German man walked too close to the pride while taking a picture and the lion killed him before we could hear his screams."

I'm convinced! Maybe even Brian will hesitate.

"However, the most dangerous animal in Africa is the hippopotamus. The jaws are so powerful they can bite a man in half instantly. Even the crocodile swim away from baby hippos."

My hand reaches inside my pocket and finds a loose button that rolls around in my palm. I am thinking I will keep the metal frame of the vehicle between myself and the savage creatures of Kenya.

"Stay inside the safari bus unless we tell you otherwise."

No arguing from me but Brian's face looks defeated.

Several cameras poke their lenses through the opening in the top of our moving metal cage in order to capture shots of the lions that soon will find themselves displayed in wood frames on living room bookcases around the world. The lions sit quietly enjoying the cool of the evening, occasionally shaking their head to rid themselves of persistent savanna flies.

As the safari vehicle rolls on I crane my neck to get one last glance at the majestic creatures. A full-grown male opens his gaping mouth and stretches into a drawn-out yawn revealing dagger-like fangs.

Our bush bus moves across the plains in the direction of the river as dusk descends. In the cooling air fireflies blink on and off just beyond the vehicle. I roll the button around in my pocket and consider how far I have come from the New Jersey Pine Barrens on the other side of the world.

When we reach the river we are allowed to venture out of the safari bus in search of a closer view of crocodiles and hippopotami. I hesitate, thinking of the words "the most dangerous animal in Africa," but finally leave the vehicle resolving to stay with the guides and their guns.

Standing near the water's edge I see a lethargic-looking hippopotamus. She is soaking beside her young, while slowly grinding her enormous jaws just twenty yards away. Picturing those incredible jaws snapping a full grown man in half gives me new respect for this creature, which I had previously pictured as big-hearted, playful characters in children's books.

I lay my hand on Brian's shoulder to point out a crocodile gliding past the mother and offspring. He looks in the direction I point but moves uncomfortably away from my touch. Note to self, "Brian not comfortable with casual touch."

Back in camp Brian unzips the door of the tent we decided to share solely out of monetary concerns. Although the canvas walls and roof shelter two queen size four-poster beds dramatically draped with mosquito netting that overflows onto a stone floor, I am concerned that more luxurious accommodations will set Brian into another tirade of his favorite mantra. But he seems relaxed and to be genuinely enjoying himself.

Coming out of the full bathroom I notice my roommate has politely left the tent to give me some space. The tent zipper is slightly open. I notice a figure squatted on the ground. Quietly I open the zipper just enough to catch a glimpse of Brian holding an ailing brilliant blue butterfly on a stick close to his face. Soft whispering comes from him in tones I suspect he rarely shares with humans. I zip the tent back down and give him the same courtesy he gave me.

At dawn the air is cool and fragrant with an earthy aroma. I swing my backpack over my shoulder and climb the three steps into the awaiting Cessna Caravan, and within minutes we are sailing hundreds of feet above a large herd of graceful gazelles.

Near the end of our flight in the single engine Cessna, I notice Brian's tension seems to increase in direct proportion to our descent into Nairobi's Wilson Airport.

"We'll probably be in Mogadishu tomorrow at this time. Hard to imagine," I say trying to crack his thickening shell.

"We goddamn better be. I can't take another day waiting to do what I came halfway around the fuckin' world to do."

Brian is back. A calm smile moves across my face. I find comfort in the company of a good friend I have known less than 48 hours. I remember the butterfly and wonder if his thick exterior and cutting words protect the sweetness of a gentle heart.

As we enter the surreal luxury of the Jacaranda Hotel Simon's Toyota Corolla pulls up behind us. He signals with two high-pitched beeps. Leaving the car running, he steps out, wearing another crisp white button down shirt and jeans. This time, however, he sports a marine-blue baseball cap with "IMC" inscribed in white letters.

"Hey, we're going to dinner tonight. See you here at eight?"

It's more of directive than a question.

"Yeah, sure," I say, looking at Brian to verify.

Brian just stared blankly and asked, "What the hell's going on with our transport plane?"

"It's in the works for tomorrow. Don't have a definite time yet. There's been fighting around the landing strip at the airport in Mog."

Brian turns and disappears into the Jacaranda without responding.

"So, I'll see you then," Simon instructs.

"Yeah, eight o'clock," I agree. "We'll be right here."

At 7:55 p.m. I stand at the spot where Simon said he would meet us. No sign of Brian. I am not surprised. A casual dinner with the people keeping him from his mission does not seem to fit my friend's current demeanor.

On the way to dinner Simon asks me about Brian.

"What do you make of him?" he asks with a skeptical tone.

Uneasy with the motive behind the question, I struggle for a benign answer.

"He certainly is passionate about getting started in Somalia," I reply, hoping that will be the end of this line of questioning.

"Yeah, but, I don't know. I wonder if IMC should send him at all. What do you think?" Simon asks.

I am thinking, "How am I supposed to know?" So far Brian has, although gruffly, been able to verbalize my confusion and frustration better than I have. What are we doing at a luxury hotel when thousands suffer from starvation and war in the next country?

"I am probably not the most qualified person to answer that question, but as far as I can tell Brian seems compassionate and dedicated," I say with a slight tone of annoyance.

My head turns to look at the scene out the window hoping he will take this as the end of this conversation. A sign announces the "YaYa Center," an expansive shopping mall dotted with a dozen other signs advertising every pricey outlet one would find in the States. The three-story burnt orange brick building is lined with a black security fence around its parameter. It houses a supermarket, used bookstore, several clothing boutiques, a shoe repair, and our destination—a Korean restaurant.

Inside the restaurant, ten men and women sit around a large round table draped with a fine linen tablecloth. On top of the table sits a centerpiece made up of beautiful orchids. All ten are grasping their drinks and engaged in boisterous laughter. They stop when Simon and I reach the table. He introduces me, rattling off everyone's name, their job description and the humanitarian organization to which they belong.

Exotic Korean food richly displayed on delicate fine bone-colored china is served. Plate after plate is brought to the table until it is filled with more than our crowd can manage in a week. It is painfully clear to me that Brian made the right decision. Although the abundance continues to be disturbing, it is impossible to deny that I am beginning to enjoy this lifestyle.

"Mary." I look up and see a rugged-looking man with piercing blue eyes sitting two chairs down.

"If you have any problems in Somalia just find SAVE," he says in a British accent.

Others add to his words of wisdom by giving me information

about USAID, SCF, UNICEF, MSF and warn me of the USF. They throw around names of warlords as if they are well-known film stars. They discuss Somali clan structure overestimating my knowledge of African culture.

Throughout dinner the feeling of inadequacy begins to sweep through me winding into overwhelming confusion and doubt. For the first time I wonder if I have made a huge mistake.

That night, after a copious meal served with buckets of intimidating information, sleep teases but never settles in to stay. Simon's 5 a.m. call pulls my sleep deprived eyes away from the glowing travel alarm clock on my nightstand.

"Mary, you leave in an hour," he announces.

"Be ready outside the hotel."

He hangs up before I can ask any questions.

Outside the Jacaranda the lovely softness of the early dawn light inadequately prepares me for the stench of a burning rubbish pile. It is an otherwise gorgeous Kenyan morning. Once more my luggage goes in the trunk of Simon's Toyota but this time I get in on the left.

The regret of departing this exotic country so soon has already left me. Along the route cool Kenyan breezes and choruses of tropical birds revives my excitement. After what seems like an hour of weaving through traffic circles and curvy roads we pass something familiar, the main road to Jomo Kenyata Airport into which I flew just three days ago. We continue on until we reach the outskirts of the city overlooking a valley of tin roofed slums. Not far from the tenements on the opposite side of the road is Nairobi's second international airport, Wilson. It resembles a nondescript office park with one-story mismatched building covered with thatched and tin roofs. Although signs above the doors indicate various aviation offices, there are no airplanes in sight.

Simon turns a corner and stops the car at a private air terminal where I am the only passenger.

"Where's Brian?" I ask assuming until now that he would meet us here.

"He got on a cargo plane very early this morning," Simon answers.

"It will just be you."

A slight uneasiness threatens my excitement but is distracted by Simon.

"You are only allowed 15 kilos of luggage, Mary," he says and casually adds, "You may have to start unpacking."

Nowhere in the IMC literature was a specific weight allowance given.

"Hey, little lady," a new voice breaks in.

A large man with protruding paunch offers a chubby hand. His beady blue eyes rove up and down my body. When he releases my grip I have an urge to swipe my palm on my trousers like a three-year-old child after an unfortunate encounter with a mud puddle.

"Don't worry about unpacking, without that other guy and less cargo, this Beechcraft King Air twin turbo can handle a few more kilos of silky panties," the man says, winking at me with a greasy smile.

"Mary, this is John, your pilot," Simon says, giving me an empathetic look.

"You're going to love this flight," John says with another wink as I board the plane.

Simon laughs and leaves me with a sarcastic, "Enjoy!"

From two seats behind the pilot I watch the relative safety of Nairobi disappear into a small clump of buildings and then into a blur on this endless African plain. Excitement and fear mix in equal parts as Kenya stretches into an endless savanna a thousand feet below the plane.

"Hey Mary, sit next to me. The co-pilot seat is getting cold," John says with a slight whine.

Determined not to make eye contact, I reluctantly move into the seat next to him and buckle my seat belt a little tighter than needed. He hands me a set of headphones with attached microphone.

"You married?" he asks.

"No," I answer, looking straight ahead.

"Boy friend?"

"No."

"Seeing anyone?"

Am I on a humanitarian flight bound for a war zone or trapped in some pathetic singles bar?

"Ever been to Somalia?" he persists.

"No, never have."

"I'm from Lebanon. Had to change my Muslim name because I got so damn tired of people suspecting I was a terrorist."

"Hey, take the yolk," he says on his way to the back of the cargo area.

Never have I been this close to the front windshield of any aircraft and certainly never have my hands gripped the steering mechanism. I push forward on what I assume is the yolk and the plane begins to dive. Fast!

John's belly gyrates in a repulsive rhythm with his boisterous laughter as he takes control, leveling us back to parallel alignment with the ground.

Sweat begins to form in beads on my forehead and one rolls past my temple. My excitement is waning and I will be happy to land anywhere to get away from this lecherous madman.

"You know…I have auto pilot, Mary. Are you a member of the mile-high club?"

Oh God, please get me safely to the land of warlords and automatic weapons.

After what seems like three weeks of flying, the King Air begins its descent just two hours after departure. Below, the Indian Ocean radiates the purest blue waters I have ever seen washing upon a deserted pristine shoreline.

As we approach Mogadishu I notice billows of smoke dotting the horizon. John is solemn during the landing, his demeanor unrecognizable from thirty minutes before. As the plane rolls along the landing strip he slips into a withdrawn concentration, abandoning any notion of amorous pursuits. I'm not sure whether to be relieved or concerned.

With John a safe distance in the back of the twin turbo unloading the cargo, I unbuckle my safety restraints. I am momentarily breathless when the Beechcraft's door opens and a furnace blast of heat jolts me from the lavish luxury of a temperature-controlled environment.

Carefully I balance my luggage as I descend the three narrow steps until my feet meet the parched white sand accumulated on the Mogadishu airport tarmac. Ours is the only plane in the silent surroundings that resemble what was once a major international airport. There are no sounds. No birds. No cars. No voices. I can only hear intermittent bursts of the rat-a-tat-tat of what must be automatic gunfire.

Without warning a Toyota pickup speeds toward me and comes to a stop just before sandwiching me between its bumper and the plane. My eyes lock onto the enormous anti-aircraft weapon mounted in the bed of the truck pointed at my face.

-6-

The Boss

Mogadishu, February 1992

Several men pile out of the Toyota sporting AK-47's slung over their shoulder like accessories meant to complement their kilt-like skirts and castoff designer tee shirts that read, "I am the Boss." One walks toward me, fingering the trigger on his weapon. He abruptly grabs my luggage out from my hand and carries it to the heavily armed vehicle. I'm unsure whether to run after him and attempt to retrieve my meager possessions or freeze and pray they decide to spare my life.

"Nahbaht," John says to the man.

"Subah Wahnoxin," replies one of the kilt-clad Bosses.

The Somalis shout at each other and then effortlessly fall into a rhythmic chant as they pass the cargo from one to another until finally depositing it in their armed vehicle. Their weapons rattle against their sweat-soaked backs until the last item has been transferred.

As quickly as possible the once-flirtatious pilot dots the last "i" and crosses the last "t" on his paperwork and preflights the King Air, also checking the fuselage for bullet holes. When he is satisfied with the level of oil, fuel and tire pressure, he pulls up the stairs, closes the plane's door and leaves me without a word.

The silence grips me. The gun-wielding men have just taken my luggage and they are the only signs of life in the otherwise deserted airport. Except for a distant machine gun firing in random patterns, no sound interrupts my heavy sense of bewilderment.

White dust bursts in clouds around me when the plane speeds past just before its nose lifts into the air. When the dust clears a gaunt man wearing a white tee shirt with marine blue IMC letters across his bony chest makes his way to me. Amid the Bosses' flurried activities I had not noticed him pacing nervously beside a dented off-white pickup truck equipped with mounted anti-aircraft weapon. He approaches, skillfully balancing a cigarette in the corner of his parched lips.

"You're Mary Lightfine I assume," he says with a British accent.

"Andrew Marclin, IMC country director," he adds, extending a slightly trembling hand.

He directs me to the pickup truck and I notice his movements are jerky and he seems afflicted with a perpetual nervousness.

We squeeze into the tight quarters of the cab and the driver starts the engine and begins to pull away before the guard on my right closes the door. Andrew tells me the driver's name is Salat and the Somali guard at the window on my right is Abdi. Casually, Andrew glances back at the enormous anti-aircraft weapon less than a foot from my head. Another Somali man, wearing an amber plaid scarf with colorful fringe that frames his light brown forehead, sits behind the weapon at the ready.

"How do you like our Mad Max?" he asks.

"We call them technicals and don't worry, you'll get used to them."

His cigarette bobs up and down as he talks.

"Okay, I'll take your word for that. Why all the guards?" I ask.

"The fighting between rival clans is erratic. To stay alive, always assume you could be a target or caught in the middle of a spontaneous gun battle. The guards are for our protection. No one with IMC leaves the compound without them. For now, they deter would-be bandits who presume we have valuable cargo since we are coming from the airport," he explains.

"By the way, I suppose my bags and I will end up together again at some point," I say trying to sound casual.

"Oh, yeah, no worries. Did John give you any trouble?" he

asks with a knowing smile.

"How did you know?"

"John does that to all the pretty girls," he replies easily, "But he's harmless."

Fending off the hyper-amorous pilot must have been my first test.

The Mad Max moves through the tall arched iron gates at the entrance to the airport and turns onto a road lined with flat, treeless terrain. Enticing scents drift from the Indian Ocean and move through the cab. Electrical poles stand uselessly at attention; the lines they once held high, now striped away and lying on the ground, like oversize snake carcasses. A downed power line drapes across the damaged fence surrounding the airport. The iron fence is torn open in several places and no longer serves any aesthetic or practical purpose.

Topless white stucco buildings become more plentiful as we move farther away from the airport. Many have gaping holes blown out by bombs and mortar fire and all are covered with random bullet holes.

"What happened to the roofs?" I ask Andrew.

"They were tin, which in wartime becomes a valuable material which is looted and sold on the street to warlords and NGO's to build their own structures."

Bursts of automatic gunfire rattle every couple of minutes.

Andrew looks at me and says, "Welcome to Somalia."

"Does the gunfire ever stop?" I ask.

"No, it's constant. However, because most Somali's are Sunni Muslim they stop to pray toward Mecca several times a day. When the loud speakers send the call to prayer there is a short reprieve. But it is short."

"You'll get used to it," he adds.

"There is no law here. Mogadishu is in a state of true anarchy. The infrastructure, the government, virtually all services are non-existent."

Along the road a Somali man and young boy lead a well-worn donkey harnessed to a cart loaded with sticks on the way into the market. The donkey's tail swishes constantly in a useless attempt to rid itself of dozens of flies circling and landing on its hindquarters. The boy and man bellow an exotic rhythmic chant in time with their steps.

Our Mad Max passes through a lively market. A woman, although leaning forward slightly, walks easily with a large woven water basket in the small of her back seemingly held in place with a strap across her forehead. Her head is covered with a light blue and orange material that frames her beautiful tawny face. Another carries an infant in a papoose of faded floral fabric wrapped across her chest. Suspended from her right hand is a yellow plaid thermos, like the one I carried to kindergarten. Small fires burn inside tiny shacks with walls made of sticks. A man wearing a long piece of cloth wrapped around his waist like a skirt sits inside stirring something in a small pot over a fire. Sparks jumping from the fire narrowly miss his toes which are hanging over the edge of his flip flops made from discarded tires. Another man stops to fill a thermos with the liquid from the pot. An aromatic earthy smell occasionally passes through the cab of our truck.

Toyota trucks, sedans and Landrovers weave dangerously fast between crowds of people, animals, and donkey carts. Almost all of the pickups have the same type of automatic weapons mounted in the truck bed and are heavy with armed men. The men have head coverings ranging from colorful fringed cloth to bath towels to shoeboxes. One man walks proudly through the market firmly dictating something to his colleague that I do not understand. His automatic weapon is strapped loosely to his chest and he has a fuzzy toilet seat cover mounted on his head.

The buildings are all large stucco fortresses adorned with hanging bougainvilleas heavy with deep purple and brilliant pink blossoms, a welcome pageant of color after the desert conditions I've seen since I landed. A young child walks under large baskets of flowers that hang over a foul-smelling pile of rubbish. He hits a small rock along the sand with a stick, sending it skidding forward two to three feet where it lands inches from a lifeless human hand. A corpse lies among the rubbish, its skin shriveling in the merciless sun. The child casually kicks the decomposing hand away from his rock and continues his game. Even in the searing heat inside the crowded truck I shiver slightly. None of my companions show any reaction.

Our driver presses the horn, sending two high-pitched signals to the men at the white fortress just ahead. Two guards peer through the small peephole in the door and seconds later open the ominous Iron Gate. We speed inside past a large sign. Scrolled across it are three hand painted letters: I M C.

The gate quickly swings closed like the drawbridge of a castle as if protecting from an approaching enemy. We enter the courtyard and park between the house and the twelve-foot stucco wall surrounding the IMC "fortress." Flowering shrubs climb the walls, stopping short of the jagged broken glass and coiled barbed wire on top around the entire perimeter. The elaborate surroundings surprise me. Palms and other tropical plants garnish the courtyard that separates two large houses, each with verandas providing panoramic views of the city. I pass under a grand arched doorway and step onto a marble floor.

I notice four or five Somalis moving briskly about. One takes my bags somewhere into the house.

"Come this way, Mary," Andrew directs.

We walk through another arched doorway into a living room area with towering twelve-foot ceilings, more marble floors and ornately carved Italian furniture.

Andrew indicates a red winged-back loveseat adorned with finely embroidered cushions.

I sit and cannot contain my confusion any longer.

"Andrew, the contrast between this compound and outside its walls is unbelievable. Frankly, it disturbs me a little."

"Okay, fair enough. Let me explain. This was once a villa owned by a well-to-do Italian family. Before the civil war, Mogadishu was a vacation playground for wealthy Europeans. When civil war erupted they fled, abandoning these buildings. At that time a Somali man commandeered the property for himself and IMC rents the compound from him."

His hands shake continuously as he hastily takes a last drag from his cigarette, grinds it into an ashtray beside a dozen tiny smashed butts that look like miniature accordions. He wastes no time lighting the next one. Nervously he steals glances from side to side while we talk as if he is waiting for someone to walk through the doorway.

"Do you know much about Somalia?" he asks as he drags desperately on his cigarette.

Before today I was confident my IMC information packet and my own extensive travel experience had sufficiently prepared me for any new cultural situation. However, all of that seems far removed from what I really need to know. I am hungry to learn more and I'm guessing that my survival here will depend on it.

"Not much," I reply honestly.

Just then a tall, slim man with deep brown eyes and light brown skin glides into the room.

"Pardon, I must interrupt," he says with an exotic Somali accent.

"Mary, this is Ahmed, our logistician," Andrew says.

He is tall and professional looking in a white collared shirt and pressed trousers. Ahmed speaks with a smooth, confident manner.

"Very nice to meet you, Ahmed," I say.

Ahmed instills confidence and calm and I almost wish he was the one giving the briefing.

"I must attend to other duties," Ahmed replies, "but first I want to get you familiar with the house. As you can see, there are two houses in the compound. Your room is in the one with the red brick," he points to the two-story building behind me.

"Your room is on the top floor, third door from the bathroom. Meals are served on the first level of the same building where you'll be sleeping. This compound is powered with a generator and water is stored in a large container on the roof."

A balding, overweight Somali man saunters in behind Ahmed.

"This is Aweis, Chief of the house staff. He is responsible for making sure the rooms are cleaned and for assigning places for people to sleep." Ahmed informs me.

"Hello... Aweis," I say, struggling with the unfamiliar names.

Aweis's shifty eyes do not instill the same sense of safety and calm as does Ahmed. I make a mental note to navigate carefully around him.

"Nahbaht," he says. I recognize this as the same greeting used by John the lecherous pilot.

"I will leave you now to finish your briefing. Thank you. I will see you again later," Ahmed says as he and Aweis leave me with Andrew.

They pass through the arched doorway as Andrew repeats his cigarette ritual—drag, grind, replace.

He begins speaking as he lights and puffs his new cigarette.

"Okay, Somalia. (puff) Yeah. (puff) Okay." His hand shakes and he has to concentrate to light the end of his cigarette. Andrew continues to look around as if he is watching for someone. After lighting up he drops the opaque yellow lighter into his pocket.

I wait. He continues.

"I'll give you some background before you go to the hospital. By the end of the thirteenth-century Somalia was inhabited by Islamic nomadic traders traveling from the ports along the east coast into Kenya and Ethiopia. Local tribes were pushed southwards where farming communities developed. Currently there are three ethnic groups in Somalia: Somali, Bantu and Arabs. And then there are hundreds of clans. The language is primarily Somali, Arabic, Italian, and English. But most speak Somali or a local tribal language."

"What brought the country to the devastation it is in today?" I ask.

"In 1991 Siad Barre's presidency was overthrown and he fled the country. Tribes from the north, in a region called Somaliland, separated from southern Somalia."

Andrew shifts his position on the loveseat and always looks ready to jump to his feet. I try not letting his nervous demeanor distract me from what he is saying.

"Throughout the rest of Somali," he continues, "politically aligned fighters with common ancestry known as clans began vying for a stronghold as the country plunged into a state of anarchy."

"Is there any formal military authority?" I ask.

"No. After 1991 any man with enough money and charisma to rally clan supporters could declare himself a warlord and anyone with a weapon has become a fighter. Today there are four principal warlords driving the civil war. One is Ali Mahdi Mohamed who, at times, aligns himself with another warlord, Osman Ali Otto...who happens to be our neighbor."

He points over my head in the direction of Otto's compound.

"Mohamed Farah Aideed is another warlord who has given financial support to Otto, and then there's General Morgan who is related to Siad Barre—the ousted president. Somalia is a free-for-all. A state of true anarchy. Anyone is a target, including humanitarian workers."

A primal voice inside pleads with me to walk directly out of this God-forsaken land.

"Oh, I'm sorry," a hesitant voice comes from behind me.

Andrew stands straight up like a freed Jack-in-the-Box.

I whip around to see what has caused such a dramatic reaction from Andrew.

A woman in her mid-forties stands in the doorway with her hand on her chest and somberly repeats, "I'm sorry."

"Mary, this is Ann," he says, dragging on his toxic pacifier. "She will take you to the hospital for a tour."

Andrew moves closer to her and seems to not know where to put his hands. He moves them from his pockets to his back and finally crosses them in front of his diminutive waist.

"Hello, Ann," I say extending my hand in greeting.

She reaches for it without moving closer, slightly touching my hand and shaking only my fingertips.

"Oh, uh, I'm sorry, hello Mary," she says, quickly releasing my fingers. Her eyes never meet mine but stay focused on the floor throughout our introduction.

Ann is the essence of mousy. Graying roots stop about a half inch from her center part and fine, wispy black hair falls around her aging face. Her jowls hang around her narrow lips like a bloodhound and her nose curves into a hook like a witch in a children's fairy tale.

These people are not instilling confidence. I need some direction.

"Andrew, what exactly will my nursing duties be at …what is the name of the hospital?" I ask.

"Digfer," they say in unison.

"I'm sorry," Ann says with a slight glance in Andrew's direction.

"Your job is to do whatever you can at the hospital," he answers.

Turning to Ann and finishing his last drag on his cigarette he says, "Ann, get Jackson and show Mary around Digfer."

Obediently, she and I start in the direction of the vehicles.

Ann tells me on the way that Jackson is the Somali guard with big black rimmed sun glasses. He was hired to provide protection during the commute and while we work inside the hospital.

I decide I'm not ready to know why we need protection inside the hospital.

In the Land Cruiser Ann and I are sandwiched in the middle back seat between two Somalis sitting by opposite windows. The guards balance their well-used assault rifles between their legs, barrels pointing toward the ceiling. Jackson sits on my right. He wears faded yellow trousers with a green stripped long sleeve dress shirt and well worn but shiny black leather shoes. His soft black curls bounce slightly under his crocheted turquoise novelty hat as we navigate the rugged streets. With his index finger he gently traces the round opening at the tip of his weapon. He gazes out the window and his thoughts seem to take him far from the inside of this armed utility vehicle. His faraway ponderings give me a sense of comfort.

"How long have you been in Somalia, Ann?" I ask, trying to find a way to connect.

"Oh, I'm sorry. Umm, one month," she answers.

We travel back through the market, stopping and starting through the maze of human, animal and automotive traffic. All seem to go in one general direction, but there are no traffic laws to obey and no police to enforce order.

An institutional brick building with white trim bustles with activity just ahead. Cars and people come and go from its entrance. A man pulls a wooden cart toward the entrance. Legs dangle lifelessly from the back and I can see the head and torso are soaked in blood.

"Is this Digfer?" I ask.

"Ha," replies the man next to Ann.

He lifts his weapon and points out the window.

"Ha. This Digfer."

Our vehicle drives through the gates past a large billboard that reads "Digfer Isbataalka." Next to it is a white sign with a red slash through a circular graphic of guns, grenades and tanks and other war related items.

"That's a first," I say to myself.

When the Land Cruiser stops, Jackson gets out to accompany Ann and me inside the hospital while the other guards stay behind to protect the vehicle.

Gaping holes in Digfer's walls reveal no structure is sacred from the onslaught of war. The four-story building weakly supports crumbling balconies covered in mold and loaded down with people of all ages. It looks more like tenement housing than a health care facility.

Barely out of the car, several Somalis approach, hands outstretched and all asking, "Magacaa?"

"What are they saying?" I ask Ann while shaking their hands as fast as possible.

"I'm sorry; they are asking your name."

I repeat my name a few times, satisfying the crowd enough to move on.

Inside the doors a stench, so unbearable it nearly knocks my breath away. It is a combination of diesel fuel, blood, urine, feces, smoke and dominating them all—rotting flesh.

"Why do I smell diesel fuel?" I ask Ann.

"Oh, it is used to clean the floors, it kills bugs," Ann says as if this is routine hospital procedure.

Every window has been blown out and shards of glass make geometric designs around the frame like some bizarre art exhibition. Flies easily make their home around every fetid wound on the countless injured bodies lining the halls. Patients lie on pieces of stained cardboard and torn grass mats. Some sleep, others wait to die.

A boy of about fourteen lies directly on the concrete. Like a landing strip at JFK, the bloody stump of his amputated leg hosts flies that circle, land, and take off again. His glazed stare pierces through me.

"Are there no beds for patients like this?" I ask Ann.

"There are forty beds for approximately seven hundred patients. I'm sorry; it could be more or less because there is no way to keep track of them. Most of the ill or injured Somalis sleep directly on the concrete floor, like this boy. When the fighting began almost everything of value was either looted or destroyed, including beds."

"Ann, the urine and feces smell is so strong. What about the plumbing?" I ask growing dizzy from the stench.

"There are no functioning toilets or sinks for the patients. I'm sorry, no waste is collected and no regular health care staff to attend to these things," Ann replies.

A man walks by stepping over maimed bodies on his way

down the hall. Nonchalantly he carries an automatic weapon and tucks a large machete in the waist of his wrap skirt. He wears the now familiar "I'm the Boss" tee shirt and carries an automatic weapon. This man is one of many who ignore the sign outside the hospital warning to leave weapons outside.

We enter an open area housing scattered wooden tables covered with green plastic tarps. Dust and flies move easily through the blown out windows, which provide the only source of light. "This must be the ER," I say.

"I'm sorry; it is known as Casualty," Ann reports.

Paint has long worn away from the walls and large sections of plaster are cracked and falling out. A man tightly holds the wrists of an adolescent boy who lies on the floor next to the damaged wall. From his waist to his calves his mangled flesh is a collage of bone fragments, torn muscle and slivers of debris. The boy stares up at me but makes no sounds in reaction to the undeniable pain he endures as the doctor peels away layers of charred skin.

"I'm sorry, Dr. Abass; this is Mary, a nurse from the U.S. just arrived at IMC," Ann says introducing me to the first doctor I have seen in the hospital. Dr. Abass is about five feet five inches tall and not much heavier than my one hundred and eighteen pounds. His dark brown skin glistens slightly from perspiration and he has a jolly, round face. Dr. Abass also has two of the warmest brown eyes I have ever seen. I like him instantly.

He gently pulls dead flesh away from a shard of glass lodged in the boy's groin and looks up at me with a gentle smile, then quickly focuses again on his patient.

"Hello, Mary," Dr. Abass says with a cute Somali accent.

"Taktar, Taktar!" a voice calls across the room.

We all look in the direction of the call. Several armed Somalis shout orders as they carry an unconscious man who bleeds profusely from the mass of lacerated muscles and mangled tissue hanging where his legs have been blasted away from his body. He will likely bleed to death.

Without a word to me, Ann rushes to the scene. Dr. Abass releases a mild sigh of frustration and turns to me.

"You have just arrived, but since Ann left I must leave you with this patient," Dr. Abass says adding, "You should have everything you need here."

My mind races, what about scrubbing first? What about a mask and a hundred other medical necessities I have taken for granted in sixteen years of emergency nursing?

But he is gone before I can say anything. When I squat at the feet of the patient, my toes stick out from the tops of my red flip-flops and brush against his motionless foot. Splayed on the floor around his feet is a metal burn tray, saline, gloves and the small forceps Dr. Abass laid on a piece of gauze stuck to the floor by a pool of congealed blood. Two sizes too big, the gloves slide easily over my hands. Dr. Abass's assistant squats next to the patient's head and continues to wrap his long, black fingers around the patient's wrists and his lean body holds the same squatting position.

I look directly into the assistant's trusting black eyes and try to ask his name.

"Ma-ga-ah" I say trying out my newly learned Somali.

He looks at me inquisitively.

Maybe he thinks I'm trying to order some kind of medicine. I focus back on our patient hoping to gain his confidence in my medical ability if not my language.

With a steady hand I retrieve the forceps and begin pulling away bits of mangled flesh and debris. A large explosion outside the hospital sends chunks of plaster flying from the walls and ceiling and landing very close to the open wound where I have just removed a fragment of splintered bone. Jackson leans against a door frame several feet away thoughtfully watching how I handle this first test.

Ann and Dr. Abass return.

"Thank you, Mary. Good job. I will continue now and you can go with Ann," he says with genuine appreciation.

My legs are numb and tingling from squatting in the same position.

"You're welcome," I say a little dazed.

Ann and I step away from them and I glance back to see that Jackson is following. Walking toward us he gives me a slight, but approving nod.

"What happened with the patient you and Dr. Abass went to help?" I ask Ann.

"I'm sorry, Mary, he's finished," Ann responds quietly.

"What does 'finished' mean?" I inquire.

Ann appears to be deep in thought and does not respond.

Roaches scurry across our path as we navigate the over-crowded halls of Digfer Isbataalka filled with dozens of wounded Somalis. Within minutes of entering this hallway screams erupt and children, many barefoot and naked from the waist down, run to cling to their caretakers. Their terror escalates as we approach and they cry, "Gallo! Gallo!" Jackson bursts out in a display of laughter I had not thought possible of this quiet man. Although relieved to see he has a sense of humor, his jocular reaction to the terror apparent in their reaction to him irritates me. Ann wrings her hands and pats several people, children and adults, on the head and speaks to them in patronizing tones.

"Jackson, why are you laughing when you have terrified these children?"

"Mary, it is you they fear. They are screaming because of you," he says between his insistent laughter.

"What? Why?" I say not understanding how this could be.

"Because you are white and they think you are something evil," he says making a sweeping motion over his face. Their mothers tell them stories about white creatures like you walking in the darkness looking for small children to eat."

"Oh, my God," I say amazed.

I lean down next to a half naked girl who has folded her mother's colorful dress around her. Tears well and stream down her cocoa colored checks and she intensifies the volume of her screaming.

Parents and observers laugh boisterously in unison with the children's piercing screams. The hallway has turned hysterical. It has become impossible to convince the children I am not interested in making a meal out them.

"Let's go," says Ann.

The scene may be funny one day but now I am glad to leave.

Ann leads us through a door that leads outside the hospital and points up to the balconies overhead. They are laden with people, many working over small cooking fires.

"Why are they cooking?" I ask.

"Oh, I'm sorry. They are the family of a patient. They stay in the hospital to care for their sick or injured relative and prepare all their meals," she says.

A handful of bloodied rags sail past us onto one of the many piles of trash strewn around the ground under the balcony. As we duck under a thorny acacia tree, a wave of bodily fluid splashes Ann when a woman above us empties a white enameled pan over the railing of her balcony. As I step back to avoid a splash, my foot slides out of my flip-flop and lands near a human foot protruding from a mound of rotting debris. Cows and goats rummage and nibble their way through the waste piles.

"These aren't by any chance the same animals we'll eat for dinner, are they?" I ask fearing the answer.

"I'm sorry, a lot of people become vegetarians when they arrive," Ann replies.

Leaving the supposed safety of the thorn tree we make our way to Digfer's main entrance. On the steps outside this entrance, lies the limp body of a middle-aged man face up on a piece of bloody paper. A ragged string is tied around his two big toes. I check for a pulse but my hand meets a cold, stiff neck. Flies crawl along his black curled eyelashes as his lifeless eyes stare blankly toward the sky.

I squat next to him for a moment and feel for a pulse. I look over towards Ann. "Why is a dead man lying on the doorstep," I inquire. "Wouldn't the emergency—uh, the Casualty be the more appropriate place for a body?"

"Oh, yes, well, if they appear comatose their families leave them here so we can care for them if they live or bury them if they don't," Ann replies. "I guess they think Casualty is only for the wounded," Ann adds.

"Oh, and Mary, I'm sorry. When someone dies in Somalia we just say, 'he's finished' when he or she passes on."

"Why?" I ask.

"The Somalis believe in Inshallah; if God wills it. They believe only Allah can decide if someone will die and declaring someone dead takes authority from Allah," she explains then adds, "I'm sorry, most Somalis cannot afford to buy a shroud nor do they have a shovel. IMC pays for someone to wash, wrap and bury the bodies in the traditional manner, before sunset.

"According to their custom a hole is dug to specific dimensions, the body is placed inside and covered with sticks so it will be touched by as little dirt as possible."

She turns slightly pointing toward a sand covered area just beyond the hospital.

"See those sticks over there in the sand," she continues.

"Those are grave markers. The taller ones mark the head and the short one is placed at the feet to indicate where the next body can be placed."

I consider the implications of the need for efficient use of space in this humble cemetery.

Insects continue to explore the crevices on the man's face. We can do nothing, however, and must abandon the body to the work of the Somali gravediggers.

Our guards lean against the IMC Land Cruiser with blood-shot eyes and glazed expressions. Putting my life in the hands of these men would have alarmed me this morning, but as we pass the sandy field packed with crudely marked graves it hardly seems noteworthy.

Throughout our trip home I am lost in thought. Suddenly I'm jolted back to reality by the shrill blast of a horn. The tall iron gates open. Within minutes we are safely inside the compound of IMC once more.

The smell of cooking meat awakens my hunger and I am glad to sit for a much needed meal. The long rectangular table is covered with a pink and white floral vinyl tablecloth. Expatriates begin to gather around it talking and laughing with each other in familiar tones and gestures. I introduce myself and receive cordial welcomes but I still feel very alone and out of place.

"Mary, how the hell are you?" a voice calls from the doorway.

Brian is strutting his way to the table with the others. I am so relieved to see someone familiar that every impulse in me wants to stand and hug him. However, I restrain myself remembering his unspoken rule about touching.

"I'm just great," I say with feigned confidence.

A fiery redhead glides to the table looking beautiful and sure of herself in a baggy IMC tee shirt, vibrant Indian wrap skirt and green flip-flops.

She is speaking fluent French with a handsome man sporting a closely cropped black beard and mustache. He has a foreign look but his native culture is indistinguishable although his face is familiar to me. They sit across the table and continue their conversation. She has a bubbly magnetism about her.

Thankfully, Brian sits next to me as the food is served.

"Just back from your tour?" Brian asks.

"Yeah, not like any hospital I've ever worked in."

"No shit," he agrees.

The house staff quickly fills the table with steaming bowls of pasta and meatballs, a large plate of chicken, yellow tins of greasy Blue Band margarine, instant coffee, and Nido whole milk powder.

The meatballs, although fully cooked, have the slimy texture of raw hamburger. Nagging images of goats grazing in rubbish piles deters me from the meat. I decide to try the chicken and find, although flavorful, chewing it is like grinding a piece of leather between my teeth.

The beautiful red haired woman introduces herself from across the table.

"Hi, I'm Donna. It's good to have you. We need lots of help," she says with an inviting smile and warm green eyes.

"Thank you. I'm Mary. It's good to meet you," I say, struggling with a leg of leathery chicken.

Giving up, I place the inedible part back on my plate.

"Are you American?" I ask her, surprised that she has an American accent without any hint of French.

"My father is American and my mother French so I grew up bilingual," she answers.

"Chicken a bit tough for you, Mary?" the slightly familiar man asks.

The table bursts into laughter. I join in laughing at my failed attempt at decorum.

"A bit," I reply, with a mouthful of leathery chicken.

"We call it bicycle chicken because it must have been a tough bird that spent its life in perpetual exercise," he explains.

"I'm Carlos Mavroleon."

"What kind of work do you do at the hospital?" I ask.

"Irritate the hell out of the health care staff with too many questions," he replies dryly.

"Here, here!" Donna says raising her glass.

"I'm a news correspondent with ABC and Nightline," he says.

"Chris and Enrique are freelance journalists," he continues pointing to two other men at the table.

"The media folks hang out with the various NGO's here in constant pursuit of their story," Andrew tells me.

Ann sits next to Andrew, who is reaching over his plate cutting his bicycle chicken into small bite-size pieces.

"Ann, please pass me the meatballs," Brian asks.

She drops her utensils onto her plate. "I'm sorry," Ann murmurs.

Although I have known Ann less than 24 hours I must have heard her apologize over a hundred times. So far I have patiently ignored her mea culpas.

"Ann, God damn it, if you run over my dog you can say 'I'm sorry' but otherwise I don't want to fucking hear it out of your mouth again," Brian exclaims. I am not surprised he has quickly reached his threshold of tolerance.

"I'm sorry," Ann replies.

Brian glares at her, muttering various obscenities under his breath.

The brief but awkward silence is interrupted as Donna begins to tell Carlos about a clan skirmish in the hospital today that involved one of the doctors being held at gunpoint. They speak in such a casual manner about the violence around them as Donna flips her thick red tresses back over her shoulder. I feel out of place and not sure what to believe. Perhaps they are just showing off a little for the new people.

"Carlos, would you mind explaining to Mary and Brian the significance of clans in Somalia?" Andrew asks, noticing my befuddled expression. "I skipped that part during their briefing today."

Carlos's deep, intelligent eyes have no trouble holding the gaze of all the women at the table—and maybe even some of the men. His features are chiseled and he has an exotic look that is hard to pinpoint. His frame is slight but muscular and thick black hair rolls on his head like ripples in a pond.

"Certainly," he replies with a lilting accent I can't identify.

"It is a confusing but ancient part of Somali culture and heritage. If you, Mary, were native to Mogadishu, all your family would be in the same clan. Suppose that Brian is also a native Somali but from another clan. If the two of you marry, Mary becomes a part of Brian's clan and if you have a daughter she might also marry into another clan. The further your family line gets away from Mary's original clan of her birth, the more likely a new kind of sub-clan will branch off. Descendents in the sub-clans are more closely related to each other than they are to the main clans. The clans will continue to subdivide as families grow until there are several main clans and hundreds of distant relatives who form the sub-clans.

"After the dictator Said Barre was overthrown, his former general, Aideed, became the primary political figure with several family-based factions fighting with him for power against other warlords. Alliances shifted constantly. There are literally hundreds of clans and sub clans. As for the warlords they might stand alone or occasionally team up with other warlords, causing further confusion for everyone."

He begins to draw a diagram to illustrate the eternal maze of the clan culture in Somalia. However, taking in more information is not possible at this point, so I only absorb bits and pieces while pretending to be listening.

Finally Aweis shows me to my room. My bags are sitting on the earth tone marble floor beside a twin bed that is covered with a thin floral sheet. The bed sits adjacent to a large picture window covered only by a gauzy fabric allowing for very little privacy from the street below. Although I am mentally and physically spent I take a few minutes to unpack my belongings into the armoire. Rat droppings inside the drawers tell me I will not be alone in this room.

I pull out the notebook paper and pens from my backpack and begin to write a letter to Dad hoping this will help me unwind from the day.

Dear Dad,

Arrived today in Mog (Mogadishu), as they say here, and got a tour of the compound and hospital in this war torn city. Everything is strange to me and I am overwhelmed by how much I have to learn. The children think I am a vicious monster out for their blood. Nothing in the hospital runs in a familiar manner. Patients lay on the filthy concrete floor with gaping wounds, dead bodies are deposited at the front door and trash is regularly thrown to the ground outside the hospital where goats and cows feast on all manner of waste. We turn around and eat those animals for dinner. Even with almost two decades of experience

I am afraid in many ways I will have to start over. Everyone else is so familiar with each other and casual about the madness of war that I fear not being able to fit in.

You have always been the inspiring humanitarian in my life and I hope your example will give me courage to face the overwhelming challenges throughout the coming year.

I'll write again when possible but I cannot call because there is no regular phone system in Somalia and the satellite phone—at eleven dollars a minute—is for emergencies only. Don't hold your breath between letters because they tell me it could take a month or more to reach the States.

I love you, Dad.

Mare

I place the letter on the nightstand and walk across the room to turn off the bare light bulb that emits an oppressive glare. Sleep does not come easily. I want to wake up from this nightmare and be in my own bed in the States, but the burst of gunfire outside my window keeps me in the reality I have chosen. On the floor some airplane peanuts spill out of my backpack. I pick one up and roll it in my hand and try to let the familiar ritual lull me to a place of comfort.

-7-

Silky Lingerie

Mogadishu, Somalia February 1992

A haunting chant beckons the sun like a man calling for his lost child. Through the gauze window covering, the bluing sky is skirted by a brilliant pink dawn. Chanting drifts from a rooftop several buildings away where a Somali Muslim calls the faithful to Morning Prayer over a microphone that makes the sacred petitions sound like they travel through a tin can.

After a sleepless night, I will my body into an upright position. My feet hit the cold marble floor crunching several peanuts on my way to the tee shirt and scrubs housed in the aging armoire. A nagging fear taps me on the shoulder, insistently questioning whether I have made an enormous mistake coming here. My best answer is to keep moving—elude this stubborn doubt with a full day doing what I know how to do.

Carlos, Donna, Ann, and I climb into the heavily armed IMC Land cruiser. Brian and two other expatriates wait for the next ride. I had not met them yesterday but have learned that the tall, thin blonde nurse with kind, blue soulful eyes is Lindsey from Los Angeles. The other slightly overweight physician sporting slip on sandals with his white scrubs tucked into his socks is called Oscar. As we pull away, the three left behind pile into another armed vehicle.

Somali guards, stationed at every window, balance automatic weapons positioned between their legs, barrels pointed toward the ceiling. Jackson sits between the open window and me, shifting the barrel of his weapon back and forth with his knees.

Donna twists her long fiery hair into a ponytail as she and Carlos carry on an engrossing discussion in French. Ann, cramped in the back, remains silent for the duration.

"Good morning Jackson," I say hoping to start some interaction.

Jackson nods and gives me a boyish grin.

Even at 8:30 in the morning the heat is an unrelenting blanket of thick, moist air. Mogadishu, situated in close proximity to both the equator and the Indian Ocean, bakes like a steamy sauna under a cloudless sky.

Cindy Lauper whines through the speakers. Our driver taps his fingers casually on the steering wheel as he navigates through the market place outside the IMC compound. Merchants lay their wares on grass mats. Somali soldiers as young as twelve carry AK-47's strapped to their bony shoulders. Their guns extend over their heads and bob sloppily against their thighs. Along the road a woman wearing a tattered floral toga with one shoulder exposed, sits on a straw mat intently focused on bundling plants resembling wilted tea leaves with short stalks. A small girl, no more than five, holds the verdant tops in place as the woman binds a cluster of foliage.

Jackson startles me when he bursts an order to the driver and vigorously points toward the woman.

"Khat! Khat!" he shouts.

The driver turns abruptly toward the woman. He slows our vehicle and in one motion he hands the child several Somali shillings and grabs a bundle of khat in the other. The wilted plants are dispersed among the guards and each begins chewing the tender leaves and stalks like Chiclets.

"Somali cup of Joe," says Donna, flashing her pearly whites into perky smile.

"What do you mean?" I ask.

Carlos fields the question.

"Khat is an evergreen plant grown in Kenya and imported here daily. It gives the chewer a buzz and glassy eyes. Donna calls it 'Somali cup of Joe' because it produces a stimulant effect—sort of like drinking maybe ten cups of expresso. It's very common in Mog."

I am wondering how safe it is for me to be packed in a large moving vehicle sandwiched between several men with automatic weapons getting buzzed.

The Land Cruiser glides through the gates of Digfer. We pass two Somali men entering the hospital compound with automatic weapons casually slung over their shoulders in plain sight of the red and white, no guns sign with a diagonal slash through all the weapons that aren't allowed. The second IMC vehicle pulls up just behind us.

Jackson waits for Brian, Lindsey and Oscar to join us, and then accompanies our group into the main hospital entrance. He chuckles to himself when two small children whimper and hide behind the long skirts of their caregivers. I try to look as harmless as I can but they respond by pointing at me, shouting, "Gallo! Gallo!"

My breath catches in my throat and I fight the urge to gag when the stench hits me like a runaway train. If ever a smell could drop a person to their knees it is the reek of rotting flesh.

Patients and their families sit on the bare concrete floor along the corridor. On our way to Casualty dozens of dark, vacant eyes follow our approach. A toddler lies listlessly in his mother's lap as she fans the persistent flies that circle the bloody bandages wrapped around the child's head. Grasping my hand to be assured of my attention, she then points to the water bottle hanging from my scrub pants and then to her throat.

"Biyo. Biyo," she says with eyes piercing into mine.

"What is she saying?" I ask Lindsey.

"She is asking for water. But we cannot give them drink or food. If we start feeding patients we soon become known as a hunger relief center and will attract hoards of folks who are not even sick. That's not what we are here for; several other organizations are doing that. Also, you have to keep yourself healthy,"

"Too risky to share water I suppose," stating what I already knew.

I look at my Eddie Bauer keychain thermometer. It reads 100°F.

But I have to summon the Iron Nurse and walk past the thirsty woman without acknowledging her request.

As we turn the corner I notice that Oscar is gone and Ann has fallen behind. She slips something out of her pocket and looks quickly in our direction before giving it to a child who eagerly places the object into her mouth.

"Lindsey, I'm sorry, will you get Mary started in the Casualty today?" Ann asks when she catches up to us. It's hard to tell whether or not she wanted me to see her give the food.

"Let's go Mary," Lindsey says without acknowledging Ann.

In one of Casualty's three rooms a loose chunk of green painted plaster falls from the wall and splatters onto the stained concrete floor dotted with pools of congealed blood. Lying prone across the exam table, a blast victim's back is splayed open on one side. A ten-inch flap of skin, peeled away from his shoulder to his spine, resembles a large steak. His breathing is labored. No less than twenty flies hover, land and linger on his mutilated flesh. Calloused heels hang slightly off the end of the wood examining table covered with green heavy duty plastic. His pleading eyes meet mine.

"I don't normally work in Casualty," Lindsey remarks as she approaches the wounded man. "I took over from Ann in the minor care area over there in the next room. This is Donna's unit but she's in the pharmacy right now."

With smooth, confident motions Lindsey attaches an IV bag shaped like an upside down plastic milk carton and picks up a fresh needle to vent the bag.

"Why did you poke the bag with that needle?" I ask Lindsey.

"These bags are poorly made. I've found that they will collapse if I don't vent them first."

So much to learn.

We move to another patient and I instinctively begin looking for a chart containing medical records.

"How long have you been a nurse, Lindsey?" I ask.

"I became a nurse in 1983. My first assignment was a Navajo Indian reservation in Arizona," she says. "If you are looking for a patient chart you won't find one. Medical records are the responsibility of the patient here."

She pulls a 4x5-inch white card stock form from her pocket and says, "Each patient is given a card like this one. The card is in English and French. There are several spaces for name address, age, and birth date.

"Look at this," she points to an outline of the human body.

"This is where we indicate where the problem is. Little boxes can be marked for observations and symptoms like fever, bloody diarrhea, level of consciousness, and skin turgor."

"Why is this one all scribbled up with treatment orders written and then crossed out and rewritten for essentially the same thing?" I ask.

"Oh, um...well, Ann changed my orders, and this is not the first time either. It really bothers me but I'm not sure what to do about it right now," Lindsey whispers.

I decide to file that information away for later and change the subject. "Why are the patient cards in English and French?" I inquire.

"Because we borrowed them from MSF, you know... Medecins Sans Frontiers, Doctors Without Borders. They're based in Paris and have more experience than IMC, so we're using their cards. MSF has a compound in Mog not too far from IMC, really gorgeous guys. I'm engaged, but you might be interested," she adds with a wink.

"I'll keep that in mind. How long have you been in Mogadishu, uh Mog?" I say clumsily, feeling intimidated in spite of having eight years more nursing experience.

Lindsey's tall slim frame glides easily to the next patient who gazes up absently at us as we approach. The young man lies quietly, only a thin straw mat between his mangled chest and the concrete floor. His dark skin has paled considerably from pain and blood loss. His massive gun shot wound was a silver dollar sized hole just below his left collar bone.

Blood soaks his light blue shirt. His undernourished mother squats beside him fanning away dozens of flies from his face with a straw fan attached to a stick like a flag. As I push half a dozen flies from my own lips I make a mental note to find a fan for myself.

Lindsey grabs scissors from her pocket. In one quick motion she snips a hole in the fabric and tears his clothing, expertly revealing the flesh and rib fragments torn away from his chest.

"I've been in Mog about a month," she replies as her skilled hands move quickly to control bleeding and equalize the thoracic pressure.

"I'll grab some saline and dressings," I offer, trying to keep my insecurity at bay.

Like a bellman delivering room service, a stately Somali woman wheels a two-shelf stainless steel cart carrying medical supplies toward us.

"Amina, cali, cali!" Lindsey beckons in search of her Somali assistant.

The cart carries an array of glass bottles; plastic IV bags with only one inch of tubing protruding from the drip chamber; gauze, cotton, and stainless steel cylinders filled with instruments several flies use as perches. No gloves in sight. Amina approaches wearing an ankle-length dirac covered with broad stripes. Her multicolored, fringed hijab covered a plum and white cotton gabsar. She hands me forceps, gauze and an amber-colored soapy antiseptic solution labeled Savlon.

"Mary, this is Amina, one of the Somali...nurses," Lindsey introduces.

"Subah wahnoxin," I respond as I smile at my Somali colleague.

"Amina, can you send Oscar or any surgeon over here to see this patient; this man needs a chest tube right away," Lindsey pleads.

Amina gives a slight acknowledgement before strolling slowly away.

I hand her the supplies and complain, "Lindsey, I didn't get any gloves."

"We don't use them for cleaning wounds," she assures me.

"Just pour the saline and Savlon around the wound. I'll clean using the forceps and gauze. It saves on gloves, which are already in short supply. Every little bit counts."

Flies scatter as I pour solutions into the flesh surrounding the opening on this stoic man's chest.

As she cleans the area Lindsey speaks in hushed tones.

"Amina is not a college educated nurse that we can verify. For now she is an IMC nurse assistant but she has attitude because it's rumored that her uncle is a powerful warlord who agrees to keep the fighting away from the hospital. So we call her a 'nurse' to keep her ego satisfied but she only performs mechanical tasks like dressing changes. Some Somalis produce forged documents claiming they graduated from nursing school, so it's hard to tell who is qualified."

The patient's mother fans the flies away as we work to stabilize the wound in his frail chest, now rising and falling with increased difficulty.

"Does IMC give them a salary?" I ask.

"No. IMC cannot pay the Somali staff but IMC is working with the World Food Program to give them food in return for their work. For now, they get some sense of security and the promise of retroactive payment."

As we finish with the patient Lindsey looks directly into his eyes and gently pats his arm, then she looks directly at me and begins another lesson. "Mary, I wish we could do more for this man, but neither of us are allowed to put in chest tubes because the Somalis know we are not doctors. So he will just have to wait like all the other critical patients. There just aren't enough doctors to help everyone here. It breaks my heart." She looks up and watches Amina move into the patient area next to Casualty.

She leans toward me and whispers, "Many of the Somali staff steal supplies and turn around and sell them in the market just outside the hospital. Some have no other way to get money for food."

From the next room someone yells, "Lindsey, I need a fucking nurse in here!"

"Must be Brian," I say.

"Gosh, he's abrupt," she says as she leaves.

"Yeah, but I think he's a marshmallow underneath it all."

Somehow she manages a warm smile and a skeptical expression.

I am left standing alone in the chaos of dozens of patients to attend, devoid of adequate war-trauma training and with no specific job description. Thousands of miles away from anything familiar, I am surrounded by casualties and flies.

I decide to try to find a place that makes sense. But where in this sea of misery can I make a difference? Beautiful dark faces line the hall calling out for help. I cannot understand them. I cannot feed them. I cannot give them the water from the bottle that hangs heavy from my waist. I cannot even find any supplies to clean their wounds. Where is Amina with that cart? Where is anyone else who can help? How can a seemingly seasoned ten-year-old organization like IMC send me here without any real support or training? I am sweltering and overwhelmed by stench and suffering. Doubt sneaks back. Have I made a big mistake?

At this moment my mind throws my spirit a bone of hope. Before leaving Ohio I went to a local thrift store with what I considered a brilliantly compassionate plan. When I imagined women in a place ravaged by war and famine, it came to me to give them something that would lift their spirits. Surely, I reasoned, nothing quells a woman's disparagement like a delicate piece of feminine undergarment.

A few weeks ago I pushed a wobbly-wheeled shopping cart around a Columbus Salvation Army. I filled it with various sizes of lacy bras, gossamer slips and silky panties. These garments of hope traveled with me across the Atlantic and now await distribution to the despairing women of Mogadishu.

A woman kneels on the floor in the hallway fanning her husband who is propped up in a corner. The man's bandages are in obvious need of changing, and she determinedly fans the flies away from the blood and oozing fluid that seeps through the thin gauze around his chest.

"Hello, uh, subah wahnoxin," I say remembering the Somali greeting I had overheard Ann using earlier.

My stomach flutters with anticipation of the joy I will see on her face. For this dutiful wife I reach into my backpack bulging with lacy gifts and remove a pale pink bra with delicate beading between the cups. I hold the silky lingerie in front of her. She responds with a blank, confused expression. I am surprised that she is not overcome with gratitude. Encouraging comprehension I push the bra toward her to emphasize the gesture of giving. She reaches for it and holds it in front of her by one shoulder strap, rounded cups dangling between us. For a full thirty seconds she looks at the bra and then at me. Each time she looks at me I nod and smile.

"Mahahtsanet," she finally says.

"Oh God, what the hell does that mean?" I say to myself, crippled by my ignorance of the language.

She never stops fanning as she stares blankly at the bra. Perhaps a brief demonstration will ignite her enthusiasm.

Gently I take the garment back and put my arms through the straps and on top of my sweaty tee shirt I place the cups over my breasts and pull the back together.

Cheerfully, I say, "See?"

I hand it back to her and again, with deadpan voice, she says, "Mahahtsanet."

"Okay, well...okay," I say feeling so restricted by my lack of language skills.

I leave the couple with a friendly wave and pass a tall Somali man with the popular "I'm the Boss" tee shirt and calf-length yellow plaid skirt I learned is called a macaawis. He witnessed my gesture while he leans against the opposite wall. He reaches for his gun as he passes in the direction of the woman with the pale pink 34 C.

Throughout the next couple of hours I decide to focus on the spirit of sharing and distribute my gifts to women nursing injured children; women with foul smelling colostomies desperately in need of changing; women wearing nothing but faded rags; and women cooking over small fires on overcrowded balconies for loved ones who may not survive the day.

After I distribute the last silky slip I find Lindsey in her step down unit.

"Ready to head back for lunch?" she asks.

"Oh my, is it already that late," I exclaim.

"Yeah, let's go. What's with you? You look too chipper for your first day. You raid the Valium in the supply room?" she says with a chuckle.

Donna bounces her petite frame towards us as we get ready to leave for lunch.

"Ann, will you join us for lunch?" Donna inquires as she twists her shiny red tresses around two fingers.

"I'm sorry; I'm going to stay here with Abdi," Ann responds.

She turns back to the five-year-old Somali child wiping the sweat from his forehead.

"His fever is breaking so I would like to stay with him instead of going to lunch. I'm sorry, go ahead," she says with an angelic voice.

"Fine, we'll send a driver back for you and Oscar. Do you have a radio?" Donna asks, twisting her full lips into a pout.

"Oh, I'm sorry, yes. Go ahead," Ann says.

Donna rolls her emerald eyes and we walk out the door stepping over the latest delivery for the gravedigger.

On the way back to the compound Carlos dialogs with Donna in French as she flashes him a flirtatious grin. Brian and I sit in the back. Every time the nonexistent shocks fail to cushion the blow of the multiple ruts in the road my body ends up a little closer to his. Each time I get closer Brian scoots himself back into the circumference of the wide berth of his personal space. While he works at keeping a comfortable distance, my mind savors my scenes of giving.

After lunch I enter the halls of Digfer with renewed confidence and purpose. My spirits have lifted so high that I almost miss the man in the yellow plaid macaawis proudly adorned in a pale pink bra covering the "I'm the Boss" message on his tee shirt.

"What the fuck?" Brian exclaims, careful not to make eye contact with the man.

"Oh my God," I whisper under my breath.

Throughout the hospital I spot the women who just an hour before owned their first intimate undergarment. The new owners of the intimate apparel are all Somali men sporting the machine gun and lacy brassier combination. Some have a machete tucked beneath the delicate waistband of a satiny slip. My mood is sinking back to its original depth.

Carlos and Donna walk past me laughing.

"What the hell?" Donna's green eyes sparkle with amusement between bouts of laughter.

"Where did they get that useless stuff?" Carlos asks disgustedly.

I keep walking with no particular destination, humiliation taking me to an even deeper feeling of desolation.

Finally I come upon Dr. Abass, the gentle Somali doctor I met the day before. Needing to confess and hopeful for absolution I take this opportunity.

"Excuse me, Dr. Abass," I say approaching.

"Yes, gahleb wahnoxin," he replies, placing his hand on the patient's shoulder when he looks up at me.

"Can I help you, Mary?" he asks with genuine concern.

Before I can speak his gentle eyes almost draw the tears from mine.

"If you don't mind I need to ask you something."

"Of course," he says calmly.

Deep breath.

"I am the one who gave away all the underwear that the men

are now wearing around the hospital. They were gifts for the women I brought from the States. I thought it would lift their spirits and make them feel beautiful. "

Patiently he explains what I had never considered.

"Mary, many of these women are from the bush. They have never seen garments like these. The only women who use these have money and are urbanized. In Somalia often a woman marries so she can survive. So her family has one less mouth to feed. A majority do not have the luxury to consider 'feeling beautiful.' Most have been circumcised and only find relations with their husband to be painful. I understand that in America women want their bodies to be desirable but most women in Somalia just want to survive."

He must have seen my eyes begin to fill.

"Mary," he continues, "you only meant good. I know this."

"Thank you Dr. Abass. I really did. I just wish I'd understood more about the culture before I arrived."

"If we learn from our bad outcomes we have done well," he reassures me with a sincere smile

"And Mary, what do you think of the new look for our proud Somali warriors?"

I appreciate the laughter he brought to the moment.

"Why do the men want to wear bras?" I ask.

"In this country the weak never keep what is given to them from rich nations. The men saw something different coming from America and they wanted it for themselves. You will see them decorating themselves with all sorts of things from the west. Start to watch in the marketplace when you drive from your compound."

He makes a mark on the patient's medical card and continues as he moves to the next bed.

"When you were not looking these men simply pointed their gun at the women who held your gifts. This happens with these American undergarments and it happens with food and medicine."

"I have so much to learn, Dr. Abass. I feel so foolish," I humbly admit.

"You are not foolish, Mary. You are a good person with a generous heart."

"Thanks. I needed that."

He ambles away but his words stay to comfort my sunken spirits.

Feeling meek and insignificant, I think of Ann. In her tour she mentioned the second floor as most in need of my attention. Maybe I can step out of this vulnerable place I am in by doing something really useful. The second floor charge nurse is a Somali man named Mohammed who is supposed to be capable and English speaking according to the notes I made yesterday from Ann's briefing. This is not the time for me to tackle the language.

When I reach his second floor ward Mohammed easily recognizes me as I am new and only one of five light skinned people in the entire hospital.

An obviously shy nature prevents his dark eyes from meeting mine. His navy blue, baggy trousers hang loosely from his slender frame. The cuffs of his pale yellow dress shirt flap unbuttoned around his narrow wrists. When he lifts his arms, the sleeves fall down to his elbows revealing smooth, hairless skin the color of heavily creamed coffee.

"Please tell me your name. I was not here yesterday, I apologize for missing you," he confesses, with very little accent.

"It's Mary. I'm told you are Mohammed, right? Ann told me to find you; she says that you are a highly qualified nurse, educated in Mogadishu before the war."

"That's right. May I show you my patients? I am just making the pharmacy order so we can make notes of what we need at their bedside."

I am impressed with his efficiency and professional manner.

"IMC donates the medicines so will you please sign for them?" he asks avoiding my eyes while making notes on his clipboard.

"Of course, but first I'd love to see your patients," I reply, feeling hope for renewed usefulness.

Mohammed slowly and carefully introduces me to each of his seventy patients. He speaks to each one and knows many of the family members by name. His gentle touch never fails to give rest on a shoulder or hand before leaving their bedside. Even with a much greater workload than any nurse in the States, he does not rush and never appears overwhelmed. Each patient is visibly moved when they see him.

A young girl about three weeps quietly on her straw mat for her mother.

"Asha," he says warmly as if she were his own child.

The gentle nurse lowers himself and sits on the floor beside her speaking soothing Somali words. He gently strokes her forehead and a final tear rolls past her earlobe as she begins to giggle. A woman approaches the girl with a small carved wooden bowl filled with a steaming brown liquid. The girl turns her attention to the woman and then back to Mohammed.

"Nahbaht gelyou," she calls to Mohammed before we move to the next patient.

"You have such a gift with your patients. They seem to adore you," I say.

He smiles warmly without responding.

"Was that Asha's mother who brought the food?" I ask.

"No. Her mother was killed when a gang of fighters raided her village. The woman caring for her is a member of her clan."

Mohammed looks back at the child, pauses and says, "Asha still calls for her mother."

When we finish our rounds and make the last note for the pharmacy order, Mohammed asks if I would mind helping him redress the wound of a man who lost three of his toes in an explosion.

"The dressing cart is there," he says pointing to Amina just as she rolls through the ward.

I notice his voice seems to shake and his long fingers fidget desperately with the metal clip on his clipboard until the papers are freed and drifting to the grimy concrete floor. Quickly his shaking hands pick up the papers that have escaped the clutch of the metal clip.

Without looking at me he says, "I will assist you after I go to the office to finish the order."

Before I can respond he is gone.

Outside the ward a man struts proudly on the balcony brandishing his Playtex D cup like a vest of armor. This humble reminder of my naiveté distracts me from Mohammed's abrupt behavior change.

Amina meets me at the toeless man's bedside and I begin to remove his fly encrusted bandage. Mohammed approaches us just as the fresh dressing is in place. He hands me a pen and shows me where to sign. I reach for the papers but they are firmly in his grip. He pulls the pharmacy orders away forcefully and I am left with only a torn corner of the paper in my hand.

"Oh, Mohammed, sorry."

I hold up the corner and say, "I think we can do without this. Let me look over the order and then I will sign."

With lightning reflexes he snatches the paper out of my reach.

"How can I sign it if you don't give it to me?" I ask feeling again like I am in some alternate reality.

Finally he hands me the pharmacy order and fixes his eyes on the floor.

I run down the list of patients and easily find fifteen new patients on the list, all with orders for Valium and pain killers.

"How can this be? There are fifteen new patients with what looks like serious conditions," I say.

"Could there be patients on this ward we did not see?" I ask gesturing around the inadequately sized ward overloaded with patients.

But it is obvious there could not be fifteen more than we have already seen.

Amina stands mesmerized by the mounting tension in this moment. Language poses no barrier for patients around us who begin to quiet and watch the American boldly confronting their caregiver.

"Mohammed, I am confused. Why did you order all this medicine?"

His eyes remain fixed on the floor and his only response is a slight side to side nod.

Amina, still nearby, makes a rattling sound with the glass bottle of brown antiseptic solution. The unusual hush that hovers around me magnifies the sound and I think of the delicate glass wind chime that hangs on my mother's farmhouse porch. Suddenly I feel that sinking feeling of being very far from home.

"There are no new patients," he says finally without looking up.

He shuffles the thin rubber soles of his worn flip-flops on the slimy floor.

"Okay," I say slowly hoping he will say something to bring

sense to this whole scene.

Still his eyes are fixed and he is silent again.

"Then why all these unnecessary drugs?" I ask.

"Dr. Saeed made me order them," he replies sheepishly.

Amina steals glances between the shamed nurse and myself.

"But why would he do that, Mohammed," I ask gruffly.

His eyes do not leave his feet and his voice lowers.

"They are for his private practice. We are not paid for our work here, so the doctors and nurses work in private clinics to survive," he explains.

"But Dr. Saeed knows these medicines are for the hospital, not to boost his profits at his private clinic. I want to see him now," I say with conviction. Clearly this cannot be acceptable.

"Where is he, Mohammed?" I demand.

The deflated champion of the people of the second floor ward walks away and without a word.

Refusing to be defeated by this situation, I decide to find the pilfering Somali doctor myself. Patients stare blankly at me as I brush past Amina and leave the crowded ward without speaking to Mohammed who has positioned himself as far from me as possible.

Just outside the ward I find a door slightly ajar. The top hinges have given way stealing the door's ability to provide privacy. My forceful knock creates a flutter of activity in the room beyond.

"Ha," a man's voice beckons.

I have to lift the door slightly to open it enough to go inside. Dr. Saeed stands from his stool where he gnaws at a few tender leaves of khat. His home is an unfinished hospital room with a few broken windows. The walls are bare except for patches of peeling paint and stucco. It houses Dr. Saeed, his wife and their three young children. The children sit on a grass mat placed on the floor in the corner of the room. Their mother stirs camel stew in a small tin pot sitting precariously atop a pile of coals burning directly on the concrete floor. The youngest child is half naked and moves behind his mother when he sees the "gallo" invade his home. The only possessions I see within the walls of this tiny make shift home include the rusting metal frame of a single bed, a grass mat, an assortment of cooking pots, and a couple of wooden stools. The scene causes me to pause. I have to stoke the fire of my indignation.

"Dr. Saeed, I need to speak with you," I say, reigniting my righteous anger.

He says something to his wife, puts down his khat and starts for the door. The little boy pulls his mother's headscarf over his face but leaves one dark eye peeking out to watch me go.

Dr. Saeed pulls the crippled door shut skillfully, shielding his family from the masses just outside their home.

Tiny veins in the whites of the doctor's eyes weave delicate red paths leading to his black pupils. He is taller and a bit stockier than most Somalis. His loosely curled hair is receding at the hairline. I notice Dr. Saeed's face beginning to shine with a thin layer of sweat.

"What is it?" he asks wringing the well-kept hands of a surgeon.

"Dr. Saeed, Mohammed ordered more medication than we need for the patients on his ward. He told me you asked him to do it because you use it for your private clinic," I say hurling the accusation.

He shifts uncomfortably on his feet and smoothes the front of his bloodstained gray scrub shirt.

"It is true," he says simply, clearly embarrassed by my discovery.

"This cannot happen. You know the drugs are for the hospital. IMC cannot provide medications for your private patients," I say driving the point, eighty percent sure this is accurate.

"I must feed my family," he says gesturing toward his feeble front door.

"It is not IMC's responsibility to feed your family. We have to focus on the care of the patients in this hospital," I reply, feeling very uncomfortable.

"It will not happen again," he says abruptly.

It is obvious he does not want to continue the conversation. With a nod he turns back to the door and returns to his semblance of privacy.

I stand alone in front of the home that is the size of my walk-in closet in the States. Why do I have the foreboding feeling that I have made another mistake?

On the ride back to IMC the voices of my colleagues, the guards, the street sounds, and the constant gunfire blend into a bland symphony of white noise. So much has gone wrong today. Every time I thought I had it right, I was wrong. I am so unprepared for this culture and what it means to live with war and famine. My thoughts consume me. Mohammed's bowed head, the small distrustful eye of a toddler hiding behind his mother, a doctor trying to feed his family inside the tight walls of their meager home.

The Land Cruiser crawls forward through the market outside Digfer unable to encourage any flow of air through the half-open window. Jackson bounces his gun between his knees. He looks down at me quietly and gives me a boyish smile. His presence comforts me.

Our vehicle finally eases through the IMC fortress gates and stops just inside its mammoth protective walls. I and the other weary expats make our way into the inner courtyard. The aromas of dinner fail to arouse my lost appetite.

Ann taps my shoulder with anemic pressure.

"Mary, oh, I'm sorry, will you wait here on the couch? We need to have a meeting in the office before dinner. I'm sorry," she murmurs.

My mind begins to panic. Surely my first day hasn't been such a disaster that my colleagues have to call a meeting to discuss the most expedient plan for my permanent departure from IMC. Even Ann is one of my judges.

I collapse into the red velvet couch where Andrew briefed me a little over twenty-four hours ago. The office door closes and I am alone. With my eyes closed I sling my bag onto the floor, now much lighter minus the underwear and bras. I bury my head in my hands and release a long sigh.

"Ça va, beautiful lady?" a man's voice says with a charming French accent.

My eyes open and see a man sitting on the couch across from me. Clear blue eyes dive into mine with provocative precision. His wind blown wavy blond hair and square unshaven jaw give him a rugged appearance. In my exhausted, vulnerable state I cannot decide if I should bathe in the blue pools or remove myself from his alluring gaze.

"Hello," is all I can manage.

"Bonjour, mademoiselle. I am Marc from your neighbor MSF," he says as he places his hands on my shoulders and gently kisses both my cheeks. He offers his hand and I take it, sinking into its warmth.

"Hello, Marc. I'm Mary from IMC," I reply, regaining my composure.

With great effort I pull off my usual self-assured persona, determined not to swoon like a thirteen-year-old girl.

"What brings you here today?" I ask.

Stick to business. Stick to business.

"I'm a nurse but my job here is to handle all the supplies in and out of Mogadishu for MSF, so guess you'd call me a general logistician or 'log' for short. I'm here to meet with your 'log,' Ahmed. MSF gives a hand to IMC since it is their first war relief effort."

"Oh, yes, I saw your patient cards today," I respond.

Come on, Mary, can't you think of anything more intelligent to add to the conversation?

Marc leans in closer, resting his elbows on his thighs.

"Mahree, you look very tired," he says, with a breathy French accent.

I feel myself close to breaking but find the Iron Nurse just in time.

"Well, I've been a nurse for sixteen years so I have experience being pushed around a hospital," I state confidently.

Only his eyes respond with an unyielding grip of truth. Smoothly his hand finds mine, tenderly cradling it as if it were an injured bird. The Iron Nurse has left the building. Tears blur my vision. I fight to keep them from spilling onto my cheeks.

"Today was my first day," I say catching a tear before it hits my face.

"And you are feeling like you do not belong because everyone else is handling the madness with ease, no?" he says tenderly.

"Yes. I know you will tell me everyone feels that way at first but I have really been an idiot today. I set defenseless women up as targets for armed robbery, shamed one of the best nurses I've ever met in front of a roomful of his patients, and self-righteously chastised a poor Somali doctor outside the pathetic hospital room he uses to shelter his family of five."

Tears run in currents and I am glad my colleagues are behind closed doors.

"Mahree, Mahree. We can all tell stories like these. You are just brave enough to tell the truth about them on your first day. Many challenges will come to you and there will not always be clear answers. But you must know one thing today."

He lifts my chin and pauses until I open my eyes so he can hold my gaze.

As he wipes the last tear he says, "I see in your eyes a person of passion who wants to live strong and full. But I want you to know today that you cannot live fully without making mistakes."

"And one more thing..." he continues.

"What is that?" I ask wiping my face.

"Do you have any more of those sexy brassieres in that bag?" he says cupping his breasts.

The laughter surrounds us like a warm bath.

The office door squeaks open and although I know my fate will be spelled out momentarily, I feel lighter and will be able to take it in with greater ease.

Donna walks out of the office looking sullen.

"Mary, will you come in here please," she orders, indicating the office.

I look at Marc and whisper, "Wish me luck."

"Beautiful ladies do not need luck," he says as he releases my hand but not my heart.

No sound comes from the office that is filled to capacity. This must be very serious.

When I walk through the doorway they are all there. My colleagues, men and women alike, are all standing at attention with lacy bras over their shirts that bear the sweat of their efforts in this desperate place.

"Welcome to Victoria's Secret Hell!" they all call out in unison.

I have never received a warmer welcome.

Maybe being here is not a mistake after all. Maybe it is living fully.

-8-

Poor Man

Mogadishu, Somalia, 1992

Dear Dad,
Three flies perch on the tip of my pen like they are surfing as I write. I have a few minutes to spend with you before we leave for the hospital.

Sorry my last letter left you hanging. In the last few months I have climbed out of the bottom of my barrel of self-pity and insecurity. Lately I find myself bonding with my colleagues and gaining a sense of purpose in a place of unending need.

Chaos seems to breed more chaos at Digfer. Unpredictable explosions and gunfire burst outside its walls, feeding a steady flow of unannounced wounded to the Casualty. Some walk in, some hobble in on "crutches" cut from the branch of an acacia tree. Others are delivered in wooden wheel barrows and deposited outside the main door. Their toes are usually tied together with a piece of ragged string. Predictable unpredictability. Perhaps weathering mom's unpredictable outbursts provided a training ground for the erratic nature of working in a war zone.

When I arrived the best anyone got for a job description was "do whatever you can." However, other expats and I identified the needs and distributed the work among us. I am responsible for the hiring and training of new local staff in cooperation with the Somali hospital officials. This is no small challenge since most of the local staff speaks only Somali, Arabic or Italian.

They receive no pay for their work. At times I am suspicious of their motives. One local staff member learned to do surgical procedures so he could sell elective surgeries in the evening when IMC expats were gone for the day. Some steal supplies so they can sell them in the market just beyond the gates of the hospital. But I am learning the paradigm of survival often overshadows what my North American standards consider ethical behavior.

One Somali doctor and nurse still avoid me because on my first day I confronted them for pilfering Valium from the IMC pharmacy. The doctor sells the drugs in his private clinic so he can feed his family of five who live in an abandoned hospital room. Since that experience I've learned not to rush in with accusations, even if I have grounds. It's better to first try to understand the situation then quietly find solutions that allow local people to not "lose face."

One quiet solution has to do with Valium, which is a very popular drug to pilfer. The Somalis use it to offset their khat-induced insomnia. Khat dependence leads to sleeplessness, which leads to Valium which leads to Valium dependence and so on. I decided to try supplying the hospital pharmacy with only injectable Valium since it is not as easily stolen and because most locals do not want to inject themselves. Drug disappearance has decreased considerably.

IMC is so full of characters. Andrew, our director, seems to have a relationship with Ann who is just the kind of "saint" you want to martyr. Brian, a gifted physician assistant, often looks like he could easily snap the neck of the next person who glances in his direction. Yet I have literally seen him give away the shirt off his back when he thought no one was looking. A few days ago I saw him quietly slip a tee shirt out of his backpack and place it on a child. The child would otherwise lay naked on a hard, wooden table while recovering from the surgery required to repair his bullet-torn abdomen. I have grown close to two nurses. One named Lindsey whose warm, caring manner soothes even the most desperate of souls. She is elegant, tall and slim with lovely blue eyes. Another nurse named Donna is bright and beautiful with gorgeous long red hair and seems to have an eye for the IMC logistician, Ahmed, a handsome, well-spoken Somali.

Journalists are becoming more commonplace and often stay in our compound. Two are staying with us at IMC. One is an American reporter named Sharon who is based in Cairo. The other is a Greek of mixed ethnicity who is a special correspondent with ABC Nightline. They are so eager for information and we are so eager to unload the emotional baggage of the war that sometimes we probably say too much.

On my first day I met Marc, an intriguing French nurse-logistician with MSF, which stands for Medecins Sans Frontieres. You probably recognize the English translation, which is Doctors Without Borders. He was very kind to me at a difficult moment but I have not seen him since. IMC is planning a party at the IMC compound in a couple of weeks and will invite MSF along with some of the other NGOs in Mog. Maybe I'll see him.

They're calling me. Time for work.

Please take care of yourself.

Love you,
Mare

Although the IMC compound is only a couple of miles from Digfer, our commute takes at least twenty minutes. We could walk faster but for security reasons we are restricted from walking outside the compound. I doubt I could find my way as the driver changes his route daily to avoid unpredictable obstacles such as thick sand, roadblocks placed by armed militias, the street market that spills into the roadway, or a blown-up dump truck lying in the road like a elephant carcass.

Today, as every day since February, I arrive at Digfer as wet with perspiration as if I just stepped out of the shower. Feeling "clean and fresh" in Somalia is now only a frustrating dream. Sharon enters the hospital with me as we carefully step over the body of a young woman. She lies stiff and cold and her big toes are bound with strips of rags. I then navigate my way through dozens of people standing just inside, bracing myself for the prevailing stench of rotting flesh and diesel fuel.

Two men yell violently at each other in the hall and three girls run up to the American reporter Sharon shouting, "*Give me one pen!*"

She takes the hand of one of them and squats to her eye level.

Looking back at me, Sharon asks, "Why do they ask for a pen?"

"They are interested in everything we bring into the hospital with us. Sometimes they might ask for your clothing or your water bottle. It's not considered rude in this culture to ask for something that belongs to someone else. Sharon, I'll see you later," I say heading up the crumbling concrete steps to the second-floor ward.

Sharon waves in my direction, still holding the hand of one of the girls.

Outside sounds of exploding mortar shells and automatic gunfire easily infiltrate shattered windows, drifting through the halls like aberrant elevator musak. In addition to looking for open beds for post-operative patients, the day's initial goal is to visit various wards and measure the extent of the previous night's complications.

When I reach the second-floor ward, a young man catches my eye as I begin my rounds. He lies on one of the few hospital beds among twenty other patients, and his pleading expression slows my purposeful pace.

I walk to his bedside and notice his once dark brown skin looks as if someone has bleached his sunken face and protruding cheekbones. After pointing to him I touch my thumb and fingers together and lift them to my mouth to ask if he has eaten. His lips are the color of heavily creamed coffee. He moves them slightly and he shakes his head from side to side. A listless hand lies across the bits of fabric pieced together to form a kind of toga that covers most of his frail body. His clothes indicate he could be from the bush. The poorest of Somali's poor.

His father stands next to him wearing a plaid macaawis and collared cotton shirt graying from daily exposure to dust and sun. The man holds a long walking stick. A cloth is tied to the end that holds a few pots and utensils, which are the extent of his material possessions. The father rests an aging hand on his son's shoulder and looks at me confirming the son's gesture. His drawn face expresses the sadness that eats away at his spirit.

The list of patients for morning rounds confirms the sickly feces smell coming from the young patient. Yussuf is an eighteen-year-old shot in the abdomen two months ago. Surgery removed a portion of his intestines and a colostomy bag attached to an opening in his left side hangs loosely, filled with runny stool bypassing his lower intestines. It smells in desperate need of replacing. The patient notes hidden under the soiled mattress indicate that the surgeon intends to reattach the bowel and reverse the colostomy when Yussuf improves. But this seems like a distant possibility for the frail boy with vacant eyes and protruding bones.

Mohammed passes me with a wide berth. Although I often work in his second floor ward, he continues to avoid me since our altercation over the drug pilfering. For my sake and the sake of the patients I want desperately to regain his trust. I unsuccessfully attempted to reestablish a good rapport during the days following my confrontation with Mohammed. I have since learned my prime mistake that first day was to put him in a situation that embarrassed him in front of everyone in the ward. He lost face. But Marc, the French MSF logistician taught me that I am one who lives fully. I choose to see my mistakes as my greatest teachers.

I hold one finger up to Yussuf and his father to indicate I will be back in one minute, hoping I have not unknowingly insulted them with some obscene gesture.

I approach Mohammed where he is squatting on the floor gently changing the bandages on a young girl's neck.

"Excuse me," I interrupt as gently as possible, "I need your help with a patient."

Without looking up he says, "Yes, I will come when I finish."

I step back slightly wanting to show respect.

As he attaches the last wrap of the bandage, he touches her arm and speaks comforting words in her native tongue.

Mohammed stands at the foot of Yussuf's bed and translates as I introduce myself and begin to ask my questions. I need to know as much about his condition as possible.

Mohammed releases a deep sigh of annoyance.

"Mary, Yussuf is a poor bush man. He cannot read or write, and he doesn't know what is wrong with his body," he says indicating the place on Yussuf's where the colostomy is attached.

"All he knows is brown fluid comes out of this hole when he eats and he is embarrassed because of the odor and is frightened by the other patients who threaten him when he smells bad."

"But does Yussuf know why the hole is there?" I ask.

Mohammed glances back at Yussuf and then at my chin, never making eye contact with me.

"He says it was there after he was shot and maybe it was from the bullet. He wants to know if it can be fixed."

I wonder why Mohammed has not explained to Yussuf what is happening with his body. But I keep my thoughts to myself and begin a more thorough examination. His pale lips, complexion and white colored mucous membranes lining the inside of his mouth certainly indicate that he's anemic. I move the worn cloth he wears away from his chest and place my stethoscope on top of the thin skin that covers his well-defined ribs. His chest is clear but because his pale skin is doughy, he is likely dehydrated. I move my hands down his chest to his abdomen and begin to palpate. When I do a brown liquid trickles into the colostomy bag.

Yussuf murmurs something to Mohammed in his tribal tongue.

"He is saying this is what happens after he eats," Mohammed translates.

This is a case where a person could quite literally die from embarrassment. A lack of understanding threatens to take the life of this young man who otherwise has a considerable chance of recovery. It seems so tragic in a place where countless die every day from irreparable damage and disease in their bodies.

Through Mohammed, I ask Yussuf to turn on his side. A small bedsore weeps a bloody drainage where countless flies entrench themselves in his festering flesh. It is obvious he has not been walking, which would have expedited his healing.

"Have you been walking Yussuf?" I ask.

He and Mohammed dialog.

"He says he does not walk because it brings out the brown liquid and he begins to smell bad."

Just then a plan occurs to me. In my backpack are several sheets of paper and two colored markers. I grab a book from the bag as well and place it on the floor beside Yussuf and begin to sketch a simple diagram of digestive tract.

An audience forms almost immediately. A patient hobbles toward us on one crutch and two others join the widening circle around us pulling their IV bags with them. They are eager to learn as I suspect the Somali doctors do not spend time educating their patients. Somali nurses most likely avoid educating patients for fear of overstepping their place with the doctor or because they simply lack the understanding and training themselves. Patients are left confused and uninformed about how to manage their recovery.

"Mohammed, would you mind explaining to Yussuf and the other patients a little about colostomies?" I ask, hopeful to regain some rapport between us.

"All right," he replies flatly, still not meeting my eyes.

Using the red marker as a pointer I review the points I want to convey. My drawing depicts a man's mouth, esophagus, stomach, intestines and rectum. Digestion 101. Another drawing illustrates the same except the intestines are separated, as they are for Yussuf and one end opens into a colostomy, serving as a temporary rectum, while the lower intestine gets time to heal.

At Digfer colostomies are as common as the flies that feast on the infirm. Facilitating the conveyance of a basic understanding will not only give hope to Yussuf and the many other colostomy patients, but might also foster a little compassion. Mohammed translates as I explain the diagram of a normally functioning digestive tract.

Still pointing to the midsection of the man in the drawing, I pause while Mohammed speaks my words in Somali to a growing crowd.

"Let me see!" a voice shouts excitedly from behind the man with one crutch, "I want to see!"

The man with the crutch shuffles over slightly and I see the face of the eager learner, whose enthusiasm is unfettered by the injury that traps him on a thin layer of foam. The hem of his traditional macaawis is pulled up above his knees exposing an external steel rod stabilizing his left lower leg. In his lap he holds an English encyclopedia. I make my way through a half a dozen attentive students and introduce myself.

"I am Ishmael," he says with precise English, "I want to learn too."

"Hello Ishmael. If I teach you, would you help Mohammed and I teach the others when the questions come?" I ask, hoping I have not offended Mohammed.

"Oh yes," he says, gripping his enormous text with excitement.

I am relieved to catch a grin of endorsement creeping across Mohammed's face. I point to the diagrams with my red marker and explain how food passes through the intestines to the rectum in a healthy patient. I trace the same path with the marker, but this time show how it goes to the colostomy bag in a patient with injuries like Yussuf's.

"Eating causes the brown liquid to go through the hole in the colostomy, but a body cannot heal without food," I explain, pausing to allow Mohammed to translate.

"Walking will heal your body faster and prevent bedsores from developing."

Ishmael, a born teacher, is already fielding questions from the audience and Yussuf's hopeful expression brings a little color to his face.

The satisfaction of the moment is interrupted when Amina abruptly breaks in.

"Mary, you are needed in Casualty," she says flatly.

I leave the diagram with Ishmael and turn to the eager crowd of students promising to return later with better drawings.

"Thank you," I say to Ishmael who is immersed in his students. He barely acknowledges my exit.

I look around for Mohammed to thank him, and hope for a sign of peace between us, but he is gone.

In the dimly lit hall that leads to the Casualty I sidestep used syringes and dried brick-red wads of discarded gauze. Ann greets me nervously moving in no particular direction. She hurriedly briefs me on three patients; all require emergency surgery but no surgeons can be found.

"I'm sorry, there is a man with a bullet wound to the abdomen and both legs, a pregnant woman with two bullet wounds to the abdomen, and an infant," Ann explains nervously.

In the Casualty, a rail thin Somali woman cradles the baby wrapped in a blood soaked cloth. The tiny infant manages a faint whine. Its arm and head hang listlessly from the woman's sheltering embrace.

Sharon lifts the tea-colored cloth swaddling the child to reveal the result of a gun shot wound in her abdomen. The bullet ripped a hole next to the bellybutton. Each time the child gulps for air, her intestines protrude through the wound left by the assailant.

The baby's eyes open and seem to plead with Sharon. The reporter loses her objective stance and begins to weep openly. Brian approaches and lifts the cloth out of Sharon's trembling hand to uncover the rest of the child's body. An intestine dangles from her mangled torso. I hand Brian an 18 gauge IV cannula and he finds a large vein on the baby's ankle, which is no more than half an inch in diameter. I hold up a blood collection bag trying to indicate to the woman that she needs to donate blood for her child. The gaunt woman stares numbly and shakes her head refusing to cooperate.

"Where are the fucking Somali doctors? How are we going to get through to this lady?" he implores forcefully, grabbing the bag from me and waving it vigorously in front of the woman.

"Try speaking Arabic with her Sharon," I say hoping this is one of the languages the woman might understand.

Although Sharon tries to communicate with the woman there is no sign of comprehension. Brian hands Sharon the blood collection bag as he secures the IV in place on the tiny ankle. The child is quiet now and seems to be losing consciousness.

Sharon becomes increasingly distraught and continues in vain to speak with the woman who just stares numbly back at her.

"I'll get a translator," I say.

Just outside the Casualty I find Mohammed.

"I'm busy," he retorts briskly to my request for help translating.

I wander the halls looking for anyone who can translate until I find Jackson leaning against the doorframe engaged in lively discussion with a fellow guard. It crosses my mind briefly there may be no one guarding the IMC Land Cruiser. That's a problem for another time.

"Jackson, we need you to translate in the Casualty," I declare.

He finishes his discussion and follows me back to the child.

Jackson looks at the woman and child and begins to ask my questions in her native language. I want to know if she will give blood to her child. Throughout their conversation I notice Jackson looking into the face of the wounded baby. He touches the back of her limp hand with his finger as he listens intently. The woman speaks for another five minutes. Finally, Jackson turns to us as if he cannot find the words.

"Well?" Brian begs.

"This woman is not the child's mother," Jackson begins.

"Last night gunmen from another clan came into her village and killed everyone they could find. She hid under the bodies of her husband and two children where she stayed, listening to the shooting and screaming of the other villagers. When the guns and screams stopped she came out of hiding, searching for any-one still alive. In the house next to hers she found everyone dead but she heard the baby's cries. She found the baby beside the bodies of its mother and brother. In the whole village, only this woman and the baby are alive."

No one moves when he is finished.

The woman addresses Jackson and he replies quickly.

"She wants to know if she can leave the baby and go," he says.

"Wait! I want to do a story. Can I talk to her?" Sharon pleads.

Jackson asks the woman. She replies briefly and then she is gone.

"What village? Wait!" Sharon calls to the woman as if she can understand.

"Medina," Jackson says.

Medina. Without the protection of her fellow clan members her chance of survival is very slim. She is alone.

"I want to do a story, Mary. Let me stay with her through the surgery," Sharon pleads.

"Sharon, if you donate the blood she needs you can have plen-ty of story," I say hoping Sharon will be a match with the infant.

I leave the baby with a Somali hospital visitor and guide Sharon onto the wooden picnic table bed in the next room. She cranes her neck to see the child. A Somali volunteer pierces Sharon's vein with a sixteen-gauge needle and her blood begins to fill the bag. Her fist opens and closes expediting the flow of blood from her body. I lay my hand on her shoulder but her eyes never leave the baby girl in the next room.

"Sharon," I state, "I've got to find a surgeon for this baby, right now. I'll be back as soon as I can."

Brian finishes connecting an IV to the pregnant woman's left arm. Her other arm dangles loosely over the edge of the wood-en table. Ann cuts the woman's shirt away from her bloody belly and Brian holds a stethoscope to the protruding abdomen listening for the baby's heart tones. Blood oozes from between the woman's legs onto the green plastic tarp covering the exam table.

"Mary, I can't do all these surgeries by myself, get a fucking Somali surgeon in here, stat!" he demands as I exit the hospital on my way to locate Dr. Saeed.

A small café near the hospital is a favorite place of respite for the local doctors. Once outside I follow a small path on Digfer's east side, worn into existence by endless foot traffic. I am mindful to step carefully to avoid piles of trash and human feces, baked by the equatorial sun.

The café is a crudely built square stucco building with unfinished wood shutters propped open beside two windows, inviting a nonexistent breeze. The fragrances of tea spices float in the air mingled with mouth watering aromas of garlic, olive oil and camel meat. Dr. Saeed and Dr. Jefferson sit on wooden stools slowly sipping tea in thick clear drinking glasses. Dr. Jefferson was in medical school before the war and has since been prematurely promoted to surgeon.

"Dr. Saeed, we have several patients needing surgery right away," I say, hoping my frustration is only minimally apparent.

"I know this," Dr. Saeed says without looking at me.

"Would you like some chai?" he asks only out of polite Somali custom.

I decline. I know he has no desire for me to join them.

Word of the incoming wounded from Medina travels quickly throughout the hospital compound. However, he does his best to ignore me, still scorned from our altercation months ago regarding his drug pilfering.

In his right hand Dr. Jefferson scoops the last bites of carrots and camel meat mixed in oily pasta. He does not acknowledge me either.

"Please. We have no other surgeons," I say and turn away from them.

Dr. Saeed methodically swirls the chai steaming in his hand. The scent of cloves and cinnamon momentarily conjures up a surreal feeling of Christmas in my mind.

I think of Sharon and of the baby at the mercy of these men. All I can do is turn and make my way back through piles of human waste. Dozens of screaming starlings light up an acacia tree with their iridescent blue feathers.

In the Casualty Ann is prepping the baby's abdomen with iodine to clean the surgical area. An IV is taped along the inside of her tiny ankle. To prevent additional fluid loss, Ann covers the protruding intestines with sterile wet saline gauze and then pours additional sterile saline over the already moist gauze squares.

A small red patch shows through on the square of gauze taped to the inside of Sharon's arm where a needle drew her blood. It now waits in a plastic collection bag lying beside the child's motionless body which is splayed out like a belly-up frog. Sharon waves away the flies that hover around the baby's torso as the tiny chest rises and falls with quick shallow breaths.

"Did you find them?" Sharon asks when she sees me approach.

"Yes, they will be here soon," I tell her hoping this is the truth.

Sharon's palm and fingers are folded around the tiny girl's hand. She smiles at me and then at the infant.

"The baby is type 'O' according to the test card," she says, "the same as mine."

"Good. That's good Sharon. I have to find some post-op beds. You can stay with her now."

I am bathed in sweat as I climb the third flight of steps searching for the illusive post-operative beds. Every window is shattered from the force of countless explosions, yet not a hint of a breeze ventures through. There they are: one, two, three, scattered throughout the third floor women's ward. This is a good sign and I am hopeful the beds will not be claimed before I can get the post-op patients into them.

In the sweltering heat of the operating room, Sharon stands dutifully at the baby's head. A white surgical mask covers the lower half of her face, contrasting sharply with the amber in her hopeful eyes. She tenderly wipes tiny droplets of perspiration that spring from the little girl's forehead. The infant wraps her fingers around Sharon's pinkie. A Somali volunteer stands between the child's left ankle and the tray of sterile instruments. He picks up a syringe and injects a small amount of intravenous Ketamine into the IV. As the anesthesia takes effect the baby slowly loosens her grip on Sharon's finger.

Dr. Jefferson, a.k.a. "the angel of death," enters the surgical suite with an unwarranted air of superiority. My heart sinks knowing Sharon will probably lose the motherless child within minutes.

I inform Sharon that I must leave them temporarily as it is my job to make sure everyone has what they need for the operations and then return to the Casualty to check for more wounded.

In the next room Brian cranes over the pregnant woman's protruding belly. He lifts the fetus out of the woman's abdomen. A hole in the tiny chest marks the entry point for the bullet that took its life. The tiny head falls limply to one side and Brian gently places the blue body on the table. He carefully arranges the baby's miniature arms, briefly caressing the tiny hand. His attention quickly turns back to the mother. He assists Dr. Saeed with securing two clamps inside the woman's exposed abdomen.

"The baby?" I ask.

I know Brian will probably answer for Dr. Saeed who rations his words with me. Brian is an exceptional physician's assistant. A few weeks ago I saw him open an abdomen, repair a torn bladder pierced by a bullet, and send the patient to a post-op bed faster than any of the trained surgeons at Digfer. What he lacks in social graces he gives without end in medical skill and compassion.

"Dead. The bullet is lodged in the fetus's chest. It saved its mother's life," Brian says.

In the corner I see a man crumpled in a bloody heap slumped against the wall and sitting among used needles and discarded gauze stained with all manner of bodily fluids. Visitors, patients and medical staff pass him as if he doesn't exist. Bright red has seeped into every fiber of his tattered shirt and pants and his lids hang partially closed revealing only the whites of his eyes.

"Who is attending this patient?" I ask, pointing to the man.

"He is a poor man," Dr. Saeed replies bluntly, as if this is sufficient explanation for his neglect.

A poor man? This is the second time today I have been given this explanation. Who among these people is not poor? It seems some are arbitrarily singled out and ignored.

In a remote section of Casualty people bustle past another

"poor man" huddled in a fetal position on the concrete floor. Blood from his chest wound drips down his leg and is now congealed in the spots between his toes. I squat next to him and gently remove his blood-soaked shirt. Then I kneel beside the silent man. My legs ache but his quiet suffering stills my desire to complain. Under his left breast I find a single small bullet wound, too small for my pinkie, with more extensive trauma to both legs and a bloody gash in his side.

Dr. Abass kneels beside me and asks, "Mary, what is this man's condition?"

Dr. Abass's presence is a great relief. Perhaps there is some hope for the "poor man."

"Multiple gun shot wounds to the upper thighs, left chest and abdomen. His pulse is rapid, breathing labored and looks like he has a hemothorax; probably got his spleen too." I report.

"Let's get him to the surgical theater right away," Abass urges.

"The surgical suites in the 'theater' are being used. We can use the 'clean' room in Casualty," I offer, not wanting to prolong this man's overdue surgery.

The "clean" room is a dimly lit, walled off, alcove less removed from the heavy traffic of Casualty. Its primary purpose is for minor surgeries that require a more sterile atmosphere. Oftentimes it was used to perform emergency surgery on the cast-off patients like this "poor man."

Although he is no taller than I and walks with a limp from childhood polio, Dr. Abass and I gently lift and carry our patient to the newly remodeled mini surgical area within Casualty. A large surgical light on wheels hangs over a green plastic covered cot where the operation will take place. Plaster bits fall from the ceiling caused by nearby explosions as we gently but quickly ready our patient for emergency surgery.

We begin prepping the man under the flickering, generator-powered light.

The man moans slightly as I cut away his clothing.

Dr. Abass places his hand on the man, soothing him with the gentle words of his native language. A few weeks ago I learned that Dr. Abass is a Bantu, a people who suffer fierce discrimination. Not so many years ago Bantus were captured from the "bush" and used as slaves in Somalia. They are still considered a class below the others. In Somalia, being lower class makes a person especially vulnerable to attack and often without adequate life-sustaining resources. At times some Somalis call the Bantu "ooji" which is Italian for "today." These Somalis consider the Bantu unable to think beyond the moment. In the short time I've been here Abass has impressed me with his humility and his compassion, yet he is continually snubbed and threatened by the other Somali doctors. Only days ago I saw him save a patient's life by correcting the placement of a chest tube improperly seated and on the wrong side by Dr. Jefferson. Dr. Abass quietly agrees to keep quiet about the mistake when Dr. Jefferson gives him a threatening reminder of his many well-armed friends.

As we work in dim light I ask Dr. Abass to explain the mystery of the "poor man" label.

He laughs easily and says, "A poor man is a person with no money."

"Of course, I know that, but everyone in Somalia seems poor to me," I reply.

"Why do you ask this question?" he inquires curiously.

"I have seen two patients today who have been labeled as 'poor' and both have been ignored or mistreated in some way."

"It could mean that the patient cannot pay for services, or possibly he is from the wrong clan or Bantu who are among the lowest," he explains.

"But services at Digfer are free. What would it matter if he cannot pay?" I ask.

"Mary, most families compensate surgeons in some way because they do not know services are free and the surgeons do not tell them."

So many unanticipated complications and variables weave in and out of humanitarian work. I wonder if I can stay ahead of them enough to have a positive effect.

We finally close the patient's wounds and double check the chest tube just as the surgical lamp flickers its last illumination.

After getting the patient into one of the post-op beds on the third floor, I am anxious to find out the status of the other two Medina victims. In the surgical suite Sharon's face tells the story. Dr. Jefferson brushes past me without a word as I enter. Sharon's tear-stained face is leaning over the tiny body. She gently kisses the cool, lifeless forehead.

When she senses my presence she asks, "What will happen to her body?"

"Since she has no family or clan to pay for a burial shroud and grave digger, IMC will cover the cost," I respond, as I gently stroke the child's face with one hand and wrap the other around Sharon in a warm embrace. Sharon slides her left arm around my waist and cradles the baby's face with her free hand.

"I want to pay for it," she says caressing the baby's cheek.

"Of course," I respond. There is nothing more to say.

As several bursts of automatic gunfire spew rat-a-tat-tat in rapid succession, just beyond the walls of the hospital, I leave Sharon to mourn a child she never knew; grieving for her family, her village, herself.

"Mary, I'm sorry, this lady is ready for a post-op bed," Ann tells me, indicating the woman with the empty womb.

"How is she?" I ask.

"She is stable and will probably make it," Ann says.

I am finally able to get back to Yussuf after Amina and I settle the childless woman into the recovery bed. The bed, provided by her family, is a piece of foam lying on the concrete floor.

Lindsey and I locate several sheets of poster-size paper at the IMC compound during lunch. I plan to use them as a part of an ongoing colostomy education program for both colostomy patients and those who might otherwise ridicule them.

In the hall outside Yussuf's ward I step over a body curled up on the filthy, blood stained floor. Inside the ward I notice Mohammed is nowhere in sight and his ward seems to be precariously running itself. Inexperienced Somali nurses are changing dressings.

"Mary! It is time for some new English words; teach me English," demands Ishmael, cradling his outdated encyclopedia.

"Not right now, Ishmael. I am looking for Yussuf," I reply.

"He is there," he says pointing to the ward entrance.

I realize the curled up body is Yussuf. When I reach him I squat down and get his attention.

"Yussuf?" I utter, stunned to find him like this.

With what must take enormous amounts of his energy reserve he smiles and grabs my arm. Our languages separate us and there is little to say.

"Cali, cali, come," I request, as I take his frail hand to lead him out of the hallway and back into the ward. His stick-like legs strain to carry his diminutive frame but he is able to walk.

"Ishmael, if you translate for me I will teach you some English words before I leave today," I say hoping he will agree to the arrangement.

"Oh yes," Ishmael replies.

"Please ask Yussuf why he is lying in the hall?"

"I do not have to ask," Ishmael responds. "His smell is so strong that one patient told Yussuf he would have to get out of our ward or be killed."

Hearing this reinforces my determination to educate the patients.

"Where is your father Yussuf?" I ask looking at Yussuf and then to Ishmael.

"After you said Yussuf should eat he got some food and he says his father is cooking outside," he says pointing to the balcony.

Like most Somalis, Ishmael raises his voice loudly no matter how far he is from his audience. Shouting all the way to the balcony presents no challenge. "Nin wayn, old man," he calls.

While waiting for Yussuf's father I pull out my poster-size paper and markers and immediately become the object of many inquiring eyes. I review the colostomy lecture from the morning, and with Ishmael's help I answer as many questions as I can.

As I check Yussuf's colostomy his father asks, through Ishmael, if he could have a new bag. The bags are designed for one use only. However, because supplies are low they are routinely reused which compromises the seal and makes cleaning virtually impossible. The resulting odor is extraordinarily offensive. Without knowing how, I give assurances that I will find one for Yussuf. I remind Yussuf's father to be sure he walks and eats regularly.

When our conversation lulls, Ishmael demands, "Now? Teach me English words, now?"

The joy in his face replenishes my hope.

Ishmael shuffles his body on his foam bed and invites me to join him by patting the newly formed empty space. The crumbling mattress, host to multiple bacteria, has lost its spring but it is the most welcoming place I have been all day.

Ishmael opens the book and lands his finger on a word in the section of B's.

"What is this word?" he asks.

I laugh a laugh that releases a thousand stress-filled moments. A laugh that does not want to end. A laugh that takes the place of finding answers to war and justice for the "poor man."

"Brassiere," I say, "the word is brassiere."

-9-

The Nomad

Mogadishu, Somalia, 1992

The past few months have left me scheming to find some daily solitude to decompress from the day's constant barrage of stimuli. Each day is spent in the sweltering heat and chaos of Digfer working around the constant demands of the hopeless. Security concerns dictate that I remain in continual close proximity to my colleagues. Day after day I find myself confined behind a wire fence at the hospital, sandwiched between my fellow volunteers in a machine-gun mounted technical or huddled around an undersized dinner table in our compound. My tiny room in the compound fails to offer refuge. I am required to share the space with one or another of the chatty journalists that have begun to descend upon Mogadishu since the world has taken notice of this war-ravaged land.

As morning light breaks on the horizon, the sound of machine-gun fire rattles in the distance. I make my way to a shower downstairs in the shared bathroom. A door stands partially open in one of the rooms I pass. I stop in my tracks and go back, push open the door, and step into its delicious vacancy.

"Oh wow," I say under my breath, astonished by my good luck.

This situation requires immediate action, as unoccupied rooms like this will not go unnoticed for long. I casually pull the door closed and make my way back to my room, hoping not to run into anyone on the way. A shower now takes lower priority to staking my claim on this new piece of property.

When I reach my room I notice that my roommate, a *USA Today* journalist, is gone. In a spontaneous moment I quickly rip my donated Norwegian comforter from the mattress, grab my two Somali stools and pull my Kenyan batiks from the wall. Somehow I manage to throw my sun bleached cow skull on top of an already bulging armload. I picked up the skull along the shores of the Indian Ocean a couple of weeks earlier. It looks like something from an old western movie from home.

Since I am the only expat to use the remains of a fallen animal as decor it will serve to "stake" my claim on the new room. I stuff my things into a bag, but the bundles of unfolded clothing are too bulky to allow the zipper to close. It will have to stay open. I give the overflow one more shove into the interior of the bag. In the doorway my eyes dart back and forth, making a quick sweep of the hallway for any colleagues who might question an armload of possessions.

The extra weight makes descending two stairs at a time more challenging. Stumbling a little on the last step, I arrive at the bottom in one piece.

I barrel into the empty room and claim the space by throwing my bag and cow skull on one of the beds. It's mine.

"Mary, the technical's waiting," Brian says in the doorway.

Good-bye breakfast. But it was worth it.

"This yours?" he asks.

I look up at him offering black lace panties.

"Found them at the bottom of the stairs," he says with a smug grin. "You weren't in a hurry to say, I don't know maybe...'RF' this room by any chance?"

Brian came up with "RF" acronym for "rat fuck" to refer to taking possession of a prized space by spewing one's belongings about its interior, or by appropriating items left behind in a newly vacated room effectively staking claim to the real estate.

"Yes," I say, snatching the underwear perched on his outstretched finger.

"Better get rid of the mattress or Aweis will put someone in here with you."

"I know but I'll have to do it before dinner. And don't get any ideas about becoming roommates," I warn sternly.

"Okay, okay. Fuck, Mary, you're in a pissy mood," he says holding his hands up in a symbolic surrender.

"I've just got to have some space. Let's go."

Digfer's main entrance has been transformed to make way for the continual need for additional exam rooms and tables. The nicety of a reception area seems surreal after stepping over the previous night's bodies just outside the main arched doorway. Inside a young Somali woman stands with a toddler on her hip. The child wears a worn over-sized tee shirt barely covering his nude bottom. The woman holds out her hand and asks me for water.

"Biyo. Biyo," she pleads.

The Iron Nurse strolls past her without even making eye contact. How can I respond to every need, every request, every heart break, and every hopeless gaze?

Dr. Abass walks slowly toward me with one arm around the waist of an emaciated man whose yellow plaid macaawis and dingy button down shirt hang on his body like weatherworn garments on a scarecrow. The man hobbles on one twig-like leg across the concrete floor made slick with diesel. With the aid of a handmade walking stick and his emaciated leg he shuffles gradually toward the wooden exam table. His foot at the end of the other leg looks like a balloon at the end of a string. The ankle has disappeared and the tips of five stubby toes protrude from the engorged foot.

I help Dr. Abass lead the man to the examination table covered with a green plastic tarp but he is too weak to climb up. The table stands eighteen inches from a wall spattered with blood and the brown stains of old urine. Dozens of flies are disturbed from their perch atop these stains of bodily waste. Several settle on my lips as I close in on their territory.

Dr. Abass's arm still supports the man while he listens attentively as the man speaks without expression, words I do not understand. Crumpled on the table is a mangled tee shirt from the previous patient. A gaping chest cavity wound required the shirt be torn from hem to collar. It reads, "I'm the," on one side and "Boss" on the other. I toss the soiled garment in the corner on top of a pile of used gauze bandages and sanitize the green table covering with Savlon, the Somali, all purpose, amber antiseptic solution.

Dr. Abass and I ease our crippled patient onto the plastic covered table. Because he is too weak to raise his oversized foot, he uses his hands to lift the leg at his calf. His light brown legs lay side by side in perfect bony symmetry except for the feet. A wafer-thin flip-flop dangles from one foot dwarfed by its oversized neighbor.

The man's voice pauses a moment, sighs then continues. Dr. Abass stands patiently by his side speaking few words. He glances down at the man's foot and then back at the fallen face of his patient. For the first time I look into the man's eyes and see miles of pain and exhaustion. To avoid an emotional reaction I focus on preparing a syringe for a tetanus shot.

"Mary, do you know what would cause this kind of swelling in our patient's foot?" Dr. Abass asks.

"I have to say I don't know. I've never seen anything like it," I reply, holding the poised syringe needle up in front of me.

Dr. Abass explains. "This man, like over sixty percent of Somali's, is a nomad. In most cases a nomadic Somali is uneducated and lives in great poverty wandering long distances across the arid savannah scrub land in search of water and grazing areas for their camels, sheep and goats. Livestock is the key to their survival. This man travels many miles on foot through the scrub, much of the time without shoes. At some point he stepped on the thorn of an acacia tree. A fungal infection spread deep into his foot where it destroyed tissue and fused the bones. The condition is called Madura foot. It is painless and progresses very slowly. This man could have been walking on this infected foot for five years or more."

"Why does he come in now?" I ask.

"Would you like to hear his story?" Dr. Abass answers with another question.

Flustered, I suddenly doubt the durability of the Iron Nurse's armor. Sixteen years ago I began an ER nursing career with idealism and good will to all patients, whom were deserving of my undivided attention. I invariably asked my patients about their personal stories during their treatment. Eventually the tragedy piled around me until I decided to build a walled-off persona and call her the Iron Nurse. Some time later I ceased humanizing my patients and began seeing them only in terms of their medical conditions. Dr. Abass's question is more than a simple one. It is an invitation to come back to humanitarian nursing, something I had not considered possible in so many years. My inability to speak the native language of my patients helps me keep a safe distance from their tragic personal stories. Surely amidst the mass of suffering in Mogadishu I could not risk opening up to real empathy? How would I function effectively?

But something makes me say, "Sure. Why not?"

In his tribal language this man shares his story.

One morning as the sun began to move across the Earth my wife and three daughters began packing our belongings. Muna, my wife, began taking down the grass hut and folding it into a bundle that would be carried by one of our best camels. It was time to sell a few of our camels in the city. I had 108 in total. I was a very rich man. We were planning to buy supplies with the earnings and return to the savannah.

That morning my three daughters were up at sunrise to collect milk for our meal. I remember my eldest smiling at me as I walked past while she gently guided the milk from our hardiest female into her pail. Nimo and little Yassim led the calves to nurse after Faduma finished with their mothers.

By the time the sun was over our head we had reached an oasis where we sat together as the camels drank. Yassim threw rocks in the water and was counting the rings that grew from the center when we heard the first shots. A group of armed bandits who were hiding behind some rocks shattered the peaceful moment. The one with a bloody bandage over his eye held a gun at Yassim's head while the others quickly guided our herd away. They left us with only one riding camel. We were suddenly very poor.

For days we walked on through the dry bush and acacias struggling to survive until finally we had to eat something. As Muna and I slaughtered our sole remaining camel we heard gunfire. The bandits were waiting for us. They quickly encircled my family. Three of them gathered up the freshly butchered meat and put it atop one of their donkeys. Suddenly the one who was missing an eye ran toward my daughters with a long machete. He grabbed their little arms and pulled them into a line forcing them to stand shoulder-to-shoulder facing me so I could see their faces. My children looked so frightened but I could do nothing because one of the bandits held me from behind with a blade to my neck. I had hoped that they only wanted only to scare us. We are harmless, simple people. Suddenly the largest of the robbers shouted something I don't remember, pulled a dagger from his belt and one by one slit the throats of my beautiful daughters. Then another man grabbed the gun hanging from his shoulder and shot my wife several times in rapid succession. Her body fell across my feet. The bandits took everything from me, my family, my food, and my future. They left me standing alone in the wilderness to bury the bodies of my devoted wife and three beautiful daughters. Now I am here so you can help me walk.

Time and place fall away and I stand locked in the depth of this man's loss. Tears well in my eyes and layers of the armor melt away. But the Iron Nurse takes charge again to protect. I refrain from weeping in public, which is considered inappropriate in the Somali culture.

I look away from the man and toward his swollen foot.

"What can we do for him, Dr. Abass?" I ask quickly, wiping my face, while he focuses on the man's foot.

"It must be amputated," he says without hesitation.

"But he is a nomad. How will he survive without his foot?" I ask.

"If we were in America, yes we could do something. But not here. Not in a war zone. We don't have the drugs to treat it. Even if we did, the treatment lasts for months and must be followed strictly. Even for a city dweller this regime would be a burden but for a nomad, during a war, impossible. No choice but to amputate."

I nod silently.

Dr. Abass faces the man to deliver the news in his native tongue, heaping salt into the gaping wounds of this man's spirit.

"Maya, maya," the man replies emphatically shaking his head "no."

He swings his enormous foot over the side of the table and moves himself to standing. Dr. Abass hands him his walking stick and he limps across the concrete floor coated with diesel. I watch him pass under the arched doorway and he is gone.

As the day wears on the camel herder's image lingers. It permeates the outward armor I hold in place, even while caring for dozens of victims wounded in this bloodthirsty city.

By four in the afternoon my spirits lift a little when our Land Cruiser finally rolls through the towering gates of the IMC fortress. I have not once thought about my new bedroom sanctuary since before the camel herder.

Lindsey swings her long slim legs out of the vehicle first as Brian and I peel ourselves off the vinyl seats and slide out. Donna's fiery red hair sticks to her damp face as she steps out behind us. Sweat rolls down my chest and abdomen when I stand in the courtyard. Perhaps I can have a few minutes of relief in the cool of my room before dinner.

As I open the door to my sanctuary I remind myself to get rid of the extra bed as soon as possible.

Inside my deep sigh turns into an exasperation!

Books, wet towels and an open suitcase are strewn across the marble floor. On the beds are piles of papers, mismatched socks and men's undershirts. I throw my bag on the floor in one of the only remaining open spaces and stomp out the door to find the owner of the debris that defiles my room.

The smells of dinner draws everyone into the main living area adjacent the kitchen. The compound has gotten crowded since Carlos's news footage awakened a sleeping world to Somalia's daily atrocities. Journalists from various print and broadcast media have descended upon the country in droves. The two spacious villas that house IMC expatriates provides enough room to sleep 26 comfortably; this leaves plenty of space for journalists with expense accounts to cover their room and board. Andrew charges them $20 per minute for calls on the satellite phone providing IMC with money for continually needed supplies.

The comings and goings of these visitors adds chaos to our lives. Most are amiable and even entertaining. However, their presence presents certain drawbacks. At the end of a long day at Digfer it is less than desirable to have microphones shoved into our faces or cameras spontaneously recording us in our less than flattering sweat-soaked scrubs. Active tape recorders resting among the cutlery on the table dampens candid dinner conversation.

I look for Aweis to give me some explanation regarding my mystery roommate. In the living room I hear someone complaining loudly about an overweight, greasy-haired reporter who is sprawled out naked on the carpet. In the adjacent room another reporter interviews an expat who struggles to condense Digfer's overwhelming despair into tidy sound bytes.

"Mary," Aweis calls from behind, "I put a journalist named John Hockenberry in your room because he's in a wheelchair and yours is the only downstairs room with an extra bed."

I wasn't fast enough with the bed disposal.

"Where is he? He left his stuff all over my room," I demand.

"He is with Andrew but will be back soon."

I excuse myself early from dinner when I realize it is camel meat. Instead, I head to the veranda with a Tusker. I'm told this African beer gets its name from an acronym representing the countries of Tanzania, Uganda, Somalia, Kenya, Ethiopia, and Rwanda.

The sun submerges below the horizon, its diminished power gives an almost pleasant balmy feeling to the air. I find a stray match and light the mosquito coil that sits on the railing. The moment is soothing in spite of Somali guards conversing in raised voices in the courtyard below and erratic bursts of machine gun fire in the distance. A much needed oasis.

In the doorway the glow of Carlos's cigarette overpowers his dark features in the dim light after the sun's surrender.

"Hi. Okay if I join you?" he asks.

Carlos is one of the journalists whose charm keeps us from seeing him as an intruder.

"Sure. I'd like that," I said indicating the spot next to me on the railing.

"You left dinner. You don't seem like yourself today. Want to talk about it?" he asks gently.

I sigh deeply not knowing just where to start.

"It was the camel meat," I say.

"Did you know in some countries camel meat is used as a mood altering drug?" he asks facetiously.

"I just couldn't eat it."

I unload the story of the nomadic camel herder and he quietly validates the hopelessness.

"I saw the camel meat and couldn't help wondering if it was the very meat sold to IMC by the bandits who left a crippled man alone in the desert to bury the family they slaughtered. We then nourish ourselves with this stolen meat so we can have the strength to treat the atrocities committed by those very bandits."

Carlos interjects, "I think Somalia is probably the worst of all the violent conflicts I've seen. You know I spent time in Afghanistan several years ago and it wasn't nearly as bad as this place. Life is so cheap here. I don't know if we'll ever fully understand. The hatred among some is startling. I've been trying for a year to get the world's attention for Somalia but most of my footage ends up on the cutting room floor."

"Until now," I declare.

"True. The world now knows what's going on here," he replies.

"That must be satisfying," I say.

"Hmm," he responds. A melancholy expression shades his face.

His mind disappears far across the darkening horizon. We sit quietly for a few moments.

Finally I break the silence with a change of subject.

"Well, I suppose it's good more media personalities are here to get the story out, but one of them spewed his stuff all over my room. They put him in my first-floor room because he's in a wheelchair."

"John Hockenberry," he says.

"Yeah, that's it. Do you know him?"

"He's a colleague of mine at ABC. I think it's pretty brave for him to come to Somalia. He'll learn a lot," Carlos replies.

"Starting with roommate etiquette. I don't care if he is in a wheelchair. It seems like a decadent luxury after seeing that camel herder hobble through the door of Digfer today."

Without electricity the darkened city comes to life through bursts of gunfire and occasional explosions. The mosquito coil glows anemically, barely able to keep up with the glow from the last dregs of Carlos's cigarette.

I empty the final drops of my Tusker before leaving my perch above the dying city. Carlos is deep in the well of his thoughts. Speaking to him now seems like an invasion, so I simply lay my hand on his shoulder briefly on my way through the arched doorway.

In the living room a man with wispy brown hair sits in a late model wheel chair positioned next to the crushed velvet settee where Andrew sits, locked in conversation. John Hockeberry's friendly face and intent listening eyes tempt me to like him, but I resist.

"Are you John Hockenberry?" I ask without a hint of politeness.

"Yes, I'm John," he says extending his hand.

I do not extend mine and his retreats back to his lap.

"I'd really appreciate it if you would come with me for a moment," I say turning toward my room.

When he wheels into the room I look directly into his eyes.

"This morning this was my room. When I got back from a long day wading knee-deep in casualties, I find my one little corner of peace in this God-forsaken city has been trashed by all of your shit."

He begins to skillfully navigate the room, rapidly picking up socks and papers and stuffing them into the pouch on the back of his chair.

"I'm sorry. So sorry," he says as he works.

"I don't care if you are in a wheelchair. If I'm going to have to share my room I expect you to keep your stuff picked up."

I sigh deeply, feeling better for a release of the tension that had mounted that day.

"I'm truly sorry. I didn't realize I was sharing this room with anyone," he comments as he finalizes his clean up effort.

Finally I sat down on my bed feeling a bit more relaxed.

"All right, thank you for respecting my request. My name is Mary, by the way," I say.

"Nice to meet you Mary, maybe we could start over. I'm John," he replies extending his hand again.

I give in to temptation and shake it this time. I'll probably find this man to be a pleasant human being, I decide.

"I'm not really a bitch. I've just had a tough day and was really looking forward to some solitude," I say with a softer tone.

"Understandable. Actually it's refreshing to be treated as an equal. So many people told me I should not come here because of the wheelchair. Although a little jarring initially, I'm glad your first response is to expect the same from me as you would anyone else," he says with sincerity then adds, "What happened today?"

"Today my first patient was a crippled man who walked

across the desert after burying his whole family who had been murdered by bandits. He refused treatment and I watched him hobble out onto the harsh streets of Mog without his family or any means of supporting himself. Your wheelchair seems like a Ferrari compared to his situation. Sorry if that seems cold," I say.

"Not at all," he says listening intently.

"The Somalis have never seen a guy with legs in a wheel-chair," I say lightheartedly, "so be careful of machine-gun wielding soldiers with a lustful eye in your direction. The city is full of double amputees crawling around on their hands and stumps. It will be like you rolled into town cruising the streets of a war zone in a shiny new BMW," I say with a laugh.

"I'll certainly heed that advice. Thank you," he says with a relieved grin.

We talk for an hour. He tells me about the accident that put him in a wheelchair for life and of his interest in getting the story out to the world about the Somali people. He shared candidly the lengths to which he had to go to prepare his body for this rugged assignment. I am thankful he was able to see past my initial greeting. I feel confident a friendship can develop.

Just as I am drifting to sleep, lulled by the intermittent buzz of gunfire, John's voice brings me back to consciousness.

"Mary, you awake?" he asks, his voice shaking a little.

"Yeah, I guess so," I say without opening my eyes.

"Does the gunfire ever stop?"

"Nope. It's the one thing you can count on."

"Oh," his voice is shaking a little more.

"You okay?" I ask my new friend.

"I don't know. I guess I'm feeling kind of alone."

"Understandable," I say trying to stay awake.

"Mary?"

"Yeah, John."

"Would you mind holding my hand?" he requests innocently.

I reach out across the short space between our beds and find his trembling hand. We stay like that in the dark for some time while violent torrents of gunfire jettison through the night air just outside our tiny sanctuary.

-10-

Jackson

Mogadishu, Somalia, 1992

An AK-47 rattles against the metal frame of our Toyota technical, next to the window Jackson guards. The driver pushes in a tape and the voice of Madonna becomes a part of the Mogadishu landscape. Jackson wears his signature green striped dress shirt and worn yellow trousers. He stares straight ahead through the large black-rimmed glasses. He lightly taps his assault rifle in time with the beat as we bounce along on our rugged route to Digfer. His brother Hersi sits in the front passenger seat, next to the driver, and taps his own weapon with the same rhythm. The heavy heat of the morning creates damp rings of sweat on our clothing.

"Hey, where's John?" Donna inquires as she twists a strand of red hair between her fingers.

"He left a few days ago with Carlos and his crew a few days ago to work on a story for some nightly news program. I will really miss him. John was always a perfect gentleman and really went out of his way to keep our room uncluttered," I reply.

"Yeah, he was pretty cool, I'll miss him too. Hey Mary, what's on your agenda for today?" Donna asks, pursing her full lips into a smile.

"Ann and I are going to squeeze in time to paint the Casualty sometime this morning," I respond.

"If you can pull her away from the media attention," Donna

whispers, gesturing with her eyes rolled toward Ann who has positioned herself in the back next to Marilyn Greene of *USA Today*. Ann's shy façade seems to disappear when in convenient proximity to a journalist's camera or tape recorder.

The technical comes to an abrupt stop just beyond the large covered landing outside Digfer. Rooftop guards keep their position on top of the technical. Jackson gets out first and holds the door open for Donna, red hair caught in a burst of wind frames her lovely face.

One by one, we peel our moist bodies away from the sticky vinyl seats and slide out of the vehicle.

Just before Jackson closes the door he answers a radio call. Andrew's voice comes through the crackle.

"We'll be back. Andrew wants us at the airport," Jackson yells in our direction waving good-bye as the vehicle pulls away. His peach fuzz mustache curves upward as he flashes his distinctly understated grin.

As we approach the Casualty entrance we sidestep around two men carrying an emaciated woman in a wooden wheelbarrow. They are probably related to her, but they dump her body without a word and disappear. Leaving a wounded family member outside the hospital door in a wheelbarrow is unthinkable to most North Americans. However, I have come to understand that Somalis are not cold, heartless people but rather humans who have learned the overwhelming torrent of death from starvation and constant violence robs some of the luxury of waiting at the side of a loved one. Many cannot afford to be away from the duties of protecting their home and other family members.

As they cross the threshold, Brian and a new expat doctor from the States named Bradford wheel her the remaining distance into the Casualty and their day has begun.

Bradford is an ER doctor with a great bedside manner, an engaging sense of humor and the first black expat I've seen in Somalia since I arrived.

Ann and I spread cream-colored paint over the grimy walls of the Casualty. When I look up to inspect my work I notice a young man in a thinning dirty macaawis standing beside me. An older man in worn trousers stands beside him. The older puts his hand on the younger man's shoulder. Their shining eyes beam at me with proud recognition, yet I am unable to place them. The younger man lifts the left side of his shirt and points to a healing incision.

"Yussuf?" I say with excited surprise.

"Subah wahnoxin," he greets with equal excitement.

It is difficult to picture this young man as the same one who was discarded to the hallway floor by his fellow patients. He looks to have gained fifteen pounds, his skin and lips are back to their healthy coloring, and his face is full and smiling.

Yussuf was the catalyst for the education program in the hospital. Since then the diagrams have taken off. Ishmael, still a patient on the same ward where Yussuf almost died, uses the drawings faithfully, and remains a trusted teacher to the other patients. I capitalized on his natural assertiveness and desire to learn, and gave him the job of teaching new patients about colostomies. He has even taught some of the Somali nurses to educate the patients. Typically, Somali nurses consider instructing patients the doctor's domain. But the nurses have latched on to the value of educating because they have seen the positive results in their patients' progress.

Knowing my limited Somali will impede our conversation, I hold my hand up and say, "Sug, sug. Wait."

I leave momentarily to find someone who can help me understand what they are saying. Yussuf and his father nod their heads in agreement.

Ten minutes later Dr. Abass and I make our way back to Yussuf and his proud father.

Dr. Abass recognizes Yussuf instantly.

"Mary, I know this man. I did the surgery to reverse his colostomy," he says greeting the two men warmly.

"Really? I didn't know you did the reversal. How long ago did you do his surgery?" I ask.

"It's only been about three or four weeks. Let me see how he looks," Dr. Abass says as he gently lifts the boy's faded tee shirt and speaks softly to him in Somali.

The boy and his father share a brief conversation with Dr. Abass.

"The incision is healing very well. The father tells me he walks with Yussuf several times a day and prepares as much food as he can find for him."

Yussuf says something to Dr. Abass and gestures toward me.

"Yussuf wants to say thank you for helping him. He has been looking for you so he could show you how well he is doing," Dr. Abass remarks.

Yussuf has offered me a gratifying reminder of what I am doing in one of the world's most dangerous places thousands of miles from everything familiar. I think of Rodrigo's little plastic sword.

Yussuf's smile infuses me once again with purpose. I am profoundly grateful to him.

His father asks something of Dr. Abass who tells me they need two blankets. They have asked me at just the right moment and I stretch the rules this time.

"Mahahtsanet," they say with grateful smiles as they turn to go with their arms wrapped around their blankets.

"Mike Lima, Mike Lima!" A serious voice announces my call sign on my radio interrupting the delightful scene.

"Base this is Mike Lima, copy," I reply, smudging paint onto the radio jacket.

"Gather the team and get back to the compound now. Security incident. Don't alarm anyone," the voice says with forced calm.

A security incident could mean anything from a death threat to someone opening fire in the Casualty department.

Technicals often speed through the streets of Mogadishu with gunman hanging off the side and roof with fingers poised on the triggers of their powerful weaponry. A few months ago a gunman sneezed while manning an anti-aircraft weapon just outside our compound, causing his weapon to fire. The bullets hit a tree, which toppled onto five other men. Three were killed. Osman Otto, the wealthy and powerful Somali and financier to warlord General Aideed, employed the sneezing gunman. Not surprisingly, the careless gunman was executed.

"What is it this time?" I whisper to myself, and release a heavy sigh.

Other technicals whiz past us as our driver races through the streets of Mogadishu toward our compound. The closer we come to IMC the louder the shouting. The crowds of gunmen thicken, many no more than ten years old.

A multitude of technicals, all holding heavily armed Somalis shouting passionately amongst themselves line up outside the tall iron gates of the IMC compound. I am afraid we will not be able to get into the relative safety of our fortress without also admitting the angry crowd. The barrels of their guns are pointed at our compound. Crowds of Somalis fill the rooftops of the surrounding buildings to get a bird's-eye view of the incident. Shots fire randomly as our technical jerks into the slightly open gates. This is not just another security incident.

Inside the twelve-foot iron gates our local Somali staff is milling about with nervous tension. A Somali man's body is lying supine on the veranda, and several Somali women are squatting beside him, crying openly. Even with all the death and pain I see every day at Digfer I have never seen the Somalis openly display grief.

When I approach the body I notice the unmistakable green striped dress shirt and worn yellow trousers, soaked with red stains. Jackson's signature hat and glasses are missing but I can see his eyes are half open staring forward, devoid of expression. The marble floor under him is stained with his blood and his wives rock back and forth wailing. Their sorrowful cries pierce the air like a knife into flesh.

Several of us kneel beside him to see if there is any sign of life. There is none and we move away from him. My eyes mist with tears as one of his wives moves to his side and takes his hand. Her colorful hijab falls away from her face and she presses his hand into her face and wails.

Suddenly several of our guards shout various commands in Somali and chaotically gather their weapons.

"Where are they going?" Marilyn Greene of *USA Today* asks, with a forced calm in her voice.

"They are going to find Jackson's killer," Andrew replies, clearly shaken.

"What happened?" I ask Andrew, remembering he is supposed to be on his way to Nairobi.

Someone from the crowd yelled, "They killed him. They killed Jackson."

"But who? What happened?" I ask.

Ann is shuffling back and forth from a group of expats and back into the compound. She looks lost and close to panic, but just keeps moving, pacing nervously and wringing her long slim fingers over her hands.

"Ann, please sit down," someone demands curtly.

"Oh, I'm sorry, I'm sorry," she says but continues to pace.

Brian and three of the Somali staff lift Jackson's limp body to a more private location so he can be prepared for burial. Jackson's arms sway slightly at his sides as they walk. A trail of bright red marks the walkway as they move away.

"Jackson and his brother went with us to the airport. While we helped the pilot transfer the newly arrived pharmacy order to the IMC Land Cruiser, he and his brother sat on top of the vehicle watching a crowd of Hawadle clan members forming nearby."

"Is Hawadle the rival clan of Jackson's, Habar Gabir clan?" I ask, still not straight on who's who in Somalia.

"Yes," Andrew answers and then continues, "from out of nowhere there was gunfire and Jackson immediately slumped forward onto his brother. His brother jumped off the vehicle and before we knew it, made his way toward the crowd with his AK-47 and a string of bullets around his neck. He looked like Rambo. We made it to him before he started firing at the crowd and pulled him back to the Land Cruiser. It seemed apparent that Jackson was dead, but we didn't want to upset his brother any further so we convinced him we had to get him back to the compound for treatment. On the way back we learned a kid in the crowd shot Jackson and ran away. In the mean time, some of Jackson's clan kidnapped an elder from the shooters' clan saying they will not return him until they hand over the kid who shot Jackson."

"So, since IMC employs Jackson, all of us at IMC are considered part of his clan and literally caught in the crossfire," Donna adds, her emerald eyes pensive.

"Quite literally," Andrew replies looking toward the compound walls as gunfire and angry shouting continues just outside.

Andrew walks away abruptly with some of the Somalis to continue to negotiate a peaceful solution. It does not look hopeful. I wonder if this day that started like so many others might be my last.

The smartest thing to do is to take cover immediately. Bullets are flying over the compound walls and rocket propelled grenades can be heard exploding just outside.

"Let's find a secure place inside, without windows," I advise the *USA Today* reporter standing next to me.

"Won't argue with that," Marilyn responds.

Several expats go to their rooms. I want to avoid windows, so I opt for the hallway extending from the IMC office, which is surrounded by thick, windowless walls. We sit with our backs leaning against the wall. I scrape small patches of cream-colored paint from my fingernails.

"You getting a little more news than you bargained for, huh, Marilyn?" Donna jokes, trying to be lighthearted.

"Yeah, this is sure one way to get a story," she says.

Marilyn's interest in getting stories is not only professionally motivated, but also comes from a sincere interest in the Somali people.

"I've only been here a week. This feels a little like baptism by fire. The violence seems so chaotic and senseless. How do you feel, having been here for several months?" she asks.

I can see her holding her hands still to keep them from trembling.

"It does seem like senseless, random killings but in fact the violence is part of an intricate organized clan rivalry. The motivation is similar to that of gang warfare in American cities. Most of the time the warfare is not directed at the NGOs, but at times we get caught in it, like in situations like this, or when we make mistakes because of our ignorance of the culture," I say.

"Have you made those kinds of mistakes?" Marilyn asks.

I can't help but laugh heartily at her question thinking of my many faux pas, like the Victoria's Secret Hell incident.

"When I first got here I noticed medical supplies were making their way out the door of the hospital, usually under clothing. One day I saw a man carrying a box filled with bandages and syringes out the front door of Digfer right out in the open. It was some kind of last straw for me. I mean, hell, the nerve of the guy."

"Did you confront him?" Marilyn inquires.

"Of course, right in front of everyone in the market just outside the hospital where they sell the pilfered supplies. I got the help of a guard, took the box from the man and even told the guards to start checking all boxes leaving the hospital."

"What did the man do?" Donna asks.

"He went away angry and humiliated. But it wasn't over. The next day the man's brother stops me and begins to threaten me because of what I'd done to shame his family. He says, 'What clan are you?' So I told him I was 'the medical clan.'"

"That's good," Marilyn says chuckling. "But why'd you say that?"

"Mary's always so quick on her feet," says Donna. "But, we've all learned how to stay alive. We can't say we belong to this clan or that because of the rivalry, and we don't want to be caught in the crossfire so we avoid directly answering inquiries regarding clan as well as religion as much as possible. It keeps us alive longer."

"Yeah, but my mouth has gotten me into trouble a little too often," I add. "Before I knew it he had a gun to my head and he's yelling threats at me. He's telling me I should not have talked to his brother the way I did. After he drove his point home he backed down."

"A close one," Marilyn interjects as the rat-a-tat-tat of machine gun fire continues.

"Well, I realized I needed some help understanding what happened. I talked with Dr. Abass, a Somali surgeon, who explained that in Somalia it is very bad to ridicule someone or point out something they did was wrong in front of other people. It's better done in private. Gives the person a chance to save his dignity. I realized my aggressive American mindset had not even taken into account the man's dignity and the fact that, although we can't allow pilfering, it is important to understand its motivation. In war and famine stealing quickly becomes a way of survival. Those supplies probably meant another day of keeping hunger at bay. I mean, to be honest, I would do the same thing in his situation," I admit.

Donna finds a package of Sportsman cigarettes and a lighter. She sucks in desperately and blows smoke with another heavy sigh. It took me a year to quit smoking and I haven't touched cigarettes for seven years. However, I'm not sure my resolve will hold with angry mobs wielding high-powered weapons just yards away.

"Donna, you're a nurse trained to help save lives and care for their overall health. Why do you smoke?" Marilyn asks.

"I quit several years ago but started again after I arrived

here," she replies.

"Why?" Marilyn inquires.

"In Mogadishu it doesn't take long to pick up the attitude that life is short and could be taken from you at any minute. Why deny myself something that could kill me twenty years from now? I could die today! Literally, we could all die today. We hear it at home, but here it is real," she says as she drags passionately on the quickly shrinking cigarette.

A large explosion rattles the wall we lean against.

"Let me have one of those," I demand.

"Me too," Marilyn says, "I've never smoked but maybe I'll try one."

"You're getting it," Donna says giving Marilyn a congratulatory pat on the back.

Donna turns her head and gazes down the hall. I notice an expression of anticipation on her slightly sunburned face. A tall Somali man with smooth skin the color of creamy Cuban coffee walks confidently toward us. It's Ahmed, our logistician. He focuses directly on Donna with his seductive chestnut eyes. He squats down beside her and speaks gently in spite of the harrowing circumstances.

"You all must stay here for the time being. Negotiations are progressing but it is still dangerous out there," he advises.

Donna moves her long fiery red tresses away from her face and Ahmed's dark, soulful eyes lock onto Donna's emerald greens.

The chemistry is palpable between these obvious lovers. Ahmed pauses for a few seconds, lost in her eyes, and then continues his report.

"What about Jackson?" I inquire.

"It is getting closer to sunset and Jackson will need to be buried. Andrew is trying to get them to take the fighting away from the IMC compound. He's also trying to get the elders from each clan to meet and discuss the situation. I'll let you know when it is safe," Ahmed says, smiling at Donna before he goes.

When he leaves we both look at Donna with inquisitive expressions.

"What?" she says innocently, unable to hide her pleasure at Ahmed's visit.

Marilyn and I hold our expressions for a few seconds and

then we all burst into peals of tension-fueled laughter. We spend the next several hours having a kind of surreal slumber party, smoking, talking about the men we've loved, dreams we've lost and dreams we've found. Gunfire rattles on like a bizarre form of Somali background musak.

When the sun begins to cast long shadows down our hallway fortress we spot Ahmed coming toward us.

"It is safe now," he says offering a hand to Donna.

She takes it and glances smugly at us as he guides her to her feet. One more round of laughter bursts from deep within us. Ahmed, although confused by our behavior, smiles with us.

When I contain myself I ask, "What was decided?"

"Both clans will take the issue to tribal court where they will have a trial. This agreement took the attention off of our compound."

In the courtyard we see Jackson's wailing wives, each purchased with many precious camels, following behind their husband's shrouded body.

-11-

Long Life

Mogadishu, Somalia, 1992

A fly flirts with the crust of my stale bread. I tear off a hardened dime-sized piece, placing it a few inches from my coffee. The insect lands on my offering and its tiny legs gather microscopic "bites" of greasy Kenyan "Blue Band" margarine in short jerky motions.

The unlikely teaming of hot coffee and the sub 100°F morning provide me the jolt I need to embrace another day at Digfer Hospital. Ann secretly withdraws a red bandana from under her shirt and wraps it around two slices of bread. Her eyes quickly scan the table looking for awareness on the faces of her fellow expatriates. She doesn't notice Brian and I exchanging knowing glances. A dull hunger remains with me as we begin to clear away breakfast. I push away from the table and dozens of flies intently feast on the crumbs I leave behind.

Yesterday, Jackson's body was laid to rest in the long shadows prior to sunset. Today the sun has risen on his grave and will once again roast the warring city of Mogadishu. I can already feel the warmth of the ground coming through the rubber soles of my red flip flops as I cross the courtyard toward our IMC vehicle for another day at Digfer.

M.C. Hammer blasts *"Can't touch this,"* from the faded black IMC Toyota Land Cruiser that chauffeurs us to the hospital. Our three Somali guards tap their fingers against their automatic weapons. I wonder if they are thinking about Jackson but do not ask.

Our driver's head is wrapped in a thin, discolored bath towel. He moves rhythmically with the music. For him the M.C. Hammer tape has become something of an anthem.

What was once surreal has become routine and the unpredictable is to be expected. I caress a smooth, pea-size pebble between my thumb and fingers and consider the relative ease with which I have adapted to unpredictable explosions, literal and figurative, lurking around every passing moment. Adaptability is the silver lining rounding the harsh edges of the unpredictability that clouded my childhood.

I told you homeboy you can't touch this.

Hammer Time continues through the dusty streets of Mogadishu. The cloudless sky allows the sun to heat my oversized scrub pants and tee shirt until sweat becomes like glue bonding the fabric uncomfortably to my skin. The Land Cruiser idles near a Somali woman huddled over a fire in the market. Her vibrant red and gold gabsar distinguishes her as a city dweller and covers her head as a symbol of modesty. The pink and white floral dirac drapes her lengthy torso loosely and falls gently around her feet. I drink in the rich aroma from the frankincense sizzling in a small white incense burner atop a pile of embers. Her long slender hand gently wafts the earthy scent onto her face and clothing. Strolling gunman casually pass. She beckons the incense. It washes over her and she is adorned even in this place of unending sorrow.

Can't touch this.

A vendor calls to uninterested passers-by offering a fair price for a plastic bag filled with fermented camel milk. Kiosks constructed from dozens of thin sticks lined up in tight formation as if before a firing squad. They dot the landscape of the market. Their roofs are constructed with bright blue and green plastic distributed by the United Nations, stolen before it could reach the displaced Somalis for whom it was intended. Above one kiosk a metal pole is positioned over the head of its Somali vendor. Live chickens with their legs tied together sit next to machine guns. Tins of cooking oil stamped "USAID" are offered for sale on a small table. The vendor approaches our vehicle and tries to broker a trade but his Somali is too fast, and the driver jerks forward for the final minutes of our commute.

At first glance Digfer appears deceivingly impressive from a structural standpoint. Given five minutes this impression crumbles. Focus beyond a glance and gaping shell holes become obvious on upper floors. Spent and unspent bullets litter the ground like confetti. A huge field of graves greets the sick and dying at the front. A group of Somalis live behind the building with their goats, and slowly starve under a stand of thorny acacia trees.

At the hospital entrance I carefully avoid the used syringes littering the ground. Stubbing my toe on a dirty needle is not a good idea from a disease avoidance point of view. My flip-flops meet the concrete floor made slick with diesel fuel and blood. Although sturdier shoes would offer more protection, flip-flops provide a pleasant relief from the oppressive heat. Along a dimly lit corridor the usual odors of infection, rotting meat, gangrene, gunpowder, bodily waste, diesel fuel, and camel broth mingle like some kind of horrid stew.

"Give me one pen," a Somali woman demands as I pass. Another grabs at my pants and demands I give them to her on the spot.

A wiry woman with an outstretched hand calls to me as I pass.

"Hilib, hilib!" she pleads.

Hilib is the word for meat. I learned this word very quickly.

A man's voice calls to me. I look around to see where the words are coming from. In a dark shadow along the hallway I barely make out a feeble looking soul on a small piece of soiled cardboard leaning against the wall's peeling green paint. His impeccable English stops me immediately.

"Help me! Help me," he pleads.

A soiled button down shirt and a tattered pair of trousers hang from his frail body. He smells strongly of excrement, probably absorbed from the noxious odors of the corridor. I crouch closer to the side of his humble nest and his bony fingers desperately reach for my arm. His glassy brown eyes look directly into mine speaking an intense language of despair.

The man is so thin I can count the ribs protruding from beneath his putrid sheet. Cheekbones distend dramatically under the chestnut skin that thinly veils his skull, lined with pulsating arteries. But the smell is the dominating feature. His overpowering odor of filth and bodily waste threatens to take my breath.

"Help. I need help," his words echo the language of his eyes.

"Are you sick?" I inquire.

"Please. I am in need of medicine," he answers.

Grasping for clues to help this man I ask, "Do you have fever, vomiting, diarrhea? Are you hurting?"

"No. It is pills I need. I need medicine."

Despite his desperation, there is no reason to dispense medication. "Where are you from, sir?" I inquire.

"I am Omar from Khartoum, the capitol city of Sudan," he replies.

"What is your name?" he asks.

"Mary from IMC," I respond.

"Mary, I came to Mogadishu one year ago, but when the war began everything I owned was stolen. I lost my job and now I have no way to get home. I have no family here. I have no one here to help me."

His command of English indicates he is an educated man and possibly migrated to Somali for a prestigious teaching position at the former Mogadishu University.

Both his hands wrap around my arm. His long, thick fingernails, encrusted with the dirt of his arduous journey, dig into my skin. It is clear he does not need medication but I cannot walk away without giving him something. It is a struggle to discern a way to help him that does not involve pills or a material gift. However, a clever idea suddenly comes to me.

"I will help you," I say. "But you have to promise to do something for me."

My education by fire has taught me many times the key to lasting impact is being in partnership with those in need.

"I'll be back," I promise.

His hands reluctantly release their hopeful grip on my arm. Outlines of his thin fingers topped with indentations like tiny crescent moons mark my forearm as I walk away.

My flip-flops slip slightly as I rise to leave him. Along the ill-lit corridor my shoulder brushes against the once white walls now spattered with blood and the occasional flattened insect.

Someone calls, "Biyo, biyo!"

"Salaam ah likum!" another calls with the Arabic greeting meaning "peace."

Amina, looking elegant in her red and black dirac and striped hijab, stops me abruptly.

"Mary, Brian wants you to find a bed for his patient just out of surgery," she declares with authority.

"Right," I say with a small laugh and a large dose of sarcasm. At Digfer finding an empty bed is like finding an original Picasso at a flea market.

Her face devoid of amusement, Amina's long, slender body moves slowly away with an air of aristocracy. Although trained on the job to provide health care, under normal circumstances she would not be qualified as a Registered Nurse. She carries her resentment toward her present position like some Somalis carry AK-47's.

Now distracted from the Sudanese man, I search the male ward for an empty bed. The ward is a wall-to-wall storehouse of disease, dismemberment and death's constant hunger.

Family members make their homes in various proximities to the ill and injured. Some lie directly on the concrete floor, others on blankets. A lucky one occupies pieces of a blood stained foam pad. On the balcony a woman stokes a fire, while sparks flutter like tiny fireflies near the torn sheet enshrouding the body of her languid child. The thick liquid in her small pot slowly bubbles. Aroma of sweet camel meat arouses a grinding in my stomach.

Across the room broken glass creates an opening in the window through which the sounds of incessant gunfire and braying donkeys flow. The only two beds in this ward sit side by side next to the window. One is empty.

I recognize the man dying in the other bed. His name is Jamal. His motionless body deteriorates from internal infection caused by several gauze sponges left in his abdomen after a colostomy reversal surgery by Dr. Jefferson, the arrogant Somali medical student posing as a surgeon. The man's flesh decays from the inside because he refuses to have the rotting cotton removed. Jamal claims that he felt better when he had a hole in his side with a bag attached. He says that Dr. Jefferson made him feel worse when he closed up the hole.

Jamal is not the first patient with complaints about Dr.

Jefferson but I can do nothing about the competency of Somali volunteers. IMC does not run Digfer Hospital, we only supervise and manage the supplies we donate, and lend a helping hand when and where we can. The hospital is run by the Somali medical director who was in place prior to our arrival and Dr Jefferson is a member of his clan.

Ishmael, Mohammed and I have all explained to Jamal why he needs another operation but he wants to leave his recovery in the hands of Allah. He lies on a traditional bed brought in by his family. The mattress is a cowhide stretched tightly across a roughly hewn wooden frame with small leather straps. Next to Jamal's traditional cot sits an empty hospital type bed, neatly made up with a sheet tucked around a foam mattress. A crudely assembled wooden cylinder sits on the empty bed. The container is painted black and the contents kept secure by a metal screw-on lid.

Thinking of the legless post-operative patient with an immediate need for a bed, I hastily grab the innocuous looking object, intending to toss it through the opening in the broken window. Heaving trash out an open window is a habit not uncommon in places where survival takes a front seat to environmental considerations. I ignore several gasps and the commonplace commotion in the background.

Misjudging its weight, the modest-looking container slips through my fingers and almost falls to the floor before I am able to balance it between my knee and my elbows. Upon regaining my grip, I prepare to give the cylinder the appropriate force to send it sailing through the window.

Just before releasing the odd package I finally recognize the commotion as a mass exodus. Amputees hobble with surprising agility, intravenous bags in hand. Mothers scramble for the exit, grabbing children by the arm. Shrill screams from nurses and wounded alike pierce the once quiet desperation while bolting for the exit.

"Bomba, bomba!" a voice hurls a frightened announcement from the balcony.

Still holding the container in my right hand, my eyes survey the ward for the would-be assailant but find the room empty except for Jamal, semiconscious in the next bed. Satisfied the exodus and protests are a false alarm, I raise the cylinder once more but reconsider the disposal. I decide that dropping the object would be a more accurate method of disposal than tossing, and requires less need to aim. I walk to the jagged opening in the window with the object still in my hand.

Carefully lifting the black canister through the opening just above my head I steady my wrists on the razor-like shards of glass, ready to loosen my grip.

"Stop! Mary, bomba!" Amina's panicked voice exclaims from behind my precarious position. She exclaims again, "You are holding a bomb!"

Sweat forms streams that run between my breasts. Blood rushes out of my head causing a feeling of imbalance turning my stance from precarious to potentially deadly.

"A bomb?" I whisper, fearing the suddenness of a scream.

Time seems to stop. Through the window I see a frail man digging a grave in front of the hospital. Earth falls in small clusters from his shovel onto the mound adjacent to a small form wrapped in a torn cloth. Death's presence settles on this place like a heavy fog.

Balancing on the cut glass my arms begin to shake and a small trail of blood slowly drips along the side of my arm landing on my toe. The fog seems to thicken.

I find the strength to lift my body higher on the balls of my feet, mindful of my rubber flip-flops on the diesel-coated floor. Anxious eyes bore into me from the illusionary safety of the balcony. Calculating every motion, my fingers I slowly lift the black cylinder up and over the jagged glass.

A collective exhale is released by the huddle on the balcony. Turning slowly and deliberately I return the bomb to its home. Amina releases a slight sigh before explaining.

"Abshir, the brother of Jamal, lives in that bed."

I understand. The bomb secures his "property."

Abshir is not sick or recovering from injury but is one of the many who stay in the hospital for refuge and as a caregiver to a family member or fellow clansman.

Yet, downstairs a fresh post-op patient waits for a bed. He lies on a thin mat in the hall outside the operating room. The mat offers the only cushion between his severed leg and the concrete floor.

With the fog lifted, my fear becomes annoyance.

"This bed is needed, Amina," I demand, my naivety mixing dangerously with my determination.

Firmly gripping the cylinder I reflect that nursing school never taught me how to efficiently store an explosive device within the walls of a hospital.

"He will kill you," Amina warns. "If you take the bomb he will kill you when he returns."

Fog drifts around my thoughts.

An amputee makes his way back into the ward from the supposed refuge of the balcony.

He finds his floor mat and slowly lowers himself, cradling his IV bag in one arm, balancing his descent along the wall with the other. His hand sends curled paint chips falling like muted green snowflakes as he slides into his "bed."

My lungs fill with air and then release it into a heavy sigh.

"Abshir can take the bomb when he returns, but the bed belongs to an actual patient," I say, confident with this compromise.

Amina's black eyes look directly into me as if they intend to transfer the wisdom gained only through knowing war as a way of life. Without a word she maintains her regal stance while remaining a safe distance from death encased in a crude wooden capsule.

Ann passes through the ward interrupting our inaction. Just before she leaves our sight I call her name.

"Ann, do me a favor," I implore.

Before she has a chance to respond I place the explosive in her empty hands and casually give instructions.

"Take this bomb to the hospital administration office," followed by a hopeful, "Okay?"

"Sure," Ann says, ever happy to serve.

The black cylinder parts the sea of people as if it were Moses's staff itself creating an unobstructed path to the administration office turned bomb storage unit.

Amina directs the post-op amputee to the bed previously held by Abshir. Blood seeps through the bandages on his bloody stump as his neighbor breathes shallowly in and out.

My thoughts return to the English speaking Sudanese man who was lying on the floor in the hall. These thoughts cradle my tired spirit as I walk out of the ward, sidestepping an emaciated young women and several clumps of hair which have been shorn off a patient's head. Some Somalis believe that tossing away the hair means tossing away disease.

Thoughts of assisting the Sudanese man freeze at the sight of a large Somali man dressed in traditional green, plaid macaawis. The hem falls against his mid-calf like an extra long lightweight kilt. The writing on his tee shirt shouts, "I am the Boss." Most striking, however, is the AK-47 he carries as he furiously barrels in my direction. The automatic weapon pointed inches from my chest holds me where I stand.

He greets me with, "I will kill you."

Abshir, I presume.

"You took my bed and my bomb."

"What bed?" I ask, buying a few minutes.

He uses the gun like a pointer to indicate the bed next to Jamal.

"You can't kill me," I say, a casual laugh masking my anxiety.

"Why not?" Abshir inquires.

So this is the day I will die. A misty fog thickens in my mind.

"You can't kill me because we are friends," I chirp forcing another laugh.

A plan formulates when I remember laughter acts as a salve to powerful anger. If he laughs he can save face with his audience.

"How are you my friend?" he demands, holding his face in a hard scowl.

"I am an IMC nurse. We bring supplies, medicines and help the wounded. If I am killed, IMC will leave and who will save you if you get wounded?"

Although I precariously maintain my nonchalant air, my eyes are pleading.

"Okay," he says with a slight chuckle.

"But where is my bomb? I want it back," he demands.

"I don't have it anymore; the hospital administrator has it in his office downstairs. You can find it there," I reassure Abshir, hoping this gets me off the hook.

In his native language, Abshir confirms my reply with his fellow Somalis living in the ward. Finally, a look of satisfaction on his face meets one of relief on mine.

Can't touch this.

With an outwardly casual gate I turn from him and stroll out of the patient-lined hall to the nearest ward, where I would be out of sight. Inside the sanctuary of the male medical ward I release the air from my lungs like an exploding balloon. I take a deep breath to be sure I am still alive. This is followed by another deep exhalation. The strong odor of rotting flesh infuses my breathing, and triggers an image of the Sudanese man.

My narrow escape renews my determination to reunite Omar with his dignity—even just for today.

Winding through the maze of corridors lined with chestnut-skin bodies of the sick and wounded, I finally come upon Omar still occupying his cardboard as if anticipating a miracle. Perhaps the cardboard would become a rich Persian rug and whisk him away to another man's life. A life of dignity and promise.

"Mary!" he calls. "Please help me."

Kneeling down, placing a hand on his shoulder I remind him. "Omar, you must do something for me."

"Mary, yes. You have my pills," his request indicative of his determination.

Holding his gaze I explain. "Sir, you do not need drugs. For you, I have something better than medicine. Can you walk?"

His sunken eyes meet my question with raw hope.

"Yes. Mary, what is greater for me than pills?"

In Sudan, Somalia and the world over, people hold a common belief that pills, injections and intravenous solutions hold the key to easing any ailment. Medications in every medium are sold on the streets to countless victims desperate for relief in any form. Hawkers promise a cure for any ailment their vulnerable customers present. Intravenous dextrose is swallowed in hope of relief and powerful anesthetics are sold as a cure for pneumonia, malaria and tuberculosis. Many die as a result of these deceptions.

"I will give you a bath."

I add, "But while you are bathing you must wash your own clothes."

If his bath becomes the envy of the ward, I know filling a tub of water is much easier to reproduce than dispensing food or money.

He nods in gentle agreement.

As Omar follows me, his torn, soiled clothing hangs precariously from his bent frame. Amina moves slowly towards us on her way to another patient.

"Amina," I say halting her laborious pace, "Will you bring a big bathing tub to Casualty, please?"

Amina protests without concern for Omar. She tosses the fallen corner of her striped hijab back over the opposite shoulder while she looks up and down at the pathetic sight before her.

"Mary, this man is poor," pointing out the obvious flaw in my plan.

To many Somalis, "poor" are considered untouchable.

Amina sees a man unable to compensate for his care with even a chicken or a few loaves of bread. She sees a man from another land and without home or clan support. As Dr. Abass explained, many native doctors and nurses will find ways to avoid accepting a "poor" patient such as Omar.

"I will bathe him. I am not asking you to touch him."

Omar's head rises slightly from the belly of his shame.

"We will be in the Casualty," I say, wanting her negative tone removed from this man's presence.

The displaced man follows closely behind, with hunched shoulders and head lowered. His bare feet slide on the slick concrete in the corridor leading to the Casualty, and his bony fingers wrap around my upper arm like a vine.

A woman pulls her child a little closer when Omar stumbles over a spent syringe. Flies hover around his face and on spots of feces smeared on his shirt. His foul odor precedes our approach, distracting attention from the familiar sounds of gunfire.

Omar is not much older than thirty-five but moves and carries himself like a much older man. His shame and disgrace compress his spirit like a thousand iron chains.

Miraculously, I find a relatively clear corner where my desperate patient hunches and waits. Resourcefulness is a survival tool and friend in a place of constant disarray. I spot the rounded rim of a corrugated tin tub protruding slightly from behind a pile of maimed chairs. A woman runs past me. The abdomen of the child in her arms is ripped open and his eyes are glazed and still. One sandal loosely dangles from his foot, bobbing only from his mother's frantic pace. A Somali doctor and

American physician assistant approach the woman and child, unaffected by their tragic familiarity with this scene. There are almost no surprises and no reactions left in them.

The scene moves to another sector of Casualty and my eyes again focus on the stack of mangled chairs. I free the tub and lift it over my head to transport it to Omar's corner. Balancing the tub on my head, I am able to grab a privacy screen with one hand. The tri-fold iron frame, covered with tattered cloth, serves more as a gesture of respect than as an actual means to provide privacy.

Three buckets of water the color of weak tea sit beside the tub. Amina reluctantly agrees to participate by filling the containers with water from the pump outside the hospital. I empty the discolored water into the metal tub and ask Omar for his garments. I am unsure if he will accept this prerequisite to the bath.

But Omar has no interest in modesty. He simply lets the soiled remnants of humility fall to the cold slick floor. His bones protrude through the shallow skin covering his bent and naked body. His skin hosts abrasions and bodily waste where a multitude of flies find nourishment. Of late, only the insects consider this man touchable.

A small crowd is forming around the edges of our unadorned little spa. A thinly veiled skeleton steps into the bath, wincing from the shocking cold. Surely it had been months since he had felt the redeeming embrace of a body of cool water. Male and female nurses begin to watch in amazement.

Omar's meager one hundred pound frame lowers until he fits snuggly with knees pulled up to his chin. Someone in the crowd then lifts his stained clothing and places it at his feet where it floats briefly before his lean fingers submerge it. My homeless friend intends to earn his luxurious gift. I sprinkle some soap powder I picked up in Kenya; it falls gently onto the garments like blue manna.

Using my hands as a container, I fill them with cool rusty water and pour the first blessing onto his shoulders. My hands roll over his skin. As the water washes over him, he lifts his face to reveal an expression so pure and joyous it ignites the crowd around him. Hands begin to come from everywhere pouring and splashing water on his arms, his shoulders, his back and his head. For this moment there is only joy. Men kill and maim beyond these walls but still this moment is joyous and real. What was one gift has become a feast of giving and receiving.

An arm reaches across Omar's chest and its hands begin to massage him with soap in slow, circular motions. I look up to see Amina's brilliant red hijab. Our eyes meet and pass a thousand words between us without a single utterance. She smiles and begins to wash the palm of his hand and the spaces between his bony fingers.

I pour water over his head slowly working out the matted places in his tight black curls. As the water continues to wash over him like dozens of baptisms, Omar grips my arm and holds my gaze. With a grin from ear to ear and a sparkle of hope in his eye, he enunciates each word, "Long life Mary. Long life."

My normal thick exterior cracks and tears catch me off guard. In this moment Omar's once crushed dignity has found redemption.

Can't touch this.

-12-

Raasel Dazzel

Mogadishu, Somalia, 1992

"Ready Lindsey?" I ask my tall blonde friend as she picks a bouquet from the hanging bougainvillea plant in the square adjacent to our transport.

"Oh, yeah, just a second," she says and runs inside to place her flowers in a glass of water on an end table next to the Italian settee.

I wait in the courtyard, watching her as she strokes the fuchsia flowers gently and smiles at their simple beauty. She and I are the only expats leaving for Digfer this early. A size-able shipment of medical supplies arrived in the IMC Mogadishu warehouse, which requires a careful inventory of the current supplies before stocking the shelves with the new arrivals.

A cheerful Somali guard, Musa, lights up when he sees us. Many of the guards, like Jackson, become our friends, and Musa is certainly among them. In the few weeks he has been with us his strained English skills show gradual signs of improvement. Today he will accompany us into the hospital, guarding us close-ly as we catalogue large quantities of valuable medications.

"Mary, Lindsey, subah wahnoxin!" he calls with outstretched arms reaching towards us.

"Good...good...how do you say?" he asks.

"Good morning," I reply.

"Yes, yes, good morning Mary and Lindsey," he says proudly.

His face tenses as we approach the wiry Somali man leaning against the vehicle's rear passenger door. A green bath towel is tied around his head with what looks like the end of a leather whip. His chin hangs down toward his chest resting on the barrel of his AK-47. As I approach he appears to be asleep. The other guards pace carefully around him as we begin to get into the car. I stand in front of him and clear my throat loudly.

He wakes and stands to the side, waiting for us get in first. I take my seat in the center rear. He gets in slamming the door hard. His gun rests between his legs just like Jackson's did when he was with us, less than a week ago. This man is his replacement.

"Nahbaht, aniga Miriam—hello, I'm Mary," I say to the new guard.

His head turns slightly in my direction, suspiciously scanning his surroundings without offering me eye contact. He slides a sprig of khat out of his pocket and places it between his teeth. His jaw clenches and slowly the plant releases its stimulant. Musa's eyes meet mine in the rearview mirror before he looks anxiously at the new guard.

"Mary, this is Raasel," he says nodding his head in the direction of the back seat.

Raasel does not acknowledge the introduction. As he chews, he tightens his grip on the gun.

An electric blue starling perches on the crumbled remains of a balcony railing adjacent to the Casualty entrance. I bat at the flies that swarm my face as I enter and they retreat to the intestines spilling from a woman whose body is held in the belly of a crudely made wheelbarrow.

We enter the hospital pharmacy managed by Ali Nur, an experienced pharmacist, formerly employed as a teaching professor at the now defunct Medical University across the street. Ali is a man with a serious eye to detail who seems to enjoy his work at Digfer.

The windows are barricaded with varying sizes of plywood. A tiny shaft of light graces the wooden table, where Ali Nur strains to see the pills spilled out on its surface. He does not look up from his work to greet us until he is finished counting and jotting notes on a scratch paper. Amina waits while he sits at a small wooden table meticulously counting pills and sliding them into a plastic bag. The windowless room offers increased security for the drugs and medical supplies, but the temperature well exceeds the recommended storage temperature for the medications. A trail of sweat drips from my temple and hangs at the edge of my jaw. The thick humidity and stagnant air combine with the daily smells of bodily waste, diesel and rotting flesh. Waves of nausea roll through me like giant swells on the Indian Ocean.

Musa positions himself at the door with a fully automatic AK-47 hanging from his bony frame.

"Good morning, Mary and Lindsey," Ali Nur says, as his face transforms to offer a friendly greeting.

He stands, hands the bag of pills to Amina, and walks toward a pile of cardboard boxes in the corner.

"These are the supplies from Nairobi," he says, opening the first box.

Lindsey and I peer inside and realize we have an arduous task ahead.

"Better get started," I say with a deep sigh.

"Last time I did this, two of the boxes were filled with paper. All the meds had been stolen on the way to Mog," Lindsey says, brushing strands of blonde hair from her perspiring face as she removes the crumpled invoice from the bottom of the box.

She begins calling the names and quantities of the medication as it is written on the invoice, waiting patiently for me to confirm their existence.

"Oh, here it is, box one, Cotrimoxazole tabs, two times 1,000, Paracetamol tabs, two times 500...." I pause when I see Amina back in the doorway.

"Mary, we need you in the male ward. You come—now! Hurry," she calls from the doorway and begins walking down the hall toward the male ward not waiting for me.

"I'll be back," I say to Lindsey, a little relieved to have a break from the dungeon-like conditions in the dim airless pharmacy.

"Sure. No problem," Lindsey replies, stretching her long legs into a standing position as she waves the invoice at me.

"What is it, Amina?" I ask when I catch up to her.

"It's Jamal," she says. Amina's usual stoicism is visibly shaken by the impending death of her friend.

A cold chill runs through me, thinking of my near miss with his brother's bomb.

"He is very, very sick," she adds.

As we scale the two flights toward the male ward I shake the dozens of hands that reach out from sick and injured Somalis dotting the stairs. Even in a life and death kind of rush, it is considered extremely inappropriate not to shake everyone's hands and give a short greeting. I have come to appreciate daily touch from multitudes of people in this culture, something I know I will miss when I return to the States.

"Nahbaht," I say shaking the hand of a woman who stops me.

"Give me one pen," she says in a demanding tone.

Recently Amina asked me for my pants, to which I responded by beginning to untie the drawstring on my scrubs. My actions were met with laughter and adamant protests from Amina. I have learned that Somalis do not have a word for "please." They have a different mind set about possessions. Somalis are more communally minded. They share with everyone in their extended family. So if one person is not using something, another can use it. When they say "give me," they're really saying "If you're not using the pen, may I use it for a while?" An important cultural nuance to understand and something I didn't immediately realize.

Amina and I step over the piles of rubbish and used pieces of bloody gauze cluttering the corridor. My anxiety increases when I enter the male ward. I have not been here since the confrontation with Abshir and his bomb. If he watches his brother Jamal die while I am present, he might not be as easily charmed away from violence this time.

Jamal's body is too emaciated to fight the peritonitis that riddles his abdomen. A fistula near his navel drains pea green pus mixed with bits of rotten gauze. Having the foreign bodies removed earlier might have saved his life, but he refused to have a third surgery insisting if it is God's will, he will live. I quickly scan the ward for Abshir before walking to Jamal's bed. Abshir is no where in sight. Jamal is probably in his late twenties, but looks like an aging man in his eighties. Ribs like a washboard move in erratic movements in response to his breathing which comes only in gasps.

Instead of Abshir, Jamal's wife sits at his side. She grips his hand as though it might prevent him from slipping away from her. Amina moves next to two young boys standing at the head of their father's deathbed. The older has his arms around the shoulders of the younger. My eyes burn with tears, I no longer think of the fear I felt the last time I was in this room. I will the Iron Nurse not to fail me, to keep me focused on the medical needs of the situation. Jamal's pale face has lost its rich coffee color. When I touch his cold skin his eyes flutter and look into mine. They tell the story of the life he has suffered, of the harshness of a Somali man's journey.

Amina looks at me. I know she is asking me to do something to stop what is inevitable.

"Amina, he is going to die," I say as gently as possible.

Confusion covers the face of Jamal's wife. She looks to Amina to translate. But Amina glares at me instead and pulls my arm, leading me a few feet from the bed.

"You cannot say this, Mary. Remember, you cannot predict when someone will die," she states passionately.

"But Amina, there is nothing I can do and he is too sick to survive," I say thinking she wants to deny the inevitable truth of the situation.

"Mary, in Somalia you cannot say when someone will die. That is for Allah. Only Allah can decide when we die. Only Allah, Mary."

It is not about denial. It is about my insensitivity to sacred beliefs.

"Oh, I'm so sorry, Amina," I say.

She escorts me by the arm back to Jamal's bedside. I kneel next to Jamal and hold his other hand, forced to acknowledge the helplessness I feel. His hand is limp and clammy in mine. We sit in silence and I experience a kind of appreciation for the releasing of control. What binds us at the bedside of a dying man does not need words or common language or culture. It requires only our presence and the communion of our pain. Jamal's wife and I hold his hands until the last struggling breath leaves his body. His lifeless eyes stare into his wife's eyes. She places his hand at his side and gently presses hers against it for the last time.

Pausing, she looks at Amina.

"He is finished," Amina says to me. "He is finished."

Jamal's family wraps his body in the blanket, lifts his limp, emaciated body and silently carries it out of the ward. Before I have a chance to take this in, Lindsey's tall frame appears behind me. Her soulful blue eyes are filled with concern; she leans forward slightly and whispers in my ear.

"Come to the pharmacy right away," she says.

Her face and tone tell me not to delay. No time to process the intense experience of death.

"Amina, will you be sure Jamal's family gets a shroud and someone to help to dig his grave so they can bury him tonight before sunset?" I ask.

She nods.

"What's going on?" I ask Lindsey, rushing to keep up with her long effortless strides as we move quickly towards the stairs.

"I overheard Raasel. I was behind some boxes in the pharmacy and I heard him threatening Ali Nur. They were speaking Somali quietly so Musa would not hear them, but I could tell Raasel was being forceful."

We shake the hands with friendly Somalis on the way down the second flight of stairs.

"Do you know what they were saying?" I ask.

"No, but I saw Ali Nur hand Raasel several packages of drugs and I'm fairly certain it had something to do with antibiotics. Raasel grabbed them and quickly left the pharmacy. Ali Nur does not know I saw them but he looked very frightened," she explains.

"All right, when we get back to the pharmacy we'll act like we are ready to get back to work. When no one is around we'll ask Ali Nur what happened."

"Shouldn't we tell Andrew?" she asks.

"Let's see what we can find out. Maybe getting Ali's version of the story will help."

Ali Nur's hands shake as he nervously counts pills. He fills a bag without making notes on the ledger and hands it to the waiting nurse. When the nurse is a safe distance from the pharmacy we turn to Ali Nur. He is moving around the room like an absent minded professor. He jots notes at the table and abruptly walks to a shelf. He removes some medication, stares into space and seems to forget what he is doing. He then puts the medication back in the same place.

"Are you okay Ali Nur?" Lindsey asks with characteristic gentleness.

"Oh...uh...yes...fine," he answers nervously gripping his palms together.

"Uh...my throat is sore," he adds lifting his hand to his neck. "I must go home."

"Are you sure you are okay?" Lindsey asks again.

He looks down at his feet and mumbles something we do not understand.

"Ali, please tell us what happened. Maybe we can help," I insist.

Clearly he is not going to tell us. His entire body is shaking and he keeps saying he must go home.

"All right, Ali Nur, we'll finish here. Go ahead," I say accepting the futility of our questioning.

Ali Nur quickly locks up and leaves the pharmacy without any good-byes.

Lindsey and I decide the best action is to get back to IMC to let Andrew know the situation.

"What will we say to Musa and Raasel about going back this early?" Lindsey asks.

"Good point," I say. "Let's tell them we have to go back to finish some paperwork at the IMC compound."

Musa accompanies us through the hospital. We do not risk telling him about Raasel since we do not know the clan dynamics between the two of them. Outside we find Raasel reclining his wiry body against the IMC vehicle, once again sound asleep. Since he is armed we wake him gently and explain that we need to get back to the compound.

Lindsey and I slide in between Raasel and Musa. Our driver lurches the vehicle forward and the five of us ride back in total silence except for the distant rat-a-tat-tat of AK-47's until the Land Cruiser pulls safely into the compound gates.

Musa follows us to Andrew's office where Andrew chats with Ahmed about a report they are working on.

"Andrew, come over to the house for some coffee," I say knowing Musa will not follow us into the residential part of the compound.

Andrew sits beside us at the long dining table. He retrieves a crumbled package of Sportsman cigarettes from his back pocket. His lips curl around the end of the cigarette and he cups the end, skillfully lighting and puffing.

"You two look a little anxious. What's up?" he asks as the tip of the cigarette glows red.

Aweis walks into the dining room, lifts the lid off of the water filter and replenishes our supply. Next to the cooler flies crawl on a bowl of raw camel meat someone forgot to take into the kitchen. Aweis waves his hand at the flies and they move away quickly, but return to the meat within seconds.

I look at Aweis and then back at Andrew. Andrew and I exchange knowing glances and he says, "Let's take our coffee to my private office."

He closes the door once we are inside his bedroom, otherwise known as his private office. It is filled with an eclectic collection of donated desks, filing cabinets and mismatched chairs. A single bed sits in the corner. Piles of papers and two ashtrays filled with dozens of tiny cigarette butts rest on its rumpled sheets. Lindsey explains what she witnessed in the pharmacy and Andrew's face becomes drawn with concern.

As he draws the life out of his second cigarette I say, "I just have a bad feeling about Raasel, Andrew. Ali Nur was really shaken."

"Did you mention this to Musa?" he asks.

"No. I didn't know enough about his clan affiliation. I thought maybe it would get complicated if he were with Raasel or Ali Nur's clan."

"He's not with either. I'll speak with him right away to explain the situation," he says.

I stand from my dented folding chair, Lindsey from her rickety wooden office chair, and we make our way out of the smoke-filled office.

"Oh...wait...uh, why don't you two hang around here in case I have some questions? It's almost lunch time anyway," Andrew says.

"All right, we'll be in the kitchen," Lindsey advises as she strides out into the hall.

Another Land Cruiser pulls into the courtyard as we are leaving Andrew's office. Ann, Brian, and their guards spill out of the vehicle still engaged in some disagreement. Lindsey and I look at each other and chuckle. Brian continually tries to make sense of Ann.

"Fuck it, Ann. Just fuck it," he says as he blows past us.

"Oh, I'm sorry, excuse me," she says moving past us on her way into Andrew's office.

"Why are you going in there Ann?" I ask trying to minimize interruptions as Andrew finds a solution to the potentially volatile situation.

"Oh, I'm sorry," says in her soft southern accent.

She moves a piece of wispy black hair away from her eyes.

"Uh, I'm going to ask Andrew if I can get him anything before lunch. He's probably not eaten and with his diabetes... you know....I'm sorry, I just want to be sure he's okay," she says as she heads for his office.

"He's a grown man, Ann," I say.

Ann is in the office and does not acknowledge my statement.

"Give it up," Lindsey recommends under her breath.

I let out a frustrated sigh and decide she is right. Andrew is also capable of telling Ann to leave while he considers his options with Raasel.

Lindsey and I saunter into the kitchen to find what's on the menu for lunch. The tinny radio blasts a mixture of static and the American Top 40 from an old cassette. As I lift the lid of the pot, I can see Raasel in the distance sauntering into the office as Musa steps out giving him a wide berth.

A powerfully uneasy feeling passes through me watching Raasel but I'm relieved to see he is unarmed. Musa paces just outside the office.

"What's for lunch? I could eat a whole camel?" Brian says walking into the dining area located in our house across the courtyard from Andrew's office.

"Bam! Bam! Bam!"

Screams and gunfire rip through the air just as I am directing Brian to the camel meat steaming on the table. Crashing sounds come from Andrew's office followed by Raasel bursting through the front door clutching a large handgun. Musa rushes into the office and the rest of us push away from the dining table letting our chairs fall to the marble floor.

"Oh my God!" I say as we run toward Andrew's office in the

main house.

Inside Andrew's chair and desk are thrown to the floor and papers are strewn like confetti. Several bullet holes mark the wall just beyond Andrew's overturned office furniture, but we can see neither him nor Ann.

Ann emerges from behind the desk lifting Andrew who goes limp in her arms. Brian and Musa make a path through the overturned furniture. Andrew leans his head on Ann's shoulder where she cradles it with her hand. Gingerly they stand up and step through the office out on to the veranda.

"Is he gone?" Andrew asks.

"Ha. Yes, I saw him run through the gates," Musa replies reassuringly.

"Sit down here," I say to Ann and Andrew who lower themselves carefully onto the settee in the courtyard.

A crowd of guards and expats gather around. Andrew lies down and Ann guides his head to rest in her lap. She smoothes his hair away from his forehead over and over again.

"Are you hit?" I say moving in to examine them.

"No. No. He missed us," Andrew said as his breathing begins to calm.

"What happened?" Lindsey asks, her blue eyes filled with apprehension.

"It was clear that Raasel was stealing penicillin from the pharmacy. So I called him in and told him we would not need him after all. I made up some excuse about having too many guards and even handed him one month's severance pay. Didn't want to tell him the real reason for fear his response would be violent," Andrew explains.

"Guess that plan got rat fucked," Brian says.

Andrew does not respond to Brian's comment. He fumbles in his pocket for the package of cigarettes. His hands shake as he removes the last one, lights it and takes an exaggerated first drag.

"Why did he start shooting?" I ask.

"Who knows, he just lifted his gun in my direction and started shooting. Ann was already in my office at the time and ran towards Raasel screaming for him to stop. I grabbed Ann and we stumbled to the floor behind the desk. Before he started shooting again Ann recognized Raasel as the brother of a recent patient. She reminded him that IMC had saved his brother's life so why shoot the IMC director. He hesitated and then shot into the wall a couple more times and ran out."

"Did you see him leave?" Lindsey asks the guard that was one of those huddled around Ann and Andrew.

"Yes. He ran out of the gate. But he stood outside with his gun in the air shouting he would be back to kill people of IMC," the guard replies.

"Listen, we are all in danger. Raasel's out there angry as hell and will probably be pleased to make anyone from IMC the target of his need for revenge. Obviously he has a drug business and needs a connection with IMC. I think we're all back for lunch so let's stay in the compound for the day. I'm going out to see the clan elders about a traditional court hearing for Raasel," Andrew announces.

"Did you find out why Ali Nur was upset?" Lindsey asks.

"Yes, evidently Raasel threatened to kill Ali Nur's sister if he didn't hand over the penicillin. Apparently, Raasel is known for his extensive extortion schemes. He was even threatening Musa," he explains, pointing at Musa who seems equally shaken.

Andrew's body begins to shake uncontrollably in a likely diabetic episode.

"Oh, I'm sorry," Ann says, heaping three teaspoons of sugar into her tea.

With great drama she quickly stirs the sugar into the tea and begins to spoon-feed it to Andrew.

Fifteen expats surround the dining table filled with ample platters of camel, carrots and spaghetti doused with garlic oil. Every set of eyes is on Andrew, hoping for news from his visit with the clan elders. He takes a long drink from his cup of Nescafe and taps his cigarette on the edge of the ashtray. Andrew begins to answer the question everyone is asking with their eyes.

"The elders refuse to do anything. They are afraid of retribution from him as well. In fact, they said IMC would have to pay Raasel another several hundred dollars to settle the case. They said this is the only way anyone can be safe from him."

"Fuck that shit! How can you let them tell you that," Brian explodes.

"You cannot apply the legal system we are all familiar with to Somalia. We have to respect their culture if we expect to be able to make any difference at all. Believe me, I'm pissed off too, but in the end it is the best way of assuring that he drops his vendetta."

That night I lie in bed for several hours trying to make sense of a situation that seems hopeless. I'd watched a man die before his family and almost lost two of my colleagues in our compound where it's supposed to be safe. I imagine Ali Nur huddling with dozens of his family in a bombed out shelter that is their home where he keeps a tight watch on his little sister. Andrew had to pay a man not to kill us. All of us are caught up in the cycle of oppression here that leaves most Somalis struggling for survival.

-13-

Leyla

Mogadishu, Somalia 1992

Lindsey pushes the toast around her ornately painted Italian china showing no intention of using it to nourish her body. Her long blonde hair has lost its luster and her expressive blue eyes seem so mournful. Lindsey's colleagues and I see she is becoming thinner, a mirror image of the patients we serve.

"Are you going to eat that?" Ann asks Lindsey, pointing to the uneaten breakfast.

Lindsey hands it to her without answering. Ann takes the stale, dry toast and liberally spreads it with greasy Blue Band margarine.

"You've got to eat something," I say to Lindsey. "I am getting so worried about you."

She doesn't answer. Across the table Sharon hands her half-eaten second piece of toast to Ann whose handouts form a tower on her plate. Although she's been told by Andrew not to, she no doubt will smuggle the food to Digfer to feed one of her patients.

"Lindsey, are you hearing me? How are you going to fight off an infection if you get one? You've got to eat," I insist.

"Mary, you are a good friend. I know you care, but I just have no appetite. I can't stop thinking of one of my patients."

"Who," I ask, fearing what she will reveal.

"Leyla," she answers.

Lindsey continues, "She is a gentle twelve-year-old girl who wastes away in front of her family. I cannot get her to eat anything. Yesterday, I offered to get anything I could for her to eat. She tried to squeeze my hand as if to offer me hope and whispered in my ear that there was something she would eat. She asked me to bring her an apple."

She quickly wipes a tear welling in the corner of her blue eyes. No other words are needed. We both know apples are an exotic luxury, absent in a place where people die every day at the hand of gun-wielding bandits who extort even for a bland mixture of cooked grains. Last week a man shot a woman carrying a bag of rice on her head. When he turned the woman's body over to claim his stolen rice, he looked into the face of his wife who was carrying the food back to their home.

The morning is heavy and unusually cloudy as the rainy season is beginning. Sitting next to Jackson's brother makes his death real. Hersi sits against the Land Cruiser's window where he sat not long ago when he and his brother were colleagues. He stares out into space chewing khat and lost in thought. There is no rhythmic tapping in time to the music this morning.

Donna is sitting next to me shifting in her seat.

"God, what is the problem Donna?" I ask.

"There's something...sticking...into my back," she says reaching behind her to investigate the annoyance.

Donna leans forward and a bit of red hair falls into her face. I see it. The barrel of a rocket launcher is poking through the small space between the seats.

"Shit, it's a rocket launcher!" yells Sharon, the journalist, from the back seat of the IMC vehicle.

She and Ann are sitting close to some weapons hidden under an old towel.

"Stop. Stop the pickup!" I shout to the driver.

He jerks the pickup to an abrupt stop in the middle of the dusty road. A technical flies past with half a dozen Somali fighters hanging off the sides and roof. Our guards get out of the vehicle and Donna and I take this opportunity to move quickly away from the barrel of the rocket launcher.

Ahmed, our logistician, and Hersi jump out and head to the back of the pickup where Ann and Sharon have plastered their bodies against the windows as far from the weapon as possible.

Ann's pockets bulge with her breakfast bounty.

Ahmed shouts angrily at Hersi who shouts back while they reposition the weapon. When they get back in the Toyota, Ahmed speaks rapidly in Somali to Hersi.

"He did not put the rocket launcher away," Ahmed tells me.

He pounds the butt of his weapon on the floorboard and shouts more Somali criticism toward Hersi who ignores him.

We are stunned into silence until Ann begins to talk with Sharon.

"You really cared about that little baby that died a few weeks back, didn't you Sharon?" Ann asks.

"It was very hard for me to watch her die. I might even have adopted her," Sharon replies.

"I'm sorry. When we get to the hospital I will show you a little girl who was orphaned a few days ago when her mother was killed by a grenade blast in her village. The child wanders along in the market outside Digfer," Ann says.

I give my tall, slim friend Lindsey a worried glance. We both sense this could take a disastrous turn.

There was another side to Ann's personality that only those close to her on a daily basis could detect. Others, especially the reporters, did not see her darker side. But most of us on the team did see it—a word, a gesture or a behavior would creep out unexpectedly and warn us. For the most part Ann seemed passive and kind, but she was driven by something we couldn't identify and she had an overwhelming need to needed. Ann also had a will of iron that hid itself quite well.

"Ann, how do you know the child's clan isn't caring for her?" Lindsey inquires.

"Oh, I'm sorry, there is no one looking after her. She just wanders the market looking for food," Ann says, checking the bulges in her pockets.

Our vehicle comes to a jerking stop in front of Digfer Casualty. Two well-armed men carry in a Somali fighter whose worn dress shirt hangs open at his sides revealing several gunshot wounds to his chest. Lindsey and I follow them in.

Ann and Sharon walk into the market just outside the hospital where I see Ann lifting a small girl and delivering her into the arms of the American journalist.

Oscar, the IMC surgeon, and Brian take the injured man to a

table where he is pronounced dead. The men disappear before hearing the fate of their comrade.

Last month I was given the dubious promotion to hospital staff management. In addition to my nursing supervisory duties, I monitor the fuel level for the generator that sporadically powers the hospital. My Somali counterpart is a large man named Ali Abdi. He is tall and broad shouldered with a paunch that pushes out from his plaid dress shirt. Only powerful men have paunches in Somalia and Abdi is considered one of the elite. However, this distinction is lost on me as I am only interested in running the hospital as smoothly as possible.

Managing the fuel level is a constant battle as fuel is the highest valued commodity in a war machine. Because there is no electricity in Mogadishu, the hospital's massive generator provides power to sterilization of essential instruments, refrigeration of medications, and the pumping of water for surgery, into the storage tanks on the roof for a gravity feed when needed. Providing light only for the surgical suites during the day conserves fuel. The shattered windows of the hospital provide natural light for the wards. At night, without electricity, Digfer remains dark, so surgeries are not performed after sunset. Emergency surgeries after nightfall are sent to the MSF hospital several miles away, which operates with an expatriate surgeon on call twenty-four hours per day. Lately however, reports are coming to IMC that lights have been seen beaming through windows at night, prompting my desire to inspect the fuel levels first thing in the morning. Since IMC donates the diesel used in the generator, and fuel is in short supply, I want to manage it wisely. Ali Abdi has avoided this inspection for three days. Yesterday he claimed a cat got into the electrical system and chewed the wires so we could not check the generator. It is rumored that he is pilfering the fuel to sell or trade to augment his many possessions. His pilfering goes beyond a need for survival and my patience is running thin.

While looking for the illusive Ali Abdi, I notice Ann in front of a group of *Time* magazine photographers. She dramatically wipes the brow of her pet patient, a three-year-old Somali boy named Abu, and looks into the cameras with contrived vulnerability. Abu's mother watches as Ann sneaks him several pieces of the toast she collected at breakfast. Although he is capable of walking, Ann carries him around the hospital like a puppy.

"Mary," Lindsey calls from across the ward.

"What is it?" I ask when I approach.

She is looking over the patient charts Ann prepared while Lindsey took some time off in Nairobi last week.

"Ann's doing it again," Lindsey says flipping through the charts.

All of the patient orders Lindsey had meticulously made before she went to Nairobi had been changed. Each one crossed out by Ann's hand and replaced with unnecessary changes. One order required a patient to be given aspirin four times a day. Ann changed it to Acetaminophen. Each of the unnecessary changes is trivial and intended to make Lindsey appear incompetent. Lindsey is one of the finest IMC nurses at Digfer and takes great pains to be sure her patients were well cared for. She does all she can to ensure the comfort and healing their wounds and illnesses. Her ward is the cleanest in the hospital, free of foul-smelling debris and bodily waste found throughout the rest of Digfer.

On numerous occasions Ann had undermined and embarrassed Lindsey by rewriting her patient orders without reason.

Lindsey's soulful blue eyes are filled with humiliation. "Will you talk to her Mary?" she implores.

"Lindsey, if I say something she'll just know she got to you. Let's just make sure she doesn't take care of your patients next time you're out on R&R," I suggest.

"All right. You're right, I guess," she agrees. "Do you have a minute? I want to introduce you to someone."

"Sure," I respond.

Ali Abdi still eludes me, so I might as well meet Lindsey's patient.

We walk a few yards to the bed of a young girl who looks to be about twelve. Her frail arm is hooked to an intravenous tube that drips fluid slowly into her veins. Next to the patient an older man continuously waves flies away from his child's gaping mouth while he watches his beloved offspring slowly die. Ashen skin is pulled back tightly across protruding cheekbones, giving her the appearance of a starving refugee.

The ailing child and Lindsey seem to connect in an unseen place, beyond the hollowness of war and hunger. Somewhere they alone seem to understand.

"Hello Leyla," Lindsey's slim fingers cradle the girl's hand in her own.

"Lindsey," the girl says to her ally.

Recognizing her friend brings the girl's dewy eyes to life, momentarily released from the reality of her emaciated body. Her lips curve in a frail smile.

"Lindsey, Lindsey," she says.

"Leyla, I want you to meet my friend, Mary," Lindsey says, never taking her eyes from the girl.

"Leyla came in a few weeks ago with a gunshot wound to her leg," Lindsey explains to me.

Leyla's withered leg is wrapped in bandages crawling with flies.

"She began to have a massive infection in the wound after surgery. I've been trying to get her to eat but she will not eat anything—except an apple. I need to find her an apple"

I picture Lindsey fidgeting with her toast this morning and begin to understand as I watch the bond between her and Leyla.

"Lindsey," Leyla whispers.

Lindsey leans her tall frame towards the girl and a few blonde stands of hair fall onto her chest. Lindsey holds her face close to Leyla's mouth. She whispers something in her native tongue.

Lindsey looks up at the father who interprets.

"She is talking crazy. I do not know what she is saying to you. She says she wants her apple," he states.

Lindsey's blue eyes fill with tears but she holds back not wanting to lose control of her emotions in the ward.

"Her father wasn't here when Leyla asked me for the apple," she tells me.

Lindsey turns to the father again and says, "She told me she would eat an apple."

He looks down at the floor. There is nothing for him to say.

Lindsey's soulful eyes turn hopeful as she pleads, "Mary, please help me find an apple?"

Holding together my Iron Nurse armor I say, "Inshallah." If God is willing. An Islamic term we hear daily in a place where so much is out of our hands.

"I have to go Lindsey," I say gently.

"Thank you, Mary," she says still holding the girl's tiny hand.

Outside an operating room a group of children gather round and hold their little hands out asking for food. They try to put their hands in my pockets. Their bare bottoms are half covered by their tattered tee shirts. I tell them I have nothing to give but they point down the hall to Ann still carrying Abu. They've seen her feeding him and naturally wonder who will give them slices of buttered toast.

I am interrupted from confronting Ann when I hear Brian say, "Fuck this shit!" The lights in the operating room flicker and finally give up completely. Brian and Dr. Jefferson must finish surgery in the dark on their unfortunate patient.

Ali Abdi darts out of another room and I am finally able to corner him. His size, taller and broader than most Somalis, combined with an air of importance gives him an intimidating presence.

"Ali Abdi!" I call to him running to catch him.

"Yes, Mary, what is it today?"

"The generator just went out. I want to go check the fuel level. Someone said they have seen lights on in the hospital at night and now we've run out during the day—in the middle of surgery. This cannot happen, Ali Abdi! Come with me now," I say insistently.

In one motion, Ali Abdi reaches under his shirt and raises a handgun to my face.

"You, come with me," he orders.

I have no choice but to follow him, hoping to devise a plan on our way to some undisclosed location. He keeps his weapon hidden as we pass people in the hall. Soon we are outside the hospital and walking toward the small outbuilding that he makes his personal living quarters.

My mind is racing thinking of the brutal rapes committed against some nurses from Irish Concern, a small relief organization from Ireland. I also remember the stories from MSF of some Somali women they treated, who were raped. I was told that the rapist opened their circumcisions with a knife then the rapist doused the women in diesel and set them ablaze. Death, I decide, is preferable to Somali-style rape.

The private entrance to his tiny home is unbolted, and the door stands open a few inches. Several pairs of large, dark hands gesture rapidly and voices belt out forceful Somali words. Through this narrow opening I also see handguns laying on the floor beside their owners. Ali Abdi opens the door and two automatic weapons come into view.

"Get inside," he commands, nudging me with his handgun.

He closes the door behind us and engages the bolt.

"This is it," I think, "I will either be brutally raped or die trying to escape."

We step over a pile of flip-flops discarded by the men in bare feet sitting cross-legged on the floor. Their macaawises are hiked up around their knees as they sit in a circle drinking from thick juice glasses. In the center of the circle, like a statue of a god, stands an antiquated Sixties-style Osterizer blender half-full of a creamy white concoction. My eyes follow the electrical cord powering the appliance to the persistent humming of his private generator, running on fuel stolen from the surgical suite.

I stand frozen, like a block of ice, in this brief moment of indecision.

Ali Abdi's home is meager by Western standards, but by Somali standards, it is a luxury apartment. The walls are lined with shelves, stocked with canned food and bundles of khat. In the corner next to his bed is a tangled mound of metal hospital equipment that he will most likely use to trade for additional luxuries.

Slowly my foot eases toward one of the handguns and I start to scoot it in my direction.

Abdi grabs my arm with a jerk. "Sit down."

Just before I sit the barefoot man next to me in a white koofiyad grabs the gun I was trying to conceal.

What now?

"Mary, do you want a milkshake?" Ali Abdi says, stuffing his own gun into the waist of his macaawis and covers it under his untucked shirt.

"Uh, okay," I say wondering if this is some perverted ritual performed as a prelude to violent rape.

As I scan the rest of the men in the room they each nod a friendly smile and slightly raise their drinks toward me. Abdi reaches for the a can of Nestlé's Nido whole milk powder sitting open on the shelf above the huddle of men. He sprinkles powder into the blender and adds some unfiltered water. The blender buzzes to life and the milk powder mixes with water laden with unhealthy organisms, which seems of little consequence at this point. He pours me a glass and hands it to me.

"Have some khat," offers my hospitable host and adds, "It's good quality, just arrived from Kenya this morning."

I begin to realize with relief that this is just another of Abdi's elaborate avoidances. He is counting on my fear to keep me from addressing the issue of the generator fuel while locked in a room with his armed drinking buddies.

He has estimated correctly. As I finally stand, he laughs uncontrollably and begins speaking to the men in Somali. The men turn to me and join in the jokes no doubt made at my expense. Abdi has won control again but I have no desire to stay at the party and even the score. With great humility I thank my host for his hospitality and leave the milkshake consuming Rambos behind a closed door.

I stroll back to Casualty taking several deep breaths and feeling deeply grateful for escaping a close brush with death, or worse.

When I arrive back at Digfer the generator is back on line, but there are no Somali doctors in sight. Most leave when the generator shuts down, opting to go their private clinics where they can see their paying patients. A woman lies on a table outside the empty operating room. Her abdomen is ripped open and her intestines hang in shiny coils over the side of the table. Flies delight on her exposed organs. Her heavy eyelids allow irises to peek through like tiny half moons. She lies alone, no one to advocate for her, no one to ensure her care, and no one to hover anxiously around her failing body. As I approach, her eyeballs roll slightly upwards. She moans faintly when I touch her clammy skin. Still no doctors in sight, I pull gloves from my pocket to examine her distended abdomen and discover she is probably six months pregnant. It appears to be a botched cesarean section, probably performed by an inexperienced medical student. Sand is encrusted in the dried blood spattered on her chest and legs. She needs a moist cover for her exposed viscera but the supplies are two floors above. However, the surgical supplies in this unit are locked up to prevent pilfering. I decide to race two floors up to the surgical supply storage. Perhaps I can find some help on the way.

On the second floor I notice a commotion in Lindsey's ward around Leyla's bed. But there is no time to stop. When I return to the silent surgical suite with a bottle of saline and some gauze, the woman is not on the table. She is lying on the floor where she fell with no one to notice. Her eyes stare lifelessly up at me. Her family left her to die not because they are heartless, but because the harsh reality of war did not afford them the luxury of waiting by a loved one's bedside.

When we return, half a dozen Somali men are standing at the tall IMC gates outside the compound when our technical returns for the day. They speak angrily with the guards. Andrew comes through the gates and gestures for us to wait as he approaches the men. After some exchange he lifts his radio and his voice comes through inside our vehicle.

"Ann, do you know anything about a small girl taken outside the hospital today?" he asks.

I pass Ann my radio so she can respond.

"Oh, I'm sorry, there was a little orphaned girl that has been there for a few days. I told Sharon about her and she is going to look after her, maybe adopt her."

There is a pause and then, "According to these men the child belongs to the clan even though her parents are dead. The clan is considered her guardian and they are accusing IMC of kidnapping."

"Oh well, Sharon took the child to stay with her at ICRC," Ann replies.

Andrew explains the situation to the guard and we can see him telling the men. Hurriedly they leave the front of the compound and our technical moves safely inside.

At dinner Ann is still collecting food and stuffing it inconspicuously in a bulging napkin beside her plate. Lindsey's chair is empty which worries me because she cannot afford to miss another meal.

After dinner I find Lindsey's door ajar. I knock and the door swings slowly open. She is lying on her bed in a fetal position in the darkening room. I sit next to her and I smooth my hand across the side of her face, wet with tears.

"Do you want to talk?" I ask gently.

After a few minutes she sits up and says, "She's gone."

Her shoulders shake with her silent sobs.

"She's gone and there was nothing I could do. Nothing."

"Leyla's gone," I say quietly acknowledging Lindsey's loss.

"Just before she died she said, 'Lindsey, Lindsey, I'm going to die, where's my apple? Lindsey, good-bye.' Her child eyes looked at me once more and then they were lifeless. She was gone."

I hold Lindsey's thin frame for a long time and we both cry for Leyla. Lindsey says she will carry Leyla with her always. And I know she will. Leyla's death will not be lost to the senseless tragedy of the war.

-14-

Party Time

Mogadishu, Somalia 1992

"Mary! Watch out!" Donna screams, her flaming tresses streaming from the passenger window as I make a sudden change in direction.

The IMC technical I am driving screeches around the corner and swerves to miss a pick-up truck loaded with armed Somalis. A few fire rounds from their AK-47's into the sky. In the passenger seat next to me the displaced hired driver braces himself. When his khat falls to the floorboard he releases a string of Somali expletives.

Lindsey and Donna are in the back between our two guards releasing many months of stress and tragedy in the form of hysterical laughter.

"Girls just wanna have fu-uh-n!" the voice of Cyndi Lopper blasts from the tinny speakers of the IMC technical.

Her lyrics could not be more accurate. Today is Friday, our day off, and the guards have advised us not to travel more than a two-mile radius from the compound because of sporadic fighting on the outlying roads. Tomorrow will be the fifth consecutive Friday we've traveled only within this confining radius. The twelve-foot concrete walls surrounding the IMC compound, studded along their perimeter with shards of protruding broken glass, are beginning to feel like a prison. Between Lindsey's sad loss of Leyla, our near-death experience when Jackson was murdered, and all of the horrors facing our long days at Digfer, have left us desperate for some diversion. After a long day, I invite Lindsey and Donna to join me on an errand to ICRC to pickup some cold boxes, much like beer coolers, used for refrigerating vaccines. Tonight they will house drinks for the IMC party.

IMC has invited expats from several NGOs, journalists, and Digfer staff to an evening of diversion. There isn't a soul who could not use it, especially Lindsey, my tall slender friend, for whom since Leyla's death, I've grown increasingly concerned. Her blue eyes even more soulful then ever. She retreats to her room every chance she gets and continues to wither away. Eating is so painful for her. She continually laments having so much in comparison to a little Somali girl whom Lindsey could not even grant her dying wish. A wild ride in a commandeered IMC technical and a party to plan are medicine for all of us.

Donna and Lindsey are still laughing when I pull the vehicle into the open gates of our compound and quickly get out of the driver seat before Andrew has reason to give me a security lecture.

The delicious aromas of stewing goat and camel meat curl around us as we enter the courtyard.

"Mary, let's use the skulls as décor," my perky friend Donna suggests when we pass the collection of goat and wildcat skulls. An expat named Jerry, who served briefly as a logistician, left behind an eccentric collection of wild animal skulls. None of us could think of what to do with them.

"We can put flowers in the eye sockets. They can be centerpieces," I say fingering what was a goat's visual portal.

Once more, laughter spills out in boisterous rounds.

In the kitchen Aweis holds the edge of a large pot with a dirty tee shirt. He stirs several pounds of pasta on the kitchen stove boiling in giant aluminum pots. David, the newly arrived logistician from California via Kenya, dances in the kitchen with a miniature boom box to the guttural voice of Tom Waits.

With great passion David sings our favorite line far off key.

"I'm an innocent victim of a blinded alley and I'm tired of all these soldiers here. No one speaks English, and everything's broken."

David arrived a couple of weeks ago to organize the IMC

logistic and administrative affairs. I find him a pleasant addition to our IMC family. David can carry on an intelligent conversation, and five minutes later display a sharp, bizarre wit. As he does his kitchen dance with the boom box, his thick, long dark curls delicately swing with him. His impish brown eyes hold my gaze and he finishes the dance with a curtsy in his blue paisley knee-length cotton dress. It is unbuttoned to his belly button exposing swirling hair covering a muscular chest.

"Mary, my dear!" he says, allowing me to cut in on the boom box.

He swings me around the kitchen, dips me and asks, "Did you order me a grip from our office in Nairobi?"

"What are you talking about?" I query, smiling up at his flickering chestnut eyes.

"A grip, you know, did you order me one? Because I am losing mine," he says with one more turn and lets me go.

"What are we having, Aweis?" I ask peering over the pot.

David is frolicking in the hall breaking all of Brian's personal space by inviting him to dance. Not surprisingly, Brian walks away from the opportunity to dance with a man in a blue cotton frock.

"Lobster, fish and roasted goat," Aweis replies, "I sent Ahmed to buy samosas in the market."

"It appears we have plenty of spaghetti," I say looking down into the steaming pot of pasta.

Another pot is full of boiling water waiting for the lobster in a large dish on the table.

Aweis grimaces as he approaches the platter.

Although Mogadishu is a coastal city and many of its inhabitants are severely undernourished, most refuse to eat seafood.

"Fish is for poor people," many Somali's would say.

Bantus are among the only Somalis willing to eat from the Indian Ocean's bounty. IMC and other NGOs provide business for the Bantu fisherman. We eat everything they can catch in their rickety fiberglass boats.

Abdullah, a slender nineteen-year-old kitchen assistant, bursts into the kitchen screaming and shoving me aside. He makes a quick escape through the back door with David following close behind waving a live lobster in the terrified teen's direction.

"What are you doing, David?" I ask amid rounds of laughter.

"I can't believe gun-wielding Somalis are so afraid of these bugs," David replies plopping the lobster into the waiting pot.

Aweis stands plastered in the corner.

"Stop, it's not funny," he says in a shaking voice, "not funny at all."

David takes this as his cue to pick up another lobster and wave it in the air.

"Okay, stop," I implore through giggles, "I think you've done enough terrorizing for one evening.

"Oh no, just getting started!" he proclaims waltzing out of the kitchen.

I put the last of the lobsters into the pot and Aweis ventures out of the corner to finish cooking. It is time for a shower, so I make my way out of the kitchen hoping there will not be a line.

Donna sashays coyly to me in the hall in her new hand-tailored matching ensemble. Many of us buy fabric while on leave in Nairobi and commission a local tailor to construct an outfit according to a picture in a book or magazine. Donna's dress looks like a brilliant sunset on fabric. Its fit and the stunning mixture of colors flatters her flaming red hair and emerald eyes, but pushes the outer limits of modesty, even considering the relative privacy of the IMC party. The vest-like top is closely fitted over Donna's full breasts. Her slim waist is exposed at the midriff, and the ensemble is accompanied by a long fitted skirt. Modesty is sacred to the Somalis so I am uneasy about their reaction to Donna's exposed middle.

"How do I look?" she asks twirling around like a college girl waiting for her date.

"Wow Donna, you look incredible," I answer.

Her rosy cheeks are aglow; I decide not to burst her bubble by mentioning the modesty issue.

Leaning to my ear, she whispers, "Do you think Ahmed will like it?"

"Well, he's due back any minute with the samosas; why don't you ask him," I suggest.

While Lindsey and I collect bougainvillea from the garden, Aweis creates a dance floor by moving the household furniture to the brick courtyard.

Aweis's kitchen assistant places the final plate of camel meat on the long banquet table. There is just enough room for a wild-cat skull as a centerpiece. Its fangs protrude over a plate of goat kabobs.

After seven, the guests begin to trickle into the courtyard. An MSF group brings a bottle of French wine and cheese they normally keep stored safely in their extensive warehouse. The French women wear jeans so tight they appear to be sprayed onto their petite bodies. They walk nonchalantly past Andrew, who continues his briefing with several journalists sitting on the Italian velvet settees. Carlos Mavroleon listens intently as he chews khat and drinks an orange Fanta soda. Alcohol is forbidden for the Muslims. Khat, on the other hand, although a powerful stimulant, is permitted since it is a substance found in nature.

A chipper nurse from Irish Concern, named Sally, arrives with colleagues. She swings her wavy auburn hair as she bounces through the courtyard, carrying a guitar and a set of bongos.

Sally stops me, flashes her expectant green eyes and asks about David.

"Have you seen David?" she asks meekly, attempting to mask the crush she has on him.

"I think he's upstairs getting ready," I say pointing toward his room.

She leaves her friends and heads up the stairs, taking them two at a time.

A shapely French nurse with glossy long blonde hair approaches me two minutes later as I am chatting with some of the guests from Save The Children.

"Excusez-moi, Mahree, these are for the dancing," she says casually handing me cassette tapes of the French groups known as Alpha Blondie and Yello.

"Merci," I say and hand them to Donna, who takes them to the boom box near the dance floor.

Within seconds the mesmerizing rhythm of French Reggae fills the courtyard, and the small group of journalists who gathered for a briefing has no choice but to disband in favor of the growing party atmosphere.

"Could you tell me, where is David?" the French nurse asks me as her inquisitive amber eyes scan the area.

I point toward his room just as I had for Sally minutes ago.

"I will look for him, but if you see him tell him Magali wants him," she said saying her name slowly and clearly so I will not forget.

She takes slow, regal steps toward the stairs, sensually swaying her hips hugged by her French jeans. I note that they both know where to find his room. David will have his hands full tonight—literally. I considered pursuing him myself but am not interested enough to engage the mounting competition.

On the dance floor, one of the newer Physician Assistants is well on his way to becoming quite drunk. He dances in my direction, barely staying on his feet. His large, sweaty palms rest on my shoulders and he leans into my ear.

"Mary, I'm so lonely. Will you go out with me?"

Nothing could be more unappealing, so I think of a way to distract him.

"Otto, remember, we're in a war zone. There's no place to go on a date."

His body is leaning against mine and swaying to the French beat.

"Pleassseee," he implores.

Now he's really getting disgusting. I manage to get a grip on his shoulders and push him away from me.

"Come on Otto. You're going to Nairobi tomorrow for R&R. Surely you'll meet someone there," I say reassuringly, and move off the dance floor out of his reach.

Donna's bright outfit and flaming hair give her away as I scan the crowd for my friends. I spot her sitting on the couch in extremely close proximity to Ahmed. Both are chewing khat, which has an astringent affect on the inside of the chewer's mouth. Donna washes her herbs down with a glass of whiskey but Ahmed, faithful to Islamic teaching, drinks tea with the botanical stimulant.

"Mary, join us!" she calls.

I sit next to her and she offers me some khat and a whisky chaser.

David and Magali descend the stairs with broad smiles on their faces. He playfully grabs her well-rounded butt on their way down. As they get closer, I can see she's missed a couple of buttons on her blouse. When they reach the bottom of the stairs

Magali leaves David to greet some late arriving men from MSF. One of the men looks vaguely familiar but I can only see his profile.

David takes this opportunity to slip onto the dance floor where Sally, who suddenly appears from the banquet table, does not hesitate to join him. With a playful charm David swings her tiny body easily, sending her auburn locks off her shoulders.

Andrew approaches me with a bottle of tequila in one hand and a saltshaker and lime in the other.

"Come on Mary, get up," he says beckoning me to the dance floor.

My body sways a little as I rise to join the dancing. Apparently I have underestimated the effects of mixing khat and whiskey. When I regain my balance Andrew saunters toward me.

"Mary, have you ever been body slammed?"

Several journalists move in next to us. They are dancing with some unfamiliar Somali women dressed in tight mini skirts and tube tops. The rich natural coloring on their faces is marked by dark blue eye shadow and bright red rouge, probably given to them as a gift from the journalists that accompany them. They look like twelve-year-old American girls trying on their sexuality for the first time.

"Well, Andrew, I have to say I don't know, since I have no clue what a body slam is."

Fearing it has something to do with the tequila, salt, lime and a part of the body, I distract him before he has a chance to illustrate its definition.

"Who are those women with the press? I've never seen Somali women dressed like that. It's got to be dangerous for them," I ask.

He glances in their direction.

"I have no idea who they are," he says raising the tequila bottle over my head.

"Could they be prostitutes?" I say, still trying to distract.

"Possibly, they came from the hotel where most of the media is staying. Why don't you go ask them?" he says.

When I turn to look in their direction I see Brian dancing with Magali. He comes to life on the dance floor. All his pent up passion spills out in flawless movements around his French partner. Out of the corner of my eye I see David casually leading Sally into the bathroom, confirming my suspicions that this will be a very busy night for our new colleague.

Without warning, a cold liquid douses my shoulder. Before I have a chance to react, Andrew sprinkles salt on the tequila and then rubs the lime into my skin.

"What are you doing?" I ask laughing.

Instead of answering he licks the mixture off my shoulder and chases it with a shot of tequila.

"Now you've been body slammed!" he says enthusiastically before moving on to educate the next woman.

A hand lands on my shoulder and I am poised to give Otto the brush off.

"Otto, I told—" I stop short when I recognize the man in front of me.

Marc leans in to kiss both my cheeks in a traditional French greeting. The music changes to the slow melody of the Beatles classic "Yesterday."

"Will you dance with me, Mahree?" he asks pulling me closer to him.

Instead of answering, my body responds to his by moving with his lead. I have looked for Marc since my first day when he tenderly talked me through my insecurities and helped me understand mistakes as expressions of a life fully lived.

"It is good to see you. Marc, right?" I say knowing his name, but not wanting to appear as excited as I feel.

"Oui. I am pleased to find you again," he says.

His breath feels warm on my face when he speaks.

"It's been awhile. Where have you been?" I ask.

"MSF sent me to Hargesa for several months to set up a feeding center and Maternal Child Health clinic for refugees. I am back in Mog now until I return to France."

A smile crosses his face covered with the sexy stubble of several days without shaving. He easily recognizes my obvious delight at this news. Our bodies move easily together and I am transported in this moment from the reality of war.

The gentle, melodic respite is violently interrupted by an enormous explosion. The force shakes the compound and lights up the air in a cloud of orange fire. Several smaller blasts follow in immediate succession and the night is filled with the smell of gunpowder.

The pop of a champagne bottle breaks the temporarily frozen partiers, who respond with hearty cheers as they are sprayed with the bubbly liquid. Although the city appears to be ablaze not far from our compound, most continue partying, accustomed to the violence and unwilling to give up the party's sweet distraction from life in a war zone.

"Let's go to the roof and see what's happening," I suggest, interested in the events outside the compound and anxious to find some space to be alone with Marc.

He grabs my hand and we bound up to the roof together.

On the second floor Otto steps in front of us into the hallway sporting Mickey Mouse boxers. He is rubbing his eyes and appears disoriented.

"I was trying to sleep but someone keeps slamming the doors," he complains angrily.

Marc and I look at each other and laugh.

"Go back to bed, Otto," I say moving quickly past him.

In relative privacy we huddle on a corner of the roof and watch as the fuel depot in the port is consumed in flames. Smaller explosions and gunfire continue in the area between the compound and the nearby village of Medina.

"What do you think caused it?" I ask.

"Sometimes locals try to steal petrol from the pipeline. This could spark an explosion. Or it could have been intentional— part of a warlord's war strategy."

Millions of stars and a brightly burning petrol fire light up the sky in a city without electric power. Marc pulls me in close to him and we embrace under a canopy of stars oblivious to the explosions of war. Every rooftop is filled with Somalis looking down into our party, which is more of a novelty than the multiple explosions that rocked their perch.

"What are you thinking of, Mahree?" Marc inquires gently brushing the back of his hand across my face.

"I am thinking of how guilty I feel watching all these people looking into our party that overflows with food and drink. It all seems so decadent knowing they don't know if tomorrow will give them enough food to feed their children."

"Oui, I have had to consider this same thing in every country MSF has sent me," he reminisces.

"How do you deal with it?" I query.

"I have learned that it is human nature to need to stop and play whenever we can. If we do not, we cannot go on offering aid in this kind of environment. It is not fair. This is true. But NGOs must give expatriates a break or they will not be able manage the emotions and everyone will all have to go home."

"Humanitarian work is so much more complicated than I thought it would be," I mutter.

He takes my hand without responding and gently kisses the tips of my fingers.

"With the all the fighting, it's too dangerous for you to go home," I declare and with a deep breath I risk an invitation.

"Stay with me tonight."

-15-

The Beach

Mogadishu, Somalia, Friday, November 13th, 1992

My eyes open with a startling suddenness. No gentle transition from the surreal experience of a dream state to the three-dimensional world of consciousness. A dog barks desperately outside my window. I peel the sheet, soaked with perspiration, from my bare torso, not able to loosen my mind from a violent nightmare's hellish images. Torrents of crashing waves heavy with human appendages and arsenals of machine guns haunt my conscious mind.

I notice a note is scrawled on the blank side of a gauze wrapper leaning purposefully against my backpack:

Je t'aime
Marc

My nightmare momentarily took the previous night from my mind. The party, the explosions, the Frenchman, the passionate night spent in this bed, away from the harsh reality of war. I look out the window and again see Marc in the distance walking the dusty street toward the MSF compound. The dog continues, non stop, with its rhythmic arf, arf, arf. His ribs protrude grotesquely with each heaving bark until a spray of machine-gun bullets abruptly ends its misery.

I place the sheet that serves as my curtain over the window and swing my feet to the cold marble floor. My fingers caress Marc's note before I grab my towel and pull a sarong around myself and make my way to the shower.

Outside my door two guards lean against the wall chewing khat and talking with Donna and Andrew, who press them for information.

"Do you think we can travel today? How is the fighting along the road to the beach?" Donna asks with pleading green eyes.

The guards mumble something to each other in Somali. Their expressions appear doubtful.

"Look, it's been five weeks. I haven't heard of any fighting. We can just go for a couple of hours and come straight back. We'll take as many guards as we can get on the technical," I interject.

"Mary, I'll tell you what, I'll send Ahmed and Musa to check out the situation," Andrew says. "They'll come back and give us their evaluation. So go take your shower and leave them alone."

Reluctantly, I leave the guards and walk to the shower. Water runs over my body and I wince slightly at its icy touch, far from the warm embraces of the previous evening. This is the fifth Friday my colleagues and I are kept like prisoners in our compound because of the likelihood of fighting along the road to Gezira Beach's fine powdery sand and deserted coastline. Attempting to push nightmare beach scenes from my mind, I fantasize about lounging without a care on fine sand with Marc and all of our colleagues.

Ahmed and Musa finally return as we are clearing the dishes from breakfast. Everyone's plate is empty and Ann piles her harvest of leftover bread into the bag she hides inconspicuously under the table. It will be easy for her today as most expatriates and Somali hospital staff will not be at Digfer since Friday is the Muslim holy day. Fridays do not offer a great deal of care for patients. In spite of our coaxing, Ann refuses to take a day off. At one time I felt guilty about watching her go off to work on our only day of rest, but I have learned the importance of pacing myself. Exhaustion only diminishes one's ability to give good care.

"Well?" I ask as they approach.

Ahmed and Musa walk past me and Andrew pulls them aside where they have a short hushed discussion. Donna and I exchange hopeful glances.

"All right, get your bathing costumes!" Andrew says with

obvious British heritage.

In my room I throw on my under-used bathing suit and decide to make a quick trip to the MSF compound to invite Marc and his colleagues. It is safe enough today to walk the two blocks between our compounds, but I have to carefully consider my clothing. In keeping with cultural and Islamic traditions I slip a long loose-fitting dress over my bathing suit and cover my head with a hijab. The cotton head covering is as long as I am tall, and striped in vibrant shades of red, green, yellow, and purple. The excessive amount of fabric not only covers my head, but also my arms.

The guards open the mammoth iron gates of the compound and I shudder remembering my dream. Quickly I repress its ominous memory. To reassure myself I position my radio in a fold of my cotton dress and look back at the IMC guard Hersi accompanying me. The two of us walk past a Somali woman who sits at a small table just outside the compound selling tea and cigarettes. Sand grinds between my toes and fine clouds of dust circle my ankles as we move around a pile of bloody rags along the sandy street. A boy runs along the walls of the Save the Children compound alongside a bicycle tire he propels forward with a stick. I think of the children all those Saturdays, turning "trash" into treasures at Bob's Mobile Service Garage workshops. Dad would be impressed with the resourceful nature of this Somali boy, creating a toy from trash he found along the streets of a war zone.

My eyes fill with tears thinking of my father holding Artie at the beach on the day of my brother's death. A sense of dread envelopes me and I quicken my pace to shake this irrational sense of fear. Today will be extraordinary. A much needed departure from reality along crystal azure waters with an intriguing Frenchman.

A small rock pelts my back and legs.

"Gallo, gallo!" a group of children yell at me.

One of the boys dressed in mismatching trousers and a tee shirt holds several pebbles in his hands. It looks like the oldest one is about eleven. His thin belly and last few ribs show under the torn tee shirt many sizes too small. He disperses the pebbles among his friends and they throw them toward me.

"Gallo, gallo!" they say again.

"Maya! Maya!" Hersi chastises.

My guard picks up a stick and swings it at the children fighting violence with violence. A never-ending cycle. The children finally run away giggling.

"What were they saying?" I ask.

"Gallo...it means infidel or stranger. They know you are not Muslim and not Somali. There is no school and no one watches the children since the war started."

I think about the oldest boy with the small striped tee shirt. He will continue to wander the streets for a few more months until a warlord puts a high-powered assault weapon in his hands, and promises enough food to feed his family. Food is finally pouring into Somali from around the world but young bandits employed by various warlords continually hijack it. The donated grains meant for starving Somalis is stolen by gangs of young men under the direction of their warlord. Humanitarian aid becomes nourishment for warlords' bandits fighting for control of a country without a government or infrastructure.

Across the street three Somali fighters begin yelling at each other around a tiny kiosk where a woman sells tea and cigarettes. The woman retreats when a man with a white tee shirt wrapped around his head raises his gun and begins firing in the air.

Yoousssssffffffff. A bullet whizzes past my face just before we reach MSF.

"I'm looking for Marc Jolie," I inquire of the guards once safely inside the compound.

"He is in the warehouse. I will show you," says the man. I walk with him along the wall of the compound. Hersi stays behind chatting with the MSF guards.

A brick wall surrounds what was once the Iranian embassy. Patterns in the wall facilitated the required modesty for Iranian women by allowing those inside to see out but blocking the view from those passing on the outside. This allows the French volunteers to place mattresses on the veranda and sleep in relative privacy. A lanky Frenchman with loose black curls falling around his shoulder lies peacefully next to a beautiful Somali woman who sits by his side gently stroking his hair. Two other volunteers sit in chairs on another part of the veranda smoking cigarettes and deeply engrossed in French dialogue. We walk through the kitchen where two Somali men cook with the guidance of an expat who passionately explains the art of stirring a sauce at just the right temperature. Rich aromas fill me with the most delicious scents I have experienced in Somalia.

We continue through the kitchen door to the outside where the guard points to an attached building. I walk through the door and find rows and rows of shelves stacked with medical supplies with neat French labels. Movement a few rows down catches my attention and I see Marc unpacking a box. His rugged unshaven face gives him the look of Indiana Jones meets Harley Davidson.

"Bonjour, Marc," I say.

"Ah, ma chérie, Mahree. Ça va?" he asks laying his clipboard on the shelf to stand. He holds my shoulders and kisses me lightly on both cheeks.

"It is nice to see you. What are you doing here?" he inquires.

"I wanted to invite you and your colleagues to go with us to Gezira," I say suddenly fearful that maybe I appear too anxious.

"Pour quoi pas? Why not!" he exclaims excitedly and adds, "Wonderful. It would be marvelous. I have to finish here and then we can discuss it."

Silently, I release a sigh of relief. I sense no hesitation from him. Instead he moves me against a stack of 4 x 4 gauze bandages, presses his body against mine and covers my mouth with a dozen gentle kisses.

"I am sorry I had to leave you so early this morning. A large order from Kenya arrived yesterday and I knew it must be catalogued and added to the inventory as soon as possible."

"Hmmm. Next time, maybe, you can stay longer," I say before accepting more of his delicate kisses.

He moves back and says, "I am so sorry. Is there something I can get you? Some tea? A Tusker?" he asks.

"No, no. I am fine. Let me help you and then we can talk about the day."

We walk over to a stack of boxes marked, MSF-France/Mogadishu. He moves one of them against a shelf and slices it across the top with a box cutter. Reaching under the packaging he pulls out a package of ten number 16-F Foley catheters and hands them to me, pointing to a space on the shelf.

"We'll stack these here," he says placing the catheters next to a small pile of others that are identical.

Easily we form into a small assembly line of two. Squatting next to the box he hands them to me and I stack them on the eye level shelf.

"This warehouse is amazing. So organized and well supplied. MSF seems to be so savvy about humanitarian aid inside a war zone. At IMC we are always referring to MSF to see how to do things more efficiently," I comment.

"Oui. MSF started in 1971 and has had many years to learn effective practices."

"How long have you been with MSF," I ask.

"Since 1984, I started organizing donkey caravans that transported medical supplies into remote areas torn by the war in Afghanistan. We had to go into areas where the fighting was very heavy. There were no paved roads through the mountains. It was very cold and I had to sleep in a small, one-man tent during the night. One morning I opened the tent and found a man sitting just outside. He was obviously hungry and shivering badly. In his arms he held a baby that looked about 18 months old wrapped in a black and white head scarf. I only spoke a little Dari but the father's face spoke for him. He looked desperately at his child and then handed her to me. When I opened the cloth, I saw the child did not move, its face very pale and sunken with emaciation. This baby was starving to death.

"I got some oil, sugar and skim milk powder from the supply bags on the donkey and mixed up a formula for the child and then inserted a nasogastric tube for the feedings. For several nights I let the man and his baby stay with me in the small tent. I gave the man some of my clothes and shared my food with him. To keep the infant warm we slept with her between us, staying very close to share our body warmth with her. We woke several times every night to feed her. The father learned to insert the tube into his daughter's nose himself and two days later she was able to drink through her mouth. Life came back into her and one day I woke to find the formula, the father and his baby were gone. In their place he left the keffiyeh that had swaddled the child. I still have it."

It is impossible to think of words to respond to his story. He tells the story with such humility and obvious compassion. I am falling deeply for this Frenchman.

After a few moments I say, "I am very intrigued with MSF. Do you think they would take me when I finish my time in Somalia?"

"Well, Mary, you know, it would be very difficult for you if you cannot speak French with any of your colleagues. You must learn to speak French first."

"You are from Paris, right?"

"Oui."

"What do you know about the language schools in Paris?" I say hoping this will perhaps win me a personal invitation to his country.

"No, I am sorry. I do not," he responds quickly and closes the empty box. His tone changes slightly and he seems uncomfortable talking about me being in France.

He takes my hand and leads me away from the new stack of 4 x 4 gauze.

"Will you stay for lunch? We can talk to everyone about going to the beach," he asks conspicuously changing the subject.

It may be too early for discussing a future together; I will just have to be patient for now. Living daily with the constant possibility of death has taught me something about enjoying each day to its fullest.

"Yes, I would love to stay," I reply.

All my senses are energized by the food spread on the long rectangular table and the sound of lively French conversations between colleagues filling the chairs that surround it. Marc passes a plate of camel slowly cooked in a thick brown sauce. It is tender and full of richness I did not know possible of such an animal.

"This food is amazing. Our camel tastes nothing like this. How do you do it?" I ask Marc.

"The French take cooking as seriously as we do our lovemaking," he responds with a modest wink. "We spend time training our Somali cook who has been a brilliant student."

The greasy Kenyan Blue Band margarine is absent from the table, instead it is replaced with the smooth European spread Nutella. It glides on my bread like chocolate silk.

A Somali woman sits across from me. She looks at me and our eyes meet briefly. She and I are the outsiders as the whole table is engrossed in several conversations, none of which we can understand. The tall man with the long, curly pony tail is in intense conversation with several of his colleagues. Although I cannot understand the subject, I can tell it has a serious tone and seems to have something to do with the woman because they periodically look in her direction as they are talking.

Marc sees that I am interested and begins to translate as much of the conversation as he can.

"They are speaking of Nur," he says, glancing at her.

The Somali woman has delicate thin lips and a slender nose. Her vibrant skin is the color of creamed coffee. She seems cared for but remains an outsider to the conversation of which she is the topic. "She and Pierre, our anesthesiologist, have been lovers for some time. In a few weeks he will return to his wife, Jeanette, in France and he is concerned about the situation Nur will be faced with when he leaves. She knows about his wife, but still believes she will go with him because according to her culture he can have two wives. Of course, he believes Jeanette will have other ideas about such an arrangement."

"What will happen to this girl?" I ask.

"This is the problem. Expatriates sometimes do not consider these things until it is too late. Because of strict Islamic tradition her clan will not take her in since she has been with a man that is not her husband. If her family is strict she could be stoned to death, but even in the best case scenario she will not be eligible for marriage. She could be destined to starve on the streets," he says.

Nur's survival is dependent on this man who will soon be thousands of miles away. She cannot be more than nineteen years old. I can only imagine the devastation ahead for her.

The conversation seems to trail off and Marc finds an opening to discuss the proposed beach trip. He speaks to his colleagues in French but thoughtfully keeps a hand on my arm to let me know I am still a part of the discussion.

"It is agreed. We will meet you at IMC in one hour," Marc assures.

Everyone raises a glass in celebration of the trip. Pierre leans over to kiss Nur on the forehead. I have to turn away when I see her face innocently clinging to mistaken hope.

"Good. I'd better get back to organize the transportation and guards," I say.

He closes his hands around mine. "You go ahead to take care of getting the vehicles. Plus tard," he bids, as he kisses my cheeks.

I say good-bye to my new French friends, each also giving me quick kisses on both my cheeks.

When Hersi and I walk through the gates of IMC, David sidles up next to me in the courtyard and says brazenly, "Oh la la, my little Mary. Did the party end well for you?"

I only send him a wink and a smile. He, of all people, does not need any details.

In the kitchen Donna and Lindsey excitedly pack a few snacks for the trip.

Several strands of gleaming red hair descend upon my shoulder as Donna leans toward my ear. She whispers softly, "Ahmed is coming with us."

That ominous feeling of trepidation comes over me again when I see her face beaming. I put my hand on her shoulder smiling, hoping her excitement will help me push it away. I should be thrilled with the prospect of a day off along the pristine shores of the Indian Ocean with my friends and an exciting new man in my life. But the dread still comes in waves, like the nightmare I am trying to forget.

After confirming our transportation and guards I pack a few things into my backpack, including a small plastic bag to serve as container for the shells I will collect.

By two-thirty the accompanying NGOs, MSF, PSF (Phamaciens Sans Frontieres), and AICF (Action International Contra la Faim) have arrived and we begin piling in two mini buses. The driver has the only seat, so ten people sitting upright fit easily on the metal floor of the vehicle.

I lean in the corner behind the driver. Marc sits close to me and pulls my legs onto his lap. He chats with Pierre who is unaccompanied for this trip.

"I'm going to fucking swim out to the reef," Brian announces with bravado.

"Brian, you know there are sharks out there," Lindsey implores with genuine concern in her expressive blue eyes.

"Carl from CARE told me they killed two expats before we got here. He knew both of the victims. Evidently the reef is full of sharks," I comment with irritation.

"It's low tide. Sharks can't get in from the reef. I'll be fine," he states nonchalantly.

Influencing him is impossible so I abandon the attempt.

"I'll stick to shell collecting, thank you. I get enough death-defying activities Saturday through Thursday. Not on my day off," I say as another wave of alarm washes over me, dousing my excitement.

After an uneventful twenty-minute ride our entourage of two technicals, filled with armed guards plus two mini buses, pulls onto the thick, white sand of Gezira Beach. We step past dozens of giant sea turtle shells dotting the shoreline. The breezes off the Indian Ocean soften the brilliant sun. Warm water washes over my toes as I take in the deep azure blue that seems to stretch for eternity.

In the distance a Bantu man is talking with the IMC expat doctor, Bradford. Bradford, a handsome black man from the States, negotiates the price of lobster while ignoring David, who twirls a French girl riding on him piggyback. The Bantu man takes orders for the lobster he sells for about 3,500 shillings (50 cents U.S.) each.

"Pierre, let's get some lobster. Do you want some Mary?" Marc asks.

"Yeah, I'll take a couple back to IMC."

As they leave, Brian runs past and dives into the surf. He is the only one brave enough, or perhaps reckless enough, to swim past his hips. Sharks are rumored to come very close to shore because at one time a slaughterhouse operated a mile up the coast.

"Watch out for the Portuguese man-of-war, Mary," he calls back to me.

"What? Watch for what?" I holler back.

But he is gone and I decide surely I am not the one to be concerned. I wade into the warm water and begin scooping it generously onto my shoulders.

"Mary!" Donna calls from shore, her thick mane whipping wildly in the ocean breeze.

She and Lindsey are laughing and pointing down the beach at a small group of young children. To honor the customs of modesty most of the women from the NGOs wear one-piece bathing suits. Local children, interested in mimicking us, take off their tee shirts and step into the sleeves leaving the neck open, creating an ideal portal for their dangling genitalia. The effect is as humorous as it is immodest.

"Owww, shit!" I scream.

My arm feels like a live electrical wire has whipped it, immediately sending a shooting pain to my shoulder and into my chest. Lindsey and Donna run over to me as I splash awkwardly out of the ocean and sit in the sand.

"Mary, what is it?" Lindsey asks, kneeling her gaunt frame at my side.

"Oh, man. It feels like hell," I say holding my arm.

Soon I have a small crowd, including the boys in tee shirt bathing suits. Marc and Pierre return quickly and Pierre says, "Let me see the wound."

Reluctantly I release my throbbing arm. It looks like someone drew an uneven line along my outer arm with a bright red marker.

"Looks like a Portuguese man-of-war. Did you see a bluish creature with long tentacles that looks like a jelly fish?" he asks.

"Pierre, I did not see anything. I was looking at these kids in the tee shirts when the pain just came out of nowhere," I say chuckling slightly remembering the sight of the little dangling penises.

"Yes, I can see why they turned your eye," Marc says, caressing my back and shoulders.

"Oh God, it feels like fire," I grimace.

"Yes, they are bastards. Their tentacles can be up to 100 feet long and even if severed from the main body, they can still be venomous for two weeks," Marc informs me.

"Splash some seawater on it. Sometimes that can neutralize the toxins. If we have some adhesive tape we can trying pulling out any toxic organisms still in your arm, and take some aspirin," Pierre suggests.

"I'll try anything. I think I have a first aid kit in my backpack," I say.

Marc retrieves a pack of his own and removes a small dropper bottle. He then sprinkles a cooling mixture of vinegar and alcohol on my arm. "I use this in my ears to prevent champignon when I swim," he adds as the burning subsides slightly.

"You get mushrooms in your ears?" I ask.

"Oh, sorry Mahree, champignon is how we call...ah, fungus, oui."

He wraps his arm around my shoulders and I lean against his chest. The aspirin takes the edge off the searing pain and I begin to feel relaxed again.

"Mary, I want to be honest with you," he says after a few minutes of silence.

I brace myself as I hold his compassionate gaze, wondering what blow I am about to be dealt. Beyond his face I see Bradford, David and several others playing soccer in the dunes, forgetting war for a moment.

"Before I left Paris I was with a woman for many years. Her name is Florence. I just wanted you to know," he says.

His statement leaves me with many questions. Is she still in his life? Is she his wife? Will he go back to her? Is this why I did not get an invitation to stay with him in Paris?

Before I have a chance to probe him for answers I hear Lindsey yelling, her blonde tresses blowing violently in the shifting wind.

"Brian, shark! Brian!" she shouts, frantically pointing toward the large fin moving toward Brian.

Several of us begin waving our arms and shouting urging him to come in to shore, but he is too far in the surf to hear us. A clap of thunder crashes across the darkening sky and we are now faced with a quickly approaching storm.

"Hey, it's getting dark. We should probably go. What are you yelling at?" asks Bradford still tossing the soccer ball from one hand to the other.

"Brian. He's oblivious to the shark swimming next to him in the wave," Lindsey shouts over the crashing surf.

The sky blackens by the minute and thunder continues to signal its warning. If we wait much longer we are vulnerable not only to the storm, but also to eruptions of violence in the darkness.

"It's getting dark. We have no choice but to go. Surely Brian will see us pulling out and have sense enough to come to shore," I shout above the roaring surf.

I push aside the throbbing in my arm as we begin to pile in the vans. Twenty expats quickly stuff towels and shells into backpacks and frantically throw them into the vans. Our guards call to each other in Somali while they help us get into the vehicles. About half a dozen pile on the technical next to the anti-aircraft gun mounted in the bed of the truck, while the rest perch alongside the rocket propelled grenade launcher. Slowly our unarmed van driver leads the four-vehicle caravan, gingerly navigating the thick sand. Through the window several of us see Brian finally running toward the caravan with all of his limbs still in tact. The van door is thrown open and he jumps in while it is still moving slowly down through the sand.

Bradford and Lindsey release a heavy sigh of relief. Pierre and Marc chat casually with some of the expats from the other French NGOs. Dark clouds hang low over the horizon and the sapphire sea has tuned into a churning black caldron. The air is suddenly eerily still as our caravan pulls onto the tiny path that winds around the dune not far from a bigger road.

Four men swiftly cut across the trail running in a crouched position cradling AK-47s.

"Not a good sign," murmurs Marc.

Immediately the men start firing rounds at our van in rapid succession. Bullets begin ricocheting inside the van.

"Everyone get down!" I order.

Bodies begin piling on top of each other trying to get as flat as they can. Pierre sits up watching the activity.

"Pierre, you have to get down," I shout just as a bullet bounces off the side of the van, narrowly missing my face.

"There're so many of them. Merde! Dozens and dozens. It's an ambush!" Pierre cries out in panic.

Our driver stops abruptly, sending our bodies flying toward the front. Shifting into reverse, he flies past our other vehicles driving backwards further away from our escape route through thick sandy soil.

A female French voice screams, "J'ai peur, I'm scared!"

Lindsey shouts, "We're going to die! We're going to die!"

The other vehicles try to turn around but get stuck in the soft soil behind us. David is in the other van about two hundred feet away with the only radio. The guards on the rooftop jump to the sand and begin shooting back at the growing army of ambushers. Bullets fly around like swarms of mosquitoes with no way of predicting where they will land.

I hear the van door open.

"I'm out of here!" Bradford yells as he jumps from the van and runs toward a small grouping of acacia trees.

"Brad! Brad! You can't go, they'll think you're Somali from the wrong clan! Brad!" I call uselessly as he runs as fast as he probably has in his life.

Marc jumps out running after him through an onslaught of gunfire. With no time to consider Bradford and Marc, our driver skillfully maneuvers the van around the other vehicles and drives as fast as possible. But there is no escaping the growing of maybe fifty or seventy angry, gun-wielding Somalis. A bullet hits just above my head, sparking a flash of red.

"Pierre, you have to get down flat!" I yell.

He is still sitting upright against the wall of the van looking out the window.

"What do they want?" someone shouts.

"Let's give it to them!"

"I don't want to die today," someone else cries through sobbing hysteria.

Through the window I see David getting out of the van and climbing to the roof of IMC's armed technical. He grabs a radio and slides his body down the side of the truck while shouting into the speaker. The ambush crowd is growing in number and our driver has nowhere to go but speed through the angry mob. The barrage of bullets increases and the walls of the van are dotted with holes. I always thought it was ridiculous when no one got hit after running through a spray of bullets like this in the movies. However, I'm living it—for the moment. Another bullet pings against the inside of the van and scarcely misses my head. I grab Pierre's ponytail and pull him to the floor just before he yells, "I've been hit!"

Pierre turns a sickly pale and beads of sweat begin to form over his face and chest. His hands tremble tucked between his legs curled into a fetal position. We are all frozen to the floor, helpless targets perhaps in our last minutes of life.

Suddenly, the force of a rocket-propelled grenade rocks our van and we fishtail over the tiny path back onto the sand dunes. Blood covers my hands as I attempt to hold Pierre's body stable while the van speeds over rocks and potholes.

After what seems like hours a faint shot rings out in the distance. Our vehicle finally stops and I wonder if we have hit a roadblock. As I brace for more gunfire I see a man in a blue helmet peering in the window. The letters "UN" are stamped plainly across the side. Tears of relief fill my eyes.

We carry Pierre's limp body from the bullet-ridden van into the United Nations peacekeeping compound and place him on an examining room table. His face is completely drained of color and blood stains his shirt around his arm and abdomen. We leave the tiny room to allow the UN Pakistani doctor to examine our friend.

Lindsey's wet hair is a tangled blonde rat's nest, clearly shaken she embraces Donna. Donna's emerald eyes overflow with tears streaking her dirty face as she wraps a free arm around Lindsey. Together we inspect the vehicle out of morbid curiosity. Holes speckle the dust covered van so it is no longer clear what its color was before the ambush. A bullet pierced the driver's door and another dangerously close to the gas tank. A third bullet entered at the exact spot where I was positioned inside and I wonder how it could have missed me.

"Just an open fracture of the elbow," the UN doctor announces to the crowd.

Although relieved, a heavy concern hangs in the air.

A UN official finally comes from one of the offices and speaks.

"We need your—," he begins.

"What about the others? What about Brad and Marc?" I plead, cutting him off.

"We must first get your statements about what happened," he informs us flatly and turns back toward the office. "Come with me."

The shaken group of expats gathers around a long conference table and the UN official begins to tediously gather our stories.

"Listen, I am really concerned about those who are still not here. One of the men is black and could be mistaken for a Somali of the wrong clan. We've got to do something," I beg with urgency.

"We cannot do anything. I am sorry," the official says flatly.

"Sorry! What do you mean? They could be kidnapped or dead!"

The official shifts slightly in his chair but his expressionless face does not change.

"We do not have enough people to handle so much fighting."

"Please, call for help," one of the French women calls out.

"We do not know where they are," he replies.

"We can show you! Our driver can help," I say, almost shouting now.

"There is no clearance for such an action. We have to get clearance."

I lie my head on the table in frustration. This is going nowhere, while our colleagues are fighting for their lives.

"Looking for me," a familiar voice calls from the door.

Marc and Bradford stand in the doorway smiling broadly. Brad's white muscle shirt is ripped and turned a dusty gray. An earring dangles precariously from his left ear and the pocket of his shorts is ripped revealing a portion of his white briefs. Marc is equally disheveled and both have thorny scratches covering their legs.

"Oh my God, it's so good to see you guys!" Donna says jumping from her chair to throw her sun burnt arms around them.

We all follow her lead until the two men are surrounded by our affectionate expressions of relief.

"What happened?" I ask Bradford, enveloped in Marc's embrace.

"I dug in under an acacia bush. It seemed outside the vehicle, away from what they were firing at would be a safer place to hide. I figured they were just after our vehicles so I wanted as much distance between me and that van as possible."

Marc listened attentively, seeming to enjoy Brad's story as if he had not lived it himself.

"Then Marc shows up and we got real cozy sprawled under that tree and didn't think much about the thorns poking at our asses," he says pausing to rub his buttocks.

"But Brad, I was so afraid they would think you were a local from the wrong clan," I interject.

"I'm getting to that. So we're sitting there in the thorny dirt waiting for the shooting to stop so we can make a run for it, when we see two pair of sandaled feet approaching. Next thing we know, we're looking up into the barrel of an AK-47. A few seconds later a dozen more guys showed up with their AK's."

"What did you do?" asks a French woman.

"I jumped my ass up and said, 'Yo, I'm American!'"

Laughter erupts and fills the small conference room.

"And I said, 'Yo, I'm a Frenchman!'" adds Marc.

They look at each other and Bradford asks, with outstretched arms, "I mean do I really look Somali?"

"Well Brad, I guess you stared into your African roots and decided you're just plain American after all!" I say with a giggle.

"Damn right," he replies.

A white UN truck escorts our bullet-ridden van back to IMC, where I can say that I have never been so glad to roll through these tall fortress gates. In the courtyard David, Brian and the others from our second vehicle are debriefing with Andrew. There are hugs all around and many relieved faces.

"David radioed from the beach something about you being a little late for dinner," Andrew says wryly.

We fall on the Italian furniture and David tells how his group ended up surrounded by close to fifty armed bandits.

"The gunmen told us to hand over our radios and the Toyota keys, but I refused until the AK-47's pointing at our chests convinced us. They got in and drove us to a building used as a kind of looters' garage where they store Land Cruisers and pick-up trucks ready to be equipped with weaponry. We got a delightful tour and then an elder showed up and began to apologize profusely. They had a quick discussion in Somali and then they drove us to UN headquarters—without our vehicle or our lobsters."

"I think they considered you liabilities rather than assets," Andrew says dragging deeply on his cigarette.

"It was all very surreal and now life couldn't seem sweeter. It's truly amazing that none of us or any guards were killed," David remarks with a glint in his auburn eyes.

He turns to Brian and without warning, grabs his face and kisses him on the mouth.

Brian explodes with "Fucking asshole!" wipes his lips and promptly stands to leave the scene.

David smiles at the crowd, throws his hands up and says, "Life is good."

It is difficult to say good night to Marc but finally he has to go. Our interrupted discussion about Florence seems unimportant at the moment.

"Je t'aime," he whispers kissing both my eyes, and then my lips.

When I'm finally in bed my arm is still throbbing from the man-of-war sting and I cannot sleep. But the pain seems insignificant compared to how wonderful life feels after nearly losing it. My colleagues and I almost paid the ultimate price for a few hours of freedom. Our desire for it blinded us from the hesitancy of our wiser Somali guards. They bent under our pressure and told us what we wanted to hear, probably believing if they did not their livelihoods were at stake. Is freedom with the promise of security even possible? Freedom rarely, if ever, walks hand in hand with security. Often it comes down to a choice. Choosing freedom means letting go of the promise of security. Letting go of the walls that keep me "safe." Walls that have become a prison. Ultimately freedom's call is stronger. It nourishes the human spirit in ways security cannot.

-16-

The Tailor

Mogadishu, Somalia, 1993

Abu's tiny body lounges in Ann's arms while his wiry fingers grip the clay "radio" he holds close to his mouth. The antenna sticks out of the top slightly askew, and he speaks Somali orders into its speaker indicated by dozens of holes poked into its earthen surface. In his other hand he holds a piece of half-eaten bread smeared with greasy Blue Band margarine, no doubt part of Ann's harvest from breakfast this morning. Clearly Abu has become Ann's favorite project. His mother rarely visits, relinquishing his care to Ann who is increasingly more like a surrogate parent.

"Ann, why don't you put him down. He must be at least six years old and obviously recovered from his sepsis. Make it easier on yourself," I suggest, knowing that it could be dangerous for the child if the others become jealous.

"Oh, I'm sorry," she says sounding like she's rehearsed her most pathetic voice.

A flash penetrates the dim hallway crowded with patients sitting on the floor along the wall. Jim, a photojournalist from Reuters, gets a shot of Ann as she wipes Abu's mouth with long, drawn out motions. She glances up at the journalist to be sure he got the shot.

"Hey Ann, it's time for lunch. Let's go," I coax. "We only have one vehicle today so we can't leave you behind this time."

Journalists love their "Saint Ann," who always provides them with a photo opportunity that enables them to make their deadline without much writing effort. However, Lindsey's efforts located deeper in the bowels of Digfer, are far more noteworthy. Her patients are better cared for, her ward is cleaner and her truly caring attitude makes her a genuine humanitarian.

A Somali woman sitting on the concrete floor leans against the wall while flies feast on a dirty mixture of bodily fluids oozing from her injured leg. Her infant child toddles in a torn tee shirt and bare bottom around her bandaged leg.

She grabs my arms and says, "Aano, aano."

She strokes her throat, points to Ann and continues her request for milk.

"Aano, aano."

Jim takes a photo of the woman with the injured leg stretching her empty hand toward me.

I know I have to refuse her. Tears burn the corners of my eyes as I walk past her. IMC is not able to provide food for the four hundred ill and injured under Digfer's roof. We know that food is essential to life and have had many discussions with Andrew about this very subject. Andrew has informed us of the security risks and explained how we would lose our ability to operate as providers of medical care if we started feeding patients. But Ann's actions understandably create confusion among the other patients when they see her bringing food to Abu day after day. We all want to feed the patients but Andrew has asked us to not to. Andrew often reminds us that what we do for one we must do for all or we will put those patients at risk. For that reason he insists that we direct family members to the nearby feeding centers rather than hand out small portions here and there.

At the end of our work day ten bodies cram inside a sweltering vehicle where the relentless late afternoon sun has thoroughly scorched the black IMC Land Cruiser. Jim from Reuters, Brian, and a Somali guard crouch in the tight quarters of the back straddling ammunition, medical bags and backpacks. Although we are heading away from the hospital, Jim continues pursuing the story of Somalia with a barrage of questions. With his personal space violated by the journalist, Brian's face becomes tense. He looks as though he is chewing a piece of tough leather. I sense him near the boiling point.

"Why is IMC not providing food for the patients? So many are obviously malnourished. Doesn't that ultimately have an effect on your work as health care providers?" Jim asks.

I decide it's time to give Brian a break so I attempt to answer from the seat in front of him.

"IMC does not provide food for the patients or the staff. You've probably seen families cooking on the balconies outside the wards. This is the only way patients are fed. If they got room and board there would be little incentive to leave once they heal, since nothing hopeful awaits them outside the hospital." I pause and look directly at Ann. She catches my glare and looks away quickly. She carefully wipes the crumbs out of the inside of her backpack.

I continue, "Casualty receives about eighty patients per day and the need for beds is continually desperate. I once had to remove a bomb from a bed that a family member was trying to hold for himself."

Donna purses her full lips seductively and adds, "Food is also a major security issue in Somalia. People fight and kill over food more than drugs. Even other organizations like CARE and Save The Children, with years of experience in food distribution, are faced with tremendous challenges attempting to distribute grain without being ambushed by mobs of bandits. It is safer for IMC and the Digfer patients to focus on medical care."

I look at Ann hoping she is taking in at least some of this discussion, but she seems to have tuned us out, gazing out the window at the active market.

Donna twists a strand of red hair between her fingers and continues, "Jim, a few weeks ago there were no beds and no floor space left for the incoming wounded, so the Somali hospital administrator had to ask a group of armed men to walk up and down the wards with him to discharge cured patients because they refused to go home. If we provided food we would have a feeding center, not a hospital."

The conversation lapses as Jim frantically records the information into his miniature composition book.

Donna winks an emerald eye at me and changes the subject, "How's it going with your Frenchman, Mary?"

"Great. He's been talking about going to Mombassa with me for some R&R. I'm hoping to catch the tailor to make some new clothes for the trip."

With the change of subject Ann decides to join the conversation.

"I'm sorry, oh, I met a new tailor in the hospital today. He is looking for work so I asked him to come to IMC during lunch today to see if anyone could give him some....Oh, I'm sorry, there he is now," she says pointing to a man outside the IMC gate.

A very thin, slightly bent man in a torn macaawis made out of an old bed sheet bangs on the gate for attention. He speaks to one of the guards through the little ten-inch by ten-inch conversation door that has just opened. They seem to be telling him to leave, and begin shouting. The man insists and put his hands inside the port hole yelling. Just as our Land Cruiser nears the scene one of the guards opens the main door a crack and fires on the man who falls in a heap onto the sandy ground just outside the compound gate.

Screams come immediately from the people in the street and our vehicle grinds to an abrupt stop. The gates fly open and more guards pile onto the street, checking for more would-be intruders. They wave our vehicle in and the driver speeds through, coming to a halt inside the courtyard. We pile out of the Land Cruiser in time to see the bloody man carried inside by the guard who shot him. The other guards quickly close the gates behind them. Confusion ensues as Andrew and Aweis run into the courtyard and the guards begin yelling at each other in Somali.

Jim hovers nearby shooting several rolls of film as we assess the situation.

"What happened?" I shout above the chaos.

"This man is a hawker. He was trying to force his way inside. We told him to leave but he said he was invited to come here. When I opened the gate he started to push me aside and my gun went off. I shot him by accident," says the guard.

"But I only shot him in the leg so he will not die," he adds quickly.

I lift his torn crimson soaked macaawis and find a bullet hole in his thigh possibly hitting an artery judging from his rapid loss of blood.

Brian looks at his leg and tells the guards to find the man's family to donate blood.

Brian and I put the man in a pick-up parked in the courtyard. Donna jumps into the truck and gently guides the man's descent into the bed.

Ann heads toward the kitchen probably hoping to grab some bread for Abu before she joins the effort to help.

"Ann, get in the pick-up, we'll need your help!" I call to her.

I want her to assume some responsibility. Our guards were just doing their job protecting us from what they thought could be a violent intruder. Ann had thoughtlessly placed the tailor in a dangerous position sending him to our compound without first notifying the guards.

The truck's engine starts and we begin to move out of the courtyard. Brad and Brian hold as much pressure as possible on the man's leg, hoping to minimize his blood loss.

"Can I come?" asks Jim loading another roll of film.

"Hop in if you can find room," I reply.

"Just stay the fuck out of the way!" Brian orders, not taking his eyes off his patient.

Jim jumps into the truck, finds a spot in the corner and continues to shoot photos.

The pickup pulls up to the doors of the Digfer Casualty and we carry the dying man upstairs to the operating theater. Jim lets his camera dangle around his neck so he can support the man's leg.

As the tailor's blood pressure drops dangerously low, we determine his blood type is "O" the same as mine. Not knowing if the search for the family will be fruitful, I ask Brian to hook me up to a collection unit downstairs. Although, I donated only four weeks earlier I made a silent promise to myself to eat an extra camel liver over the next few days. I open and close my fist expediting the flow of blood into the filling bag while other expats and some of our local Somali staff begins to line up to do the same.

The supply of electricity is so uncertain there is no way to store blood, which necessitates collecting it immediately prior to every need. This proves challenging since many Somalis are under the required weight of 110 pounds to give blood and usually they only donate to their own family or clan members.

Fortunately for the tailor, the Somalis on staff at Digfer are well fed, willing and able to donate blood, but many of us have recently donated sooner than the required eight-week waiting period. However, this man is lying on the operating table because of a shooting at IMC, so we are all willing to bend the rules.

Just as the last drops of Brian's donation fills the twelfth collection bag a breathless driver stumbles into the room.

"We found the family!"

"Great!" I say. "Send them in here."

"They are waiting in Casualty, but they refuse to give blood unless IMC pays them."

I had heard this demand once before soon after I first arrived. A father watched his dying son struggle to cling to life, refusing to give his blood unless we paid him. My reaction was intense negative judgment of this man. Reacting from a North American perspective, I had no appreciation for the intense struggle inherent in survival or the Somali Islamic perspective of life and death. A father will understandably resort to pressuring an NGO having far more resources than he will ever see in his lifetime into paying him to save the life of his son. In addition, his cultural beliefs are based on the will of Allah. If the father does nothing he rests assured the outcome is Allah's will. However, if he tries to save someone, particularly someone outside of his clan and fails, he fears that he might be blamed or he might even consider himself responsible for the death of that person.

But we cannot set a precedent of payment for a blood donation. Fortunately in this case we have collected enough for the patient. Brian and I quickly take the warm fluid-filled bags upstairs to the operating theater.

When I pass Abu's ward I see Ann carrying the child on her hip.

"Ann, we need your help. Put him down," I demand.

She follows but with him still attached. They look like some kind of eerie conjoined twins.

Amina walks up behind me and whispers in my ear.

"Abu's mother is gone," she says.

"What?" I ask.

"Yes, she told the patient in the bed next to Abu that IMC

could take better care of feeding him and that he belongs to IMC now."

"I'll deal with this later," I reply in exasperation. "Thanks."

In Ann's desperation to feel needed she has managed to turn her patients into her dependents. And now out of sheer selfishness she has managed to orphan a six-year-old boy in the middle of a war zone. But now is not the time to handle this delicate issue.

The air in the theater is thick with humidity and emotional tension. As the operating team prepares the patient for surgery their perspiration drenched scrubs turn a darker shade of blue. Three hours into the surgery we have emptied the seventh bag of blood into the tailor's arm. Donna waves her hand continuously over the patient's leg discouraging the flies from the gaping incision. Every few minutes I have to wipe beads of sweat from Brian's forehead. Dr. Saeed does not require my assistance since the Valium incident shortly after I arrived. Blood red trails trickle down everyone's legs ending up in congealing pools on the terrazzo floor.

Our patient, the tailor, begins to laugh out loud and attempts to sit up during surgery, forcing us to hold him down. With severe limitation in regard to drug supply and equipment, surgical anesthetic treatment consists of, at best, a combination of three drugs: Valium, Ketamine, and Atropine. Ketamine paralyzes the patient while still allowing normal breathing. However, it allows the patient to remain relatively conscious. Unfortunately some side effects include heavy salivation, hallucinations, violent nightmares, bouts of laughter and even singing. Valium is given to relax the muscles and ease any memory of the surgery. Atropine controls salivation so the patient won't drown in his own secretions. Today as most days we work without Valium. It is rarely found among the drugs in the locked surgical supply closet. It seems to leave the hospital as soon as it arrives and ends up a big seller in the black market outside Digfer.

I move the patient's head and wipe a sweat-soaked cloth around his face. His dark eyes stare into mine and he whispers something in Somali over and over again.

A flash temporarily blinds Brian as he ties the last suture.

"What the fuck?" he shouts squeezing his eyes open and shut

until he can focus again.

"Oh sorry. Didn't mean to blind you," says Jim who'd been inconspicuous until now.

He had leaned in for a close-up of the action and was met with Brian's unexpected rage. Dr. Saeed remains passive as he finishes up.

Brian flies at Jim, nearly spilling the metal tray and stumbles on the bloody tile. Jim steps backwards quickly as Brian reaches for his blue dress shirt in his struggles for balance on the slippery floor.

"What the hell are you doing man?" Jim yells, as he leaps through the swinging door and disappears out of the theater, narrowly escaping Brian's temper but dropping his camera in the process.

The tailor tries to sit up and inspect the commotion. I ease him back down to the table

"I told you to stay the fuck out of the way!" Brian yells towards the doors.

"I'm going to find Jim," I announce as I run out of the surgical suite, leaving Dr. Saeed and Brian alone with the patient.

"Are you okay?" I ask the breathless journalist who has stopped running.

We both settle down on a wooden bench in the hall.

"My camera is ruined and I probably lost the best shots of the day. What the hell is wrong with that guy?" Jim asks angrily.

"He's really a good guy and a great physician assistant, our best, he's just, uh...intense," I say trying to save Brian's job.

Donna appears and hands Jim some gauze to clean his hands and what is left of his camera.

"You can bet your ass I'm going to do something about this. That guy's too volatile to be in a war zone," he says stomping his way down the dark corridor.

"Shit," I say as our patient, the tailor, begins singing loudly. His songs resonate from the operating theater.

Everyone is silent on the ride back to IMC while pangs of hunger and exhaustion feed the tension among us. The double cab Toyota moves quickly across the dusty streets of Mogadishu summoning up clouds of dust into our eyes and mouths. Brian simmers in the corner of the pickup needing an extra helping of personal space. Ann does not respond to Donna when she tries to make small talk and I'm wondering how to explain everything to Andrew. Every day the complicated mixture of cultures heats a turbulent caldron of survival. Today it boiled over for a tailor, a physician assistant, a journalist, a nurse, a mother, and a six-year-old boy.

The Road to Baidoa

Mogadishu, Somalia, 1993

My hand runs down Marc's bare back as it rises and falls with the steady breathing rhythm of his sleep. First cracks of light in the morning sky signal the end of my night in his room at the MSF compound. I don't want it to end but I must return to IMC before the team leaves for Digfer.

"Bonjour," he says rolling over to greet me.

He cradles my face in his hands and kisses my nose lightly.

"Bonjour," I reply. "Marc, we need to talk about our trip to Mombassa."

He turns away and releases a long, deep breath. A sense of dread goes through me like a cold wind.

"Mary, I did not want to tell you last night—," he replies, avoiding my eyes.

"What? What did you not want to tell me last night?"

"You had such a hard week with the shooting at the IMC. I did not want to burden you further," he says.

"We will not go to Mombassa," he announces, gently smoothing a strand of hair behind my ear.

His blue eyes penetrate my dread and almost transport me from it.

"Why not?" I ask almost in a whisper.

"Because, ma chérie, I will be leaving Somalia tomorrow. I'm going home," he announces.

Tears burn my eyes and blur my vision, making him like an apparition before me. Blinking a few times I am able to hold them at bay.

"I'll be in Nairobi for a few days and then back in Paris within a week," he continues.

I pause trying to take this in without melting into a puddle of need and grief.

"I have some leave coming. I'll go with you to Nairobi. We can spend a few days together before you go," I suggest, hopefully.

He wipes a single escaping tear from the corner of my eye with his thumb.

"Florence is meeting me tomorrow in Nairobi," he says directly.

Abruptly I stand gathering each piece of clothing tangled at the foot of the bed with swift, forceful motions. The hundreds of losses I've seen over the past several months seem to well up in me at this moment. Finally, I sit on the foot of the bed. From behind a soft black and white fringed fabric is wrapped delicately across my shoulders and Marc whispers in my ear.

"I want you to have this."

I bury my face in the precious keffiyeh that once held the starving body of an Afghani man's child, and fall into Marc's arms one last time.

We do not make plans to see each other again or exchange contact information because we know, without speaking the words, that after Somalia there will never be anything for us.

Our good-bye is swift and in direct opposition to a need compelling me to stay. The deluded urge naively believes a place exists where we can hide together, away from the reality waiting for us outside the door like a vulture.

After a final embrace, I walk away without looking back.

By the time the technical pulls into the courtyard at IMC, I have wiped my last tear with the dampened Afghan cloth. It is time to summon the Iron Nurse. She can take me through another day of Digfer chaos.

Andrew approaches me balancing a cigarette and radio in his left hand.

"Mary, I need to speak with you."

"Can you give me a second to put my stuff away," I say feeling my eyes fill again.

"Actually, I need you now," he says and then adds, "Are you okay?"

"Yes. Yes, I'm fine," I say feeling the tears recede.

"Yes, well, I need you to go to Baidoa. A nurse there has fallen ill with dengue fever and was flown to Nairobi for treatment," he says.

The rest of the medical team is beginning to gather in the courtyard in preparation for their commute to Digfer. I notice Brian is not among them and fear he is in his room packing his bags after his outburst yesterday with Jim.

"Where's Brian?" I ask.

"That's part of why I want you to be the one to go," he continues in a hushed voice. "Since Mogadishu is crawling with journalists I thought it best to tuck him away in Baidoa, over two hundred and twenty-five kilometers from here. Hopefully, there his temper will have less opportunity to be triggered. I told him this is his last chance before we have to send him out of Africa."

"What's it got to do with me?" I ask.

"Might be good for the both of you," he replies with a wink.

"Oh, you know about Marc leaving, huh?"

Andrew places a compassionate hand on my shoulder and looks into my teary eyes.

"I think you'll like Baidoa," he responds.

"When are we going?" I ask.

"Brian left just before dawn on a supply truck. I'll brief you when you've packed and then you'll leave," he says.

As our technical rolls through the IMC compound gates, a heavily armed pickup loaded with Somali fighters, waving their guns in the air like madmen, zooms past. It's only nine in the morning. Within the hour their victims, and likely themselves, will be wheeled into Digfer Casualty in wheelbarrows with limbs hanging and abdomens torn open.

My mind turns to Baidoa, known as the "City of Death" because it has become the epicenter of the famine in Somalia. According to Andrew's briefing, Baidoa is located about 140 miles northwest of Mogadishu. At one time it had a population of about 50,000 to 60,000. But now starvation has claimed as many as 1,100 lives per week. An estimated 40,000 people live in the Baidoa feeding centers set up by NGO's such as Catholic Relief Services (CRS), CARE, International Committee of the Red Cross (ICRC), Irish Concern, and World Vision.

Thousands are fleeing from agricultural villages in the surrounding area once known as Somalia's "bread basket." Although recent drought has withered crops, the vicious warring bandits hold the majority of responsibility for the most devastating famine in Somalia's history. An often-overlooked war has been waged in south central Somalia as clans and sub-clans battle for control of its valuable agricultural lands. When former dictator Siad Barre was ousted in 1991, he sent General Mohamed Hashi Gani from his own Marehan clan to seize control of Baidoa. His men devastated villages, slaughtering, raping villagers and stealing food supplies and livestock. But the local people, with the help of warlord Mohamed Farah Aideed, drove Gani and his men away from the region.

However, in January 1992 Gani's group retook Baidoa while Aideed was distracted with his own war in Mogadishu. The seizure was short lived. Aideed once again chased Barre's men out of the area and the former dictator fled to Nairobi.

As Barre's men retreated they burned villages, destroyed crops and livestock, looted and raped in and around Baidoa, dumping bodies and debris in many of the drinking wells.

Getting food supplies to feeding centers anywhere in Somalia, including Baidoa is risky. Trucks transporting food are routinely looted regardless of the amount of security. It's a logistical nightmare as food arriving from all over the world meant for distribution pile up by the tons in the Mogadishu port, because relief agencies are unable to provide safe passage. International Committee of the Red Cross (ICRC) pays thousands of dollars per month for security at the Port of Mogadishu and has recruited plenty of local guards to provide protection for the NGO's operations throughout southern Somalia.

Andrew's words resonate as I consider the situation I'm stepping into.

"I cannot guarantee your safety in Baidoa. It is very dangerous. Bandits roam the area, randomly looting relief compounds at gunpoint. You already know about the ICRC expats who were killed when their main warehouse was raided. Baidoa is a small town, but maybe even more dangerous than Mog. Be careful...."

Somalia is wearing on me, and now I will be without Marc who has been my anchor for the last few months. I smile thinking of when we met the day of the bra fiasco. Although he was a relative stranger, his deep blue eyes and soothing French accent reassured me, while I waited anxiously fearing my colleagues were discussing how to send me quietly out of the country. I have never dated anyone as respectful, warm and generous a listener as Marc. Now he is out of my life just as I face new dangers where I could die alone in the burned out "bread basket" of Somalia.

However, despite its dangers and devastation I almost welcome new scenery. Perhaps patients from simple farming villages will be a respite from continual death threats from patients wielding AK-47s and grenades. Maybe in Baidoa, everyone is "poor" and I will not have to convince Somali doctors to treat dying patients who offer no potential for compensation. As the technical passes the former Iranian embassy where Marc prepares to leave Somalia, I tell myself a new place will ease the pain.

Baidoa is only 140 miles away, but the guards say the journey will take several hours. They say the dirt and gravel road is rugged and occasionally blocked by abandoned thorny tree limbs, stones and armed bandits at some check points. Boxes of supplies and three guards together with Sam, a new baby-faced logistician from Ohio, makes up our safari party.

Just outside Mogadishu the driver starts a tape and static mixes with a barely recognizable Boy George ballad. The combination fills the interior of our tired four-wheel drive as it creeps down the dusty road into the dry savannah. I don't feel much like talking so I sit back and take in the passing terrain.

Semiarid desert stretches to the horizon spotted with an occasional clumping of acacia trees and small bushes. The temperature must be over 100°F outside and at least five degrees more inside the sweltering cab of the truck. A pile of debris lies in the middle of the road just ahead. The driver carefully maneuvers his way around the pile of bones. Two skeletons lay side by side, the larger one's longer fingers lay across the chest of the smaller. Tufts of black hair grip their skulls like little caps. Our passing vehicle stirs the bits of rags still clinging to the sun-bleached bones. An empty woven water basket and a single pot, covered in a fine dust, lay a few feet from them.

"What happened to them?" asks Sam who is getting the typical introduction to the crude realities of war and famine.

"They were probably leaving the village, trying to find food in Baidoa," replies Khalid, our guard in the passenger seat.

"Oh my God," Sam gasps, brushing strands of straight black hair from his now perspiring forehead.

"There will probably be more. Thousands are fleeing their villages searching for food and water," I comment.

Our vehicle pushes on and leaves the pair behind us, lost in a cloud of dust.

A few hundred yards further on are three more skeletons sprawled out along the side of the road baking in the unrelenting sun, surrounded by spent bullet casings. No simple worldly goods lay next to these remains. I consider the camel herder, picturing him hobbling away from his slain family. Did he look back? What did he think when he passed piles of sun bleached bones on his way to Mogadishu?

The merciless heat requires us to drink generous amounts of water to replace the fluid lost in the constant stream of sweat that is soaking our clothing. Soon my body has more replacement than it needs and I ask the driver to pull over. He stops the car adjacent to a small grouping of acacias standing one hundred yards off the road. I discretely grab a few squares of toilet paper and start in their direction, hoping for a little privacy. I reach the trees and squat behind the thin trunk of an acacia. The distance gives me more privacy than the foliage. The silence is like the aftermath of Armageddon and I am the only person left on Earth. I drop my uplifted skirt to swat at something that bites my neck. I wipe the smashed insect mixed with blood on my hijab that now hangs limply over my shoulder before hiking back to the road. About halfway there I see the guards and Sam's fair skinned face creeping slowly around the Land Cruiser with their hands cupped to their mouths.

"Mary!" they call.

"Mary, where are you?"

"I'm here!" I call back, waving.

They are relieved when I appear, but Khalid looks at me sternly.

"We thought a lion or hyena got you," he says in exasperation.

"Oh, sorry. I guess I couldn't hear you," I say scratching at my neck.

"We must go," says the driver.

No one argues.

When he turns the ignition the truck responds with a pathetic click. We hold our breath, looking around at the desolate terrain. He tries three more times and the engine finally fires. We start down the rugged road once more and I decide to go easy on the water until Baidoa.

Although skeletons are becoming commonplace I grimace each time and continue to think of the camel herder. We pass what looks like an adult skeleton; loose black curls edge the skull's forehead. The hands and feet are missing, most likely carried off by wild animals. Something in the road ahead makes our driver slow. A sense of dread falls over us when we see a heavily armed technical sitting in the middle of the road.

"What is it?" asks Sam, smoothing his now damp hair away from his face.

"It looks like a roadblock," I answer.

"What do they want?"

"I don't know. Perhaps whatever they can take from us," I say staring straight ahead at five Somali fighters holding their assault rifles in front of their chest.

One runs toward our car and I hold my breath. He and our driver begin speaking to each other in forceful Somali tones. The man is pointing to his vehicle that blocks our passage. Abruptly two of our guards get out of the car and head to the back.

"Sam, you might want to be ready to crouch down on the seat," I say.

His baby face goes pale.

Just then our guards come into view rolling a tire toward the other vehicle. The gunmen's technical has a flat tire.

"Is everything okay?" Sam asks.

"Ha, ha," our driver affirms. "They are from my clan. A tire is broken. We give them one."

Sam and I simultaneously release audible sighs of relief as we finally pull safely away from the scene.

Just before dusk our four-wheel drive limps into the small town of Baidoa. Crumbling buildings pocked with bullet holes and stripped of their tin roofs, line the street. A tall, thin woman walks along the dusty road carrying a load of dried sticks, each one twice the circumference of her arm. A faded cloth once vibrantly adorned with red and black patterns wraps around her body and drapes across one shoulder. The bones of her exposed shoulder protrude sharply, stretching her dark skin. A boy about twelve squats beside a pile of trash offering pieces of charcoal for sale to the passersby. He rests his head on his knobby knees that are out of proportion to the rest of his skeletal legs.

"Khalid, why is that boy selling pieces of charcoal?" I ask.

"There is nothing else to sell. The people have nothing."

"Where does he get it?" asks Sam.

Our technical turns off the main street toward a small building with an "IMC" sign hanging on the gates that surround it.

Khalid pauses then answers the question.

"He finds pieces of wood and burns them while they are covered and they turn to charcoal."

The four-wheel drive rolls into the compound and sputters to a stop just as the guards close the iron gates. We grab our bags and the guards begin unloading the supplies we brought from Mogadishu. A short, slightly plump woman wearing a light blue IMC scrub shirt greets us as we unload.

"Just bring your things through here. I'm Rita, Project Coordinator," she states flatly, her voice bereft of any welcoming tones.

She indicates we are to go through the front door adorned on either side with a few flowering desert plants. The one-story white stucco building looks like a cute vacation cottage. Its windows are trimmed with blue shutters and matching blue lines around the doorframe. However, the bars that line up like soldiers across the thin screens of the open windows dampen their cheery potential.

The oppressive desert seems to follow us into the little house. There is no electricity or running water.

"You," Rita orders, pointing to me and then to a door, "will be in here."

"Uh, Rita, my name is Mary and this is Sam," I say hoping to stir some inkling of hospitality.

"Change if you want. We eat in five minutes," she says without acknowledging my introduction.

My room has one window, concrete floors and a twin bed. I take off my clothes and sit on the bed covered with a threadbare calico sheet hoping to cool my sweat-drenched body before dressing again for dinner. I rifle through my bag and pull out a fresh white IMC tee shirt. Folded carefully under it is Marc's black and white keffiyeh. I spread it out across my pillow. I caress its softness with my fingertips. The longing it holds seems to seep through my pores and loneliness creeps in around me like a fog.

-18-

What's for Dinner?

Baidoa, Somalia, 1993

A few doors from mine is the bathroom. A bucket of water sits under the sink not far from the toilet. As I hold one corner of the bucket and tip it towards me to dunk the cup for some hand washing water, I feel something smooth run across my toes. The bucket jerks, sloshing water on the concrete floor, when I see a green snake slithering its sleek body away from the base of the cool porcelain in search of a better hiding place. I do not move until the snake is gone and remind myself to be more careful next time.

Eight of us crowd around a table meant to seat six. The day has been long and I am more than ready for a good meal.

"Mary," a voice calls out.

Brian leans his head between two Somalis at the other end of the table. I feel the urge to jump up and throw my arms around someone familiar but I know he would not tolerate the closeness.

"Brian! When did you arrive?" I ask.

"About ten. You just getting here?" he inquires as a young Somali kitchen assistant appears in the hall with a platter of chicken.

"Yeah, about twenty minutes ago."

The chicken is placed in the middle of the table leaving plenty of room for the other dishes. But they never come. Rita picks up the platter and chooses a leg, then passes the plate to the person next to her. Hungry eyes followed the platter's journey around the table until it comes to them. When it arrives in front of me I glance down the table at the other three people lustfully eyeing the sole item on the menu. Considering my colleagues, I slice a fraction of what I want to take. The table is absent of the chatter I am accustomed to in Mogadishu. Everyone seems focused on their tiny portion of nourishment. I bite into the chicken so flavorless and tough it is like chewing a piece of old gum. My eyes land on Rita and wonder how she maintains a plump figure.

In my room after dinner I start to unpack but decide with nowhere to store my clothes it's better to leave them in my bag. At least there they'll be out of reach of slithering creatures in search of cool, dark hiding places. I lie on my pillow, wrap Marc's Afghan cloth around my face and let the thirsty cotton absorb my tears.

A hesitant knock interrupts me.

"Mary, you in there?" Brian asks.

I wipe my face and clear my throat before answering.

"Yeah, Brian, just a minute."

My hand grips the doorknob and I take a deep breath before opening.

"Hey, Mary, I want to show you something," he says already turning away from my door.

He turns back and says, "You okay?"

"Oh yeah. Just tired," I say.

"And fucking hungry, right?"

"God, you're not kidding!" I say, trying not to be too loud.

"Come on."

He takes me outside into the courtyard. Darkness is overtaking the day but appears powerless to ease the grip of the oppressive desert heat. Behind the house we take a short flight of stairs to the roof where we sit on a bare mattress.

"Welcome to my room," Brian says gazing up into the heavenly ceiling.

The surrendering sky welcomes a night sky brilliantly lit with billions of stars unspoiled by any manufactured light. We sit in the cooler air without talking for a few minutes, taken in by the beauty and by our child-like appreciation.

"Thank you, Brian. This is inspiring," I finally say.

"Fucking amazing isn't it?" he says. "Sure takes your mind off your hunger. Here, have a Tusker."

I laugh acknowledging this undeniable truth and take the beer he offers.

"I grabbed a couple before I left. Good fucking thing too. Don't think we'll see any extras in this house," he says with a hint of his signature sour tone.

"What's with that? One damn chicken for ten people?" I ask.

"It was that way at lunch too. We each had a piece of stale bread, some pasta with oil and about half a spoonful of Blue Band."

"Rita seems to be getting enough to eat. She's got to be hording it for herself," I note.

He shrugs, unable to give a better explanation.

"How was your first day?" I ask, deciding that conversation will only make my hunger worse.

Slowly and with great appreciation, I down the first swallow of what could be the last extravagance for a long time.

"It's different here. The patients are mostly farmers and nomads. They told me we'd see diseases of every kind. Malaria, diphtheria, tetanus. I saw a girl with cancrum oris today."

"What is that? Sounds vaguely familiar from nursing school."

"It eats away the flesh around the mouth and jaw. Half this kid's face was missing and flies were darting in and out of her mouth," he says.

"There is no surgeon here so I think I'll get to do a lot of surgery on my own. I think I'll really be able to do some fuckin' good here," he continues then takes a long drink.

"You know you are a better surgeon than several of the expat surgeons at Digfer. These people need someone like you. I hope you get to stick around," I say.

"What did Andrew tell you about why I came?" he asks, a little boyishly.

"He said he wanted you out of the sight of the growing press corps after you attacked Jim." I brace myself for an intense response.

But in a rare moment, Brian sits entranced by the luminous night sky, not offering any angry defensive words.

I decide to continue.

"He asked me to watch out for you," I say. "Brian, I see the way you care about the Somalis. Don't blow it for them. They need you."

He just nods his head and finishes off his drink.

"What are you scratching at?" he says changing the subject.

Suddenly I realized I had a mosquito bite on my neck.

"Oh, it's nothing. Just a small bite."

-19-

Operating at Gunpoint

Baidoa, Somalia, 1993

A two-year-old child sits in the dirt outside the hospital's one-room Casualty under the sparse shade of an acacia. He stares expressionlessly as flies crawl on his powdery white lips that give away his advanced stage of hunger. A filthy plaid cloth drapes his shoulders, over his naked chest and into his lap. His tiny feet stick straight out from the grimy folds of fabric. He is disturbingly still and alone in the scorching heat of the morning sun.

My guard, Khalid and I step over to him. Khalid gently cradles the back of the child's disproportionably sized head with the palm of his hand. He begins to speak to the toddler in his native language. The little one's expression remains dull and unchanging. A few feet away a woman squatting in the dirt says something to Khalid. Her body is wrapped in thread bare fabric, torn in several places. It hangs across one shoulder and falls between her breasts. One withered breast is exposed laying flat against her chest.

Every day for the week I have been here at least fifty patients like her squat in the dirt outside the hospital waiting for me to see them. A wise Somali nurse named Moktar and I run the Casualty. We see up to two hundred patients per day. With knees bent into a squatting position, suspending their buttocks two inches above the earth sick, emaciated, injured, and diseased Somalis patiently wait in the hot African sun with their spindly arms wrapped around their legs. Some are from rural farming villages. Others are nomadic desert wanderers. None expect a formal waiting room or even a hard wooden bench on which to wait. Without complaint they simply transform their bodies into "chairs." Most often they own nothing but the tattered rags on their gaunt bodies. This is why I have yet to see the local Somali doctor, since there is no possibility of compensation for the work.

"What did she say, Khalid?" I ask squatting next to the child.

"She says the boy has been here for a few hours. Someone brought him and then left saying his parents are dead," he replies, his eyes full of compassion. The child's hunger renders him lethargic and he does not resist the examination.

"What about his clan? Will they not take care of him?" I ask.

"He is nomad. His family was killed by bandits."

I lift the child carefully and he falls easily against my chest.

"Maybe I can get him stabilized before finding a home for him," I say.

Khalid strokes the boy's face and speaks with him softly.

The way he speaks tells me where he is from. I'll find a nomad family from his village who will adopt him," he says reassuringly.

A sudden dizziness comes over me and I almost lose my balance. When I stand with the child I have to steady myself.

Inside the Casualty Moktar is already examining a patient with a bullet wound to the leg. With nowhere else to go he allows the woman's toddler to lie curled up beside her injured mother. Both are bone thin.

"Start an IV and I will let Brian know she will probably need surgery," I say, barely squeaking out the words.

I lift my hand to my throat, which has begun to feel like sandpaper, every time I speak or swallow.

"What is it Mary?" Moktar asks pointing to my throat.

He lays a hand on my shoulder in a grandfatherly manner. This gentle nurse is invaluable and I have quickly grown fond of his soothing countenance. He is also intelligent and has taught me many new medical skills necessary for working with so few resources. A few days ago we were trying to find a way to get the nomadic patients to bring their own medical records with them when they return for follow-up. Many times the nomads go to different clinics for care so keeping records in one clinic didn't help much. Moktar decided that if we wrote basic notes on small paper and then folded the paper into the corner of the patient's dress or macaawis then it would be available for us and any other medical personnel all the time. Thus far that idea has worked well because these folks only have one garment and we share the information with the other clinics so they can do the same.

The hospital is a series of small stucco buildings serving the purpose of the Casualty, ward, and operating theater. None have electricity so I have adjusted to the tall windows that let in just enough natural light. I walk along the narrow path that leads to the ward watching carefully for debris and human waste. There is no electricity or running water or any bathroom facilities of any kind. Patients and staff must relieve themselves on the ground where the earth is often too hard to allow digging.

Despite the lack of what most would call basic necessities my experience in Baidoa offers a sense of satisfaction missing from Digfer. Because the hospital is so small, all of us need to be available to do everything from sweeping floors to major surgery. Often I am able to assist with surgical procedures and administer anesthesia when there is time. In Casualty I am able to see and treat everyone waiting for care, even the poorest of poor who often got overlooked in the chaos at Digfer. Although the need is so great and almost every patient wears the face of famine, I am finding myself making a difference with people who are truly appreciative of their care. So often I have thought of Rodrigo in Tampa who gave me his prized toy sword as a thank you. His humble appreciation inspired the path that led me here. He is with me each time I hear a patient say "mahaht-sanet." Thank you.

Brian adjusts his battery powered headlamp before scrubbing for surgery under the solar shower bag; I sterilize surgical instruments in a large pot on the sooty, wood-burning stove in the old hospital kitchen. The back wall of this building is blown out and a donkey stands napping six feet from the pot of boiling instruments. Two Somali men wander in and greet me. They stand next to the donkey and watch our movements with interest. They each wear flip-flops made of old black rubber tires, mismatching plaid dress shirts, and work slacks that come above their ankles like Capri pants. One is sporting a WWII era flight hat. Its flaps hang loosely over his ears and the sides of his long face.

Moktar has the woman with the gunshot wound to her leg lying on plywood covered in green plastic that serves as a surgical table. An orange ring of iodine surrounds her wound.

"Where's the child?" I ask him.

"With another woman who said she will watch her," Moktar replies as he waves flies from the open wound.

Just as the patient responds to the anesthesia Brian lets out a slight groan. His face turns a disturbing shade of pale green and he abruptly grabs a handful of gauze and dashes to the open window.

"I'll be right back. Fuck!" he complains, stumbling onto the ground outside the window.

"Uggghhh!" Brian's voice sounds like relief as it trails through the window.

In a few minutes he crawls more gracefully back through the window with his hands freshly scrubbed under the solar shower bag.

"Better?" I ask with a chuckle.

"I had to take an emergency shit," Brian says with typical directness.

Beds with high metal headboards line the walls of the patient ward. Evenly spaced bars line up between the rounded frames making the room remind me of a cheerless orphanage. I find an open postoperative bed and prepare it for the woman. I recheck her IV before going back to the Casualty.

I see one more patient and explain his medication dosage through drawings of a sun rise, full sun and a sunset. I circle the sun rise and sun set to indicate that one pill is to be taken twice daily. Bandits typically steal medication if they see patients carrying them in the open, so I show him how to roll the paper bag of pills in the waist of his macaawis.

A fiery raw burning sensation in my throat has increased to an almost unbearable level; I decide to go outside to see if some fresh air might help. I stand in the sun among the waiting crowds under an acacia tree. Each time I try to take a breath it ignites a fire in my throat. My joints are beginning to ache and my head is throbbing. But as I look around at the faces of these gentle people waiting in the scorching heat to see me, I know I can make it through the day.

An emaciated woman with sunken cheeks and dry withered skin stands next to a desperately thin child. The mother's shriveled skin makes her look sixty but she cannot be more than twenty-five. Her daughter, about eight, squats next to her, leaning against her mother's frail body. The child holds a faded blue veil across the right side of her face, hiding it between her and her mother's protruding ribs. I turn my head to get a better view and see the veil is hiding a massive wound.

A small cloud of dust stirs as I squat beside the little girl. I reach for her face and pause to give her and her mother a chance to understand what I am doing. The sight under the veil nearly takes my breath.

Inside the Casualty I examine her more closely. Nearly a third of her face is missing, eaten away by an unknown organism, exposing her teeth and gums. She does not appear to be in pain, but is severely malnourished and will not improve without help because the deformity hinders her ability to swallow. Some of the dry crusted sores caused by insect bites that cover her body appear infected. I lead her and her mother to the dirty surgical room used for infected and contagious cases. The room has better light and allows me to get a more in depth look at the wound. She is lying on the table when Brian comes through.

"What do you think? Cancrum oris?" I ask him.

"No way to confirm but it sure the hell looks like it," he says, gently running his hand down the length of the girls arm.

Without warning three armed gunmen burst into the surgical theater waving their AK-47's in the air, yelling at the child's emaciated mother and pushing her out of the way. While we are still stunned by their violent entrance, two of them pick up the girl and throw her on the concrete floor. The other keeps his gun pointed at my temple to keep me from interfering. He has a towel wrapped around his head like a turban and his gun belt hangs from his macaawis, heavy with grenades.

Two more gunmen burst in, their worn collared dress shirts covered in the blood of their fallen colleague. They carry him to the table and motion us toward our new patient.

Blood soaks the victim's chest, making the original color of his shirt unrecognizable. He has been shot multiple times in the chest and he is barely breathing. Brian and I both know we will be held at gunpoint until we try to save him. The mother is huddled in the corner and the girl is curled in a fetal position under the table. Blood drips from the fallen gunmen on to her tangled black hair. I make a slight move toward the girl on the floor, but the gunmen holding the gun to my temple yells something insistently in Somali and then shoves the girl's body aside with his foot.

"Mary, we both know this guy is fucked, but we're going to go through the motions anyway," Brian says slowly.

"They don't seem to speak English, so let's talk to each other with very official sounding voices and maybe we can buy some time," he continues.

"Whatever you say," I murmur, slowly lowering my hands to begin to work on the patient.

The only thing that will get me through this is adrenaline and the occasional glance I steal to check on the faceless child curled in a ball on the floor.

I start an IV and Brian sees me going for the chest tube.

"The man's lungs are quickly filling with blood, so I can put in the chest tube while you look inside his belly, if you want," I suggest.

"I'll talk you through it," he reassures me.

"Sounds good to me," I say in a professional tone as if discussing a surgical newsletter.

"This guy has lost a lot of blood. I'm surprised he has a pressure at all," I remark.

"We could transfuse him with our blood but I just donated and he's a goner anyway," I continue.

"I don't fucking want to give blood to this bastard anyway," he says still sounding professional for the Somalis who don't understand English. He makes a quick glance at the motionless girl.

I am uneasy when I see the door to the surgical room is still open. If one of the Somali local hospital staff comes in, they are likely to be killed if something goes wrong. I silently hope Moktar won't check on me.

Quickly I collect the needed equipment for the procedure and assist Brian in setting up the laporatomy. We need to determine if bullets have ripped into the man's internal organs. Although I have assisted with many chest tube insertions I have never inserted one myself. Certainly, there is nothing to stop me now.

"Okay, find the fourth intercostal space, about four fingers from the axilla," Brian coaches in a steady conversational tone.

If they realize I am not qualified to perform this procedure they will have another reason to kill me.

As my fingers explore the man's bloodied chest cavity Brian glances inconspicuously to see if I had cleaned the right spot. The scalpel shakes slightly in my hand over the man's massive wounds.

"Now make a one centimeter incision along the superior edge of the inferior rib," he says as he makes a seven-inch incision along the abdomen.

Sweat drips in streams down the sides of my face. Brian dabs blood as he cuts deeper and deeper into the man's body.

Brian continues to direct me. "Separate the muscle fibers and puncture the pleura with those Kelly forceps," he instructs.

The tone of his voice sounds like he is commenting on what he is finding in the abdomen.

The gunmen still hold their weapons on us, but I am able to work without the barrel of a machine gun against my aching head. We plug away, carefully considering our steps, trying not to step on the motionless child lying on the floor near our feet.

I feel a pop and a gush of air when I feed the clamped tube into the man's chest with another pair of forceps. After positioning it correctly, I suture it in place.

"Found the spleen," Brian announces.

"Looks all right to me," I say glancing at the organ.

"Everything's fine in the belly so far. Let's set up to auto transfuse—if he lives long enough," Brian recommends.

"How does his diaphragm look?" I ask.

"It's fine. All the injuries are above it," he says confidently.

With necessary resourcefulness, I hook up a urine drainage bag to the chest tube. The bag resembles a quart-size zip lock plastic food storage bag, without the zip. I then plug a blood collection bag into the flexible rubber section of the chest tube, just above the urine bag connection. Finally, I clamp off the drainage to the urine bag so the blood can accumulate in the blood collection bag. I make sure all is secured and positioned properly. I change gloves and hang another IV bag full of fluids. Brian has closed up the abdomen and I help him check for other possible injuries. After fifteen minutes the blood bag is full. I look at Brian before I set up the system to deliver it back to the patient.

He nods and I start the transfusion. The patient's face is turning ashen and his breathing is extremely irregular. The wounded fighter's lips are pure white. Within minutes he stops breathing.

"Brian...he's dead," I say, unsure what to expect from the gunmen when they realize we failed to save their colleague.

"Fuck," he whispers.

We look apologetically at the gunmen. They look at each other and I wince when the one with the towel turban reaches for his gun. I'm relieved to see him sling it over his shoulder. Without a word they lift the dead man off the table and carry him away, bags and tubes hanging from his lifeless body.

As soon as they are out of sight we both hurry to the side of the frightened child on the floor. I lean down beside her and check for a pulse. She has been so still I am afraid the impact of her head hitting the concrete may have killed her. When I touch her she groans slightly and rolls toward me. I can see her teeth chattering quietly.

Brian wipes the blood off the table and I lift her tiny body. Just then Moktar rushes into the room.

"Are you all right?" he exclaims. "I saw the men with guns running out," he adds.

"We're fine. I need your help translating for the mother of this child," I state.

Brian sweetly strokes the child's hair as I explain to the sullen mother that her daughter needs a feeding tube, IV fluids and penicillin. The child needs to stay in the hospital, but as Moktar translates the mother shakes her head refusing all treatment.

"Moktar, why is she refusing treatment? Her daughter will die without it," I say, my heart still racing.

"The mother says she will come back every day for treatment but she will not let her child stay in the hospital. She is afraid to stay in Baidoa at night," Moktar replies.

The mother's lost eyes look into mine. Without words I know she understands the decision will mean the child will die soon. However, I can't help but wonder what I would do if I had seen my dying child thrown to a cold, concrete floor by armed bandits.

My whole body screams in pain. My head, every muscle and my throat ring out in violent protest to the sickness that has invaded my body. Above all, my soul aches for the helpless mother and her starving, faceless child. I rub my hands across my cheeks to wipe the tears before they are noticed.

-20-

Brian

Baidoa, Somalia, 1993

A dazed look of exhaustion covers the faces of eight expats crowded around the 1960's style Formica table in the compound dining room. The two adjacent windows offer no hope for even the slightest breeze. The air is deathly still. Several fan themselves with their Corning ware plates while waiting for the evening's meager portions. Brian pinches the front of his shirt and pulls it in and out from his chest, attempting to create a slight breeze. My body shivers in waves of uncontrollable fits against some mysterious illness. The shaking only intensifies the severe aching in my joints and behind my eyes.

"Are you cold Mary?" Brian asks.

"I can't stop shivering," I say through rattling teeth.

"You've probably got the flu," Rita curtly assures me.

"It doesn't feel like any flu I've ever had," I respond.

The fanning plates go back on the table when Abdulkadir, our kitchen assistant, appears through the pantry door and places a small plate of pasta and four potatoes on the table. All eyes but mine focus on the four-serving dinner that will have to stretch to feed eight. Filling my empty stomach holds no appeal. All my energy is focused on the pain in my body that feels like bones breaking.

Abdulkadir walks to my side and unwraps the plaid cloth from his head.

"Mary, your arms. You have the red spots," he says as he tenderly lays his keffiyeh across my shaking shoulders.

I lift Abdulkadir's cloth and see a red rash covering my arms. The young kitchen assistant softly touches my arm. The rest of the table continues to pass the two platters of food around the table.

"Skin is like fire," he says with compassion.

My hand goes instinctively to my head and face.

"I think I have a fever. What do you think I have?" I ask around the table.

"Looks kind of like measles," remarks Brian between mouthfuls.

"No, I've had measles. Both kinds."

"Maybe it's malaria," Sam suggests.

"No, I say, you have the flu. Take a couple of aspirin and go to bed," Rita recommends as she sneaks an extra few strands of pasta onto her plate.

Before dawn an intense headache wakes me from a night of sporadic sleep. I will my body to get up but it does not respond and lies on the thin sheet as if paralyzed.

As the sun finally begins to stream under my doorframe I hear a knock and it opens slowly.

"Mary, you up?"

"Ugghhh," is all I can eek out.

I feel the mattress lower slightly, and my body rolls toward Brian when he sits at the edge of my bed. For an instant it feels like I am nine years old again and my father is perching beside me to tuck me into bed.

"How you feeling?" Brian asks.

"Mmmm," I respond without opening my eyes.

"Okay, stupid question."

I feel his hand on my forehead and then a cold metal object pointing against my lip.

"Open up," he instructs.

I open my mouth slightly and he slides the thermometer under my tongue.

He tenderly moves the hair away from my face. However, the mercury rises quickly breaking the rare moment of closeness he offered. He stands to check the results in the light of the doorway.

"Shit, 103°F," he announces. "Your ass is staying in bed today."

Shuffling sounds come from the door and I can hear Rita's voice talking with Brian about sending me to Nairobi. A hand reaches under my head and slowly lifts it to the edge of a porcelain teacup.

"Mary, you will drink?" Abdulkadir asks tipping the warm liquid into my mouth. The warmth soothes my throat but it takes all my strength to swallow. Abdulkadir moves the cup away from my mouth and sets it beside the bed. His lifts my arm and runs his long fingers along my forearm.

"This is dengue fever," Abdulkadir says.

"What?" says Rita with more exasperation than concern. She will have to deal with transporting me to Nairobi for treatment and manage minus one nurse, again.

"I think he's right," says Brian. "I did some reading last night. She has all the symptoms. Remember that 'small bite' you got on your neck a week ago? A bitch of a mosquito gave you one hell of a gift."

"What's the treatment?" I mumble.

"Afraid there is none. Expect a week or more in bed with symptomatic treatment and lots of fluids. Your hands and feet are going to itch like mad and your bones are going to feel like they've been put through a meat grinder. This is also known as breakbone fever," he remarks wryly.

"Oh great," I moan.

"All right, I'll radio Mog to see what Andrew thinks. We need to get you on a plane as soon as possible," offers Rita.

I open my eyelids just enough to make out Rita's plump form across the room.

"How far to the airport?" I ask.

"About 25 minutes."

My eyes close again. I cannot imagine traveling as far as the bathroom I share with the shy snake let alone a long drive.

"I'll stay here. I can't get thrown around in a technical for 25 minutes," I say in insistent whispers.

"I will stay with you, Mary," Abdulkadir says as he lifts my head once more and brings the soothing Somali chai to my parched lips.

For five days I do nothing but lie on my mattress trying not to move. Marc's scent still lingers on the Afghani cloth that lays across my pillow caressing my face. Abdulkadir rushes back three times a day from his duties in the kitchen to spend his free time by my side. If not for him, dehydration would have nearly finished me. He sits crossed-legged on a wooden stool and holds my feverish hand whispering, "Mary I'm so sorry. I'm so sorry you're sick."

As my aches subside, the rash on my hands and feet begins to itch intensely. If not for Abdulkadir placing socks on my hands and feet I surely would have worn off several layers of skin by now. This young man summons strength back into my body and reminds me of the true meaning of "nurse," and the importance of a compassionate presence.

After six days my itching has subsided to an annoying level and although a dull ache still lingers in my head, my bones no longer feel like they are being crushed. I am anxious to get back to the hospital, but am enjoying the relative quiet moments during the day while most are away. Abdulkadir is preparing dinner so I am alone with a brilliantly colored starling teetering on the windowsill outside my room. Its head jerks from side to side. The electric blue-green chest expands and its black beak opens to release his serene melody.

"Boom! Boom!"

An explosion rips through our peaceful moment and my companion is gone. I rush to the living room and find Rita on the radio calling the expats to come back to the compound. There has been a security incident in town and I hurry as fast as my weak legs will take me to the gates of the compound to investigate. Khalid runs past and jumps into the IMC technical and closes the door as the vehicle speeds toward the hospital.

The team returns within minutes followed closely by a rusted green military tank. The tank is covered in desert dust and topped with five gunmen hanging onto its ample arsenal. Just as the expats close the compound gate behind them, the tank barrels up and aims its weaponry directly towards our blue shuttered house. Angry Somali gunmen with bloodshot eyes sporting heavy assault rifles across their worn button-down dress shirts pile off the tank and begin yelling loudly. Khalid runs into the house and translates the gunmen's demands.

"They want help for their injured soldiers," he says to the medical team. "They have many wounded."

The horizon is beginning to glow with the setting sun. It will be dangerous to be out beyond the walls of the compound at night. Brian and I look at each other and then at everyone else standing frozen in the living room. Rita says nothing. None of us want to go.

Yelling continues and the tank rolls closer to the gate. Its barrel is pointing through the gate's conversation port hole. We all look at Khalid, who has become the official translator for the edgy gunman.

"They say if you do not come they will blow up the house." Although I just finished a cup of chai my mouth goes dry. I can't think of a way out.

"I'll go," says Brian.

Of course he will. It takes someone crazy enough to swim with sharks; edgy enough to threaten a journalist in a surgical theater; and compassionate enough to volunteer in a war zone in the first place. A skill set uniquely Brian.

"They will want someone to do surgery. I'm the only one who can do it," he says attempting to hide his obvious bravery behind a veil of practicality.

He grabs the radio from Rita and starts out the front door.

"Brian, you can't do this. IMC doesn't want to set a precedent that gunmen can come to the compound making demands. And who knows where they might take you," I argue.

"We don't have a choice. Either I go or we sit here and wait for them to fire that thing through our front door," he says pointing at the barrel of the tank's gun poking through the metal gates of the compound.

"I'll be all right," he adds, winking in my direction.

Complete helplessness comes over me as I watch him walk out the door, realizing he might lose his life to save the rest of us.

He checks the batteries on the radio and waves it in the air bidding us good-bye as he disappears into the night with the five gunmen. His scrubs are still covered with the bloodstains of a hard day's work.

Our worry consumes our appetite. For the first time, Abdulkadir returns uneaten food to the kitchen. I look at the clock mounted off center above the door to the kitchen. An hour has passed with no word from Brian.

"I'm going to call Brian," I say heading to the radio sitting on the desk in the living room. Abdulkadir returns from the kitchen and places a cup of chai on the desk in front of me. Silently he turns toward the kitchen. I catch his hand before he goes. I squeeze it and look at him with gratitude before picking up the radio.

Sam suggests, "Mary, why don't you try his regular call sign, Bravo Papa?"

"Brian, Brian. Bravo Papa. Do you copy?" I call into the hand-held radio.

My heart beats faster waiting for a response. Sam sits next to me, and several others begin to gather around the desk, staring into the tiny holes in the speaker.

No response.

"BOOM! KABOOM!" more explosions shake the walls and the little clock rattles against the wall.

"Bravo Papa, Brian, Brian. Do you copy?" I say with increased insistence.

"Maybe his radio is off," Sam offers. "You know how he likes to turn it off when he is busy."

An image of Brian walking out waving his radio flashes through my mind.

"It was on. I remember," I say.

"Will they take him to the hospital? Couldn't we just send one of the guards to check on him?" Sam suggests.

"They could have taken him anywhere," I speculate.

"I can't send a guard out alone in a vehicle. Besides, we need them here during the fighting," says Rita, pointing toward Khalid who has stationed himself dutifully just outside the door.

"It's also more dangerous for them if we're not with them. Last month Abukar, one of our guards, was driving without expats and was killed one mile from here when he stopped to check the tire. I guess the bandits think a lone Somali in a vehicle means he has just stolen it and it's open season or something," I add looking toward Khalid, thankful for the many Somali guards who constantly risk their lives for us.

Meanwhile, Brian rides through the dark streets of Baidoa as a hostage inside a war machine operated by violent gunmen charged up on a day's worth of khat, who are the targets of equally armed and drug-influenced rival factions. And we sit with nothing to do but wait.

I begin to wonder if we will see him again and imagine what his parents are like and how they will take the news of their son's violent death. Will they think we could have done more? Will they blame us for sitting idly by while he risked his life for ours?

Both hands on the clock point straight up. We have not heard anything for more than an hour. As the explosions outside continue our worry escalates.

"Brian, do you copy?" I yell into the radio again, trying to hold onto my remaining shreds of hope.

At this moment the living room is flooded with lights and the voices of the Somali gunmen ring loudly in the early morning hour. All of us rush to the window and see Khalid yelling at the gunmen now speeding away. With their lights gone I cannot see what is happening, but I hear the clanking sound of the metal gate opening and closing again. A figure is walking toward the front door.

"Mary, I fuckin' copy, okay!" Brian's voice comes through the speaker loud and clear.

His words echo in the doorway. His scrubs are almost all red with blood and his worn face releases the smile of a very relieved man.

"Thank God," I say and run to hug him.

Before I reach out for him I hesitate, but he reaches out his arms and pulls me to him. He forgets himself for the moment and everyone showers him with a hero's due of grateful touches of appreciation.

I look around the room at the assembly of quirky personalities and mingling of cultures. Abdulkadir's lanky arms wave in the air with exuberance. He pats Rita's plump shoulder and he and Khalid exchange energetic Somali phrases. Sam holds his palm in the air and Brian slaps it, and even allows a hug from Abdulkadir. In this moment we feel wonderful. Watching Brian and the seventeen-year-old Somali boy I am reminded of something Henry Wordsworth Longfellow once wrote: "There is a dark, invisible workmanship that reconciles discordant elements and makes them move in one society."

-21-

Afgooye

Baidoa, Somalia, 1993

Dawn crawls in my window, teasing my eyelids until they flutter, ending the final moments of sleep. It takes me a moment to remember today is Friday, my day off. Although I returned to work in the hospital two weeks ago, remnants of dengue fever stay with me. My stomach, back and legs are covered in a fading pink rash. I go to work every day still feeling weak and depressed from the draining effects of the illness. I cover my eyes with the Afghan keffiyeh and rest in its comfort for a few minutes before rising. Marc is back in Paris by now and I'm sure I will never see him again. However, the aching I feel about Marc lessens while I work with the poorest of Somalia's ravaged breadbasket.

After breakfast I hear Khalid speaking with someone outside our gates. The young Caucasian man in a cowboy hat jokes playfully in Somali. I walk into the scorching morning sun to investigate just as Khalid opens the gate for the visitor.

"Dan? Dan Eldon?"

Dan Eldon is young, maybe 20, amazing considering he's a freelance war journalist with a fearless passion for the Somali people. He stayed with us numerous times in Mogadishu. We all fell in love with his exuberance for life.

"Hey Mary, how the hell are you?" he inquires giving me a hug and lifting my body off the ground.

"What are you doing here?" I ask.

"I'm working on a story about Afgooye, a village just outside Baidoa and I'm heading over there today. Wanna come along?" he invites.

"Oh, God, I'd really like to but I've got to convince Rita first," I whisper.

Dan skips up the walk confidently.

"Leave it to me," he says.

Rita rummages through the piles of papers on the desk in the living room. When she sees us she quickly chews and swallows something she is eating as if she doesn't want to be caught.

"Rita, darling," Dan says squatting on one knee in front of her removing his worn straw cowboy hat.

He grabs her hand and kisses it softly and gazes into her eyes with his charming boyishness. I laugh under my breath admiring his workmanship.

"Hello Dan," Rita says skeptically but duly charmed.

"Rita, how are things at IMC? Heard you had a close one with an armed tank making a house call a few weeks ago."

"We made it through. What do you want, Dan?" Rita demands trying to keep control over the delightful young journalist.

Dan looks over at me and grabs my hand guiding me closer to the desk.

"I would like to take Mary to Afgooye for the day. I promise to have her home safe and sound well before curfew," he replies convincingly.

Rita looks unimpressed. She runs the house like a militant dictator forcing us to sneak out to the market in town to satisfy our constant hunger with some Somali samosas.

"Rita, Dan is very experienced in the bush and has good relationships with the local people. We'll take guards with us," I add.

She looks down at her papers as if she hopes we'll just go away. Dan glances at me with a questioning look, uncharacteristically out of words.

"You know, it would probably be good for IMC to gather information about the situation in the area villages, and we could stop by the Irish Concern feeding center as well," I say, illustrating what she could gain from agreeing to our request.

She sighs deeply and then says, "All right. But take a guard."

"Oh, Rita, you are a love," Dan kisses her hand before jumping to his feet.

"How about some sandwiches for the road?" Dan asks.

To Dan this might seem a small hill to climb but I knew he was about to be hit with a mountain of opposition.

"We can't spare food for everyone who walks in the door. This is your excursion—you figure out how to feed yourselves," she responds coldly.

"Let's go. You're about to push too far," I whisper to Dan leading him out the door.

Our Land Rover rolls slowly through town. The main dirt avenue looks like an old West ghost town. Whitewash covers the crumbling mud buildings, each inch marred by bullet holes. Only a few people walk along the deserted road. A Somali woman ambles through town carrying a load of fire wood. We pass several gaunt stick figures wrapped in rags squatting on the dry earth selling pieces of charcoal.

We pick up the scent of samosas at the edge of town coming from a lone wooden kiosk, leaning to one side and barely standing. The man inside hands us two meat turnovers each, for the equivalent of ten cents.

It takes over an hour to travel the many miles to the village along a washed out road marked with deep potholes. Just beyond a grouping of thatched-roofed huts our driver weaves around the carcass of a sun bleached car. It lies in the sand like the skeletal remains of some large African animal. Its belly rests directly on the dirt. Everything of any value was stripped long ago; its useless body is left to rot in the unrelenting desert sun.

Dan directs his driver to park beside a hut in the center of a grouping of about thirty similar dwellings. The huts are constructed with sticks woven together with mud and long thin grasses. The round roofs are topped with bent acacia branches, giving them an almost igloo shape. Villagers begin coming through the narrow alleyways between the huts to investigate. They all look like walking skeletons, with tattered remnants of once colorful wrap dresses and macaawises hanging precariously from their withering frames.

The driver stays with the car. Khalid and I follow Dan to the hut in front of us. A man bends his gaunt figure under the doorway of the hut and emerges with a broad toothless grin beaming in recognition of the young man in the cowboy hat. The two shake hands and Dan exchanges words with the stranger. He says my name and gestures toward me.

"Mary, this is Hamsa, the chief of the village," Dan says.

He includes Khalid in the introduction and the two speak to each other briefly in their native language. The chief does not wear any stately clothing or jewelry. His head is covered with a white koofiyad. He wears a simple plaid macaawis and his feet are protected from the ground with black rubber flip-flops. A woman brings four stools with rawhide seats. The chief sits and gestures for us to do the same.

"Khalid, I'll probably need you to do some translating. Do you mind?" Dan asks respectfully.

Khalid nods his head in agreement.

Villagers begin to edge up closer to us, they squat in the dirt and watch us curiously. The woman who brought the chairs comes through the door of the hut. She balances a white enameled tray with four thick glass cups. She graciously offers each of us a cup of Somali chai.

"Mahahtsanet," I say grateful for her generous gift. With occasional help from Khalid, Dan and the chief discuss the condition of the village. Adjacent to the chief's hut is a central area where people gather. Hundreds of flies hover around a drying cow carcass hanging from a wooden beam. The animal's body is carved in almost every possible place. Khalid tells me it hangs there for the whole village to come and take what they need. A woman squats at the animal's hind. She waits while a man shaves off a few bits of edible meat. Her dried, fallen breast lies across her protruding ribs and she carries a small child whose sunken eyes peer expressionlessly into mine.

We finish our tea and one of the chief's wives carries the empty cups back into the hut.

The chief stands, says something to Dan and gestures in the direction of the village.

"He is inviting us on a tour of the village. He wants us to see the conditions his people are living in," Dan says, removing his hat and wiping the sweat from his forehead.

When we stand our audience of villagers rise from their squatting positions. As many as one hundred have gathered, and all follow closely behind as we begin the tour.

"I suppose we're taking the village for a walk," Dan says caressing the young boy's head walking beside him.

Instinctively I begin to feel uneasy about crowds of desperate people. At Digfer this would mean a barrage of demands for whatever they think I might have that they want. But they do not ask. They only want to be near us as if we are celebrities. They follow quietly behind and we form a procession through the narrow path winding around the huts. Several need help walking, or hobble along with the aid of handmade canes.

I bend down to pick up an acacia twig covered with sharp thorns. Thoughts of the camel herder wander through my mind as my finger gently pokes at the end of one of the thorns.

A group of children following close behind mimic this action and begin to talk with each other through playful giggles. I smile at them and continue the game by squatting and standing again quickly. They do the same. Laughter provides a momentary escape from realities no child should have to endure.

A few tiny sprouts dot the banks of the drying riverbed. "Oxfam, one of the NGOs here, donated sorghum seeds to this village, but they have no way of irrigating. They cannot carry enough water from the river to keep the plants alive," Dan says, bending down to touch a dried sprout.

"Why would Oxfam donate seeds if there is no way to irrigate?" I ask.

"The village did have a means of irrigation but since the seeds were donated bandits filled most of the local wells with stones, dead bodies and garbage. I think farming villages like this one are especially vulnerable. When drought or fighting hits the nomadic people they can pick up and leave. But farmers are not mobile. If the crops show signs of failure, especially during drought, there are no seeds to replant because they get their seeds from the harvest. They would have to buy seeds and wait for the next rains if they have the means. Usually the farmers refuse to leave their farms until it's too late. Even then, where would they go?"

As our procession continues, we come to a place where thorny bushes hang over the narrow path. I squeeze carefully through them, avoiding the thorns that cover their branches. Without warning from the chief walking ahead, Dan and I almost stumble over the body of an adolescent lying on his back across this narrow space. Flies hover like vultures over his frail, emaciated frame and half-open eyes stare blankly into the sky. Tight, paled skin stretches over sunken cheeks. His lips are cracked and powdery white with signs of imminent death from lack of food and water.

Halting the procession, I stop and lean beside him to touch his face. It is cold as death. His eyes flutter slightly.

"Wait! Stop!" I call to the chief and the others ahead.

When they come back the chief says something in Somali to Dan and Khalid.

"Why is this boy lying here in the bush?" I ask, wondering why the chief is so casual.

The chief answers and moves on without waiting for the translation.

"What did he say?" I ask.

Dan leans down and gently touches the boy's face. He blinks hard over his watery eyes.

"The chief says to step over him."

My hand runs over the boy's knee, twice the circumference of his thigh, considering that mine may be the last human touch this child experiences. I feel his chest as it rises and falls with faint, erratic breaths. I whisper a good-bye and step over. The boy will probably be dead before the last villager passes over his body.

I catch up to Dan who seems lost in thought.

"That was horrible, Dan," I say with a quivering voice, blinking my tears away.

"Yeah. This is everyday for these people. The chief might even have known the boy was here and brought us purposely. It certainly gets the point across about the desperate hunger in his village."

The chief stops beside a charred structure that looks like it was once a windmill. He points to the structure and speaks in passionate tones, pauses and nods toward Khalid.

"He says bandits came last month and destroyed the windmill. They also took a cow the village had just slaughtered," Khalid explains.

We follow the path around the burned-out remains of the village's only power source, and find ourselves back among the huts. As we pass, we can see into one of the dwellings through its opening. A woman sits on a floor made of twigs lined up and tied together. She pours water out of a tightly woven basket onto the naked bodies of her two small children lying motionless on their backs. Their lifeless eyes are half open and a long strand of grass binds their toes together so their feet will not flop over the side. Dan and I stop in respect for the reverent Muslim ritual bathing. He takes off his hat and holds it against his chest.

The somber mother pours the water gently over her children's emaciated bodies. Tenderly she washes their ebony skin that glistens in the rays of the lowering sun. She sings a mournful song as she runs her fingers over still eyelids. Gently she slips her hands under her daughter's back and draws the limp body to her chest. Her eyes are dry. She is too dehydrated for tears.

The chief speaks quietly.

"He says these were her only children. They starved to death," Dan interprets.

With the tour complete the chief leads us back to our vehicle. He shakes our hands and we thank him for his hospitality. A few more words are exchanged before Dan gives him some biscuits and a few samosas he was saving for the return trip. The gift is a drop in an ocean of need, but the sensitive young journalist cannot bring himself to take it with him.

Our eyes stay on the village as our Land Rover drives away until there is only a cloud of dust.

"What did the chief say to you before we left?" I ask Dan.

"He asked what we would do for his people."

"What did you tell him?" I say wondering what we could possibly offer such a desperate situation.

"I told him I would tell the world about them and you would talk to people who know how to help."

The promise Dan made makes me anxious to learn more about what is being done about the desperation in this decimated breadbasket.

-22-

Twelve Meals a Day

Baidoa, Somalia, 1993

"There it is just ahead," Dan says.

The force of air through the open window forces him to hold his hand on top of his cowboy hat.

We approach a grouping of rectangular huts constructed with long dry grasses and sticks. A green plastic tarp runs along the outside like siding. The sign outside the feeding center reads, "Concern," an Irish based NGO. A deathly thin man is sitting beside a small mound covered by a plastic food sack labeled "Gift from the USA." Two tiny feet stick out from under the sack that has become a shroud.

Dan says something to the man in Somali. The man, full of sorrow, answers while stroking a tuft of the child's hair uncovered by the shroud.

When we leave the man I ask Dan what happened.

"He said his son died earlier today. The son was the last of his family to die."

Inside, a large open courtyard is an area lined with long strips of green plastic occupied by hundreds of starving children. The sight takes my breath away. They sit quietly, their tiny bodies drained of energy, while they eat or wait to be fed. A mother stumbles into the courtyard and sits on the green mat with a baby on each hip. The head and arms of one of the babies hangs away from her body, its lifeless eyes stare heavenward.

The other child's disproportionately large head lies against the mother's bony chest unflinching as dozens of flies surround his mouth and eyes. A thin, auburn-haired woman leads the mother to a small room adjacent the courtyard.

She returns shortly and greets us with her compassionate green eyes.

"Hello, I'm Sandy Brown. Can I help you with something?" she asks with a lilting Irish accent.

We shake her hand and introduce ourselves.

"Dan and I wanted to get a look at what you are doing here. He is a journalist and I am a nurse with IMC. I don't ever get to see this end of the relief work."

"Well, I'll give a brief look 'round and then answer your questions."

Along the large courtyard where family members assist in the care of their children, are several small rooms for the severe cases. In one of these rooms a Somali woman squats beside a young child. Bones protrude grotesquely from this tot who looks like a skeleton covered in thin brown skin. Other starving children sit listlessly on a thin green plastic tarp separating them from the dusty ground.

"This is Salma," Sandy says introducing a Somali feeding center aid.

Salma looks at us briefly to smile an acknowledgement and continues her care. She holds a plastic orange cup to the lips of one of the emaciated children and coaxes the little one to swallow. A few drops make it down the throat. Several trickles run down the skin that pulls tightly across the toddler's sunken cheeks.

Sandy leads us out of the room back into the courtyard.

"This center serves children under one hundred and ten centimeters, which is the average height of a five-year-old. These kids have a higher mortality rate from dehydration, disease and diarrhea. In the past two months we lost about two-thirds of our patients in this age group."

"Do all these people stay here overnight?" asks Dan, looking out over the sea of hunger.

"Only the most severe cases, like the child you saw with Salma," Sandy answers pointing back to the small room. "In the first week or so these children receive eight to twelve small feedings of high energy milk formula in a twenty-four hour period around the clock, so they have to stay. This is called phase one. When they are stronger and are past the critical stage they can be placed in a less intensive program and have about six meals a day of formula and porridge. They get less feedings but the calories are increased. This is called phase two."

"How long do the phases last?" I ask.

"Phase one lasts about seven days and during this phase we also provide intensive medical care as the child is often sick and too weak to swallow. The formula we use is only meant to gently introduce protein and calories back into their bodies. Too much too soon can cause cardiac failure. When they make it past a week and they have gained some weight, they begin phase two which usually lasts about two weeks. After this we still provide medical care and check for weight gain."

Sandy squats down to caress the bald head of a baby who appears to be about two. She continues talking as she looks into his eyes and examines his skin's elasticity.

"Finally during phase three normal solid foods are introduced and the child is watched for signs of problems. When the patient graduates to phase four he or she is sent home with a supplementary dry food, and the family is asked to return the little one weekly for checkups," Sandy adds.

We walk through rows of youngsters scooping high energy milk into their mouths from orange cups. A mother feeds her toddler who smiles at us through mouthfuls of wet porridge.

"Sandy, we just came from Afgooye where so many kids are dying. It's not far from here. Why are they not coming to this feeding center?" I ask.

"I don't know about that village; some may be coming, but we've had challenges with several of the village chiefs."

"What do you mean?" asks Dan.

"For example, one chief refused to send his village's children because he wants a feeding center just for his village. They have become fearful that there will not be enough food for all the kids, so they demand to have a center dedicated to feeding only their people."

The afternoon sun sends long shadows across the courtyard as the phase two patients receive their last daily feeding. Many women gather their offspring with full bellies and head for the hand pump to collect water for the night.

"We should go. Don't want to keep Rita waiting," Dan says.

"You're right," I agree.

After thanking Sandy we find Dan's Land Rover and start down the road to Baidoa. The Concern feeding center is closer to Baidoa than to our first stop, so the ride is considerably shorter. Dan hangs his arm out the window, trying to coax a breeze into the sweltering car. Emotionally and physically spent, we have no energy for conversation. We travel in silence lost in the intensity of the day.

It is dusk when our driver pulls through the gates of the IMC compound.

"Dan, why don't you spend the night at IMC? If you're quick you might even get a couple of bites of bicycle chicken for dinner," I suggest.

Rita waits at the door with a scowl.

"We're on time. What's wrong?" I ask.

Dan is gathering his belongings from the back of the car.

"No visitors. We're not a restaurant or a hotel," she says under her breath and stomps off into the house without acknowledging Dan.

"So what'd the queen of charm have to say?" he asks sarcastically.

I am mortified to have to turn him away after he's spent the day providing me with such an important experience.

"Dan, I am so sorry. The boss lady won't let you stay—over night or for dinner. I'm so sorry," I say.

"No worries, Mary. I always find my way," he says with a tip of his cowboy hat.

"Give me your hat and wait here," I demand.

I playfully throw the hat on my head and casually go into the house. I find Abdulkadir in the oppressively hot kitchen working on dinner. He agrees to look the other way when I steal a chicken leg from the refrigerator. I wrap it in a napkin, put it inside the cowboy hat and walk back outside.

"Here's your hat," I say holding it out to him and pointing at the napkin.

He mouths "thank you" and gives me a hug.

"Dan, thanks so much for today," I say.

I watch him walk out of the compound and wonder where he

will end up tonight. Probably on the floor of some other NGO house sharing his meager chicken leg with a new friend. He'll work on his story by flashlight late into the night keeping his promise to a desperate village chief.

Epilogue

Baidoa, Somalia, 1993

One month later I leave Baidoa and return to Mogadishu. After thirteen months of living in what many called "hell on Earth" I am twelve pounds thinner, *and* physically *and* mentally exhausted.

I've had enough anarchy, death and destruction for a lifetime. I'm finally geared up to go. In fact, I can't wait to get on the next departing plane out of Somalia. I'm one hundred percent ready to walk through the iron gates of the IMC fortress for the last time. And I'll be leaving the Iron Nurse behind, forever.

The world feels like a new place for me. I now look through vastly different eyes than when I first landed in Mogadishu and the hyper-sexed pilot delivered me into the hands of a nicotine addicted Brit surrounded by half-a-dozen heavily armed Somalis. I had walked in another person's sandals for thirteen months and now know the ethical dilemmas faced by those struggling for daily survival. I am ready to feel, love and appreciate life with renewed vigor.

The Iron Nurse's walls have crumbled and I'm not afraid to embrace every new day as a genuine gift to celebrate and enjoy. I am ready to live. My new philosophy: live like I could die tomorrow, but *now* with new found wisdom and compassion. I vow to live without regret and to respect all of humanity.

Nairobi, Kenya, April 1993

I'm alive! I MADE IT OUT ALIVE! I can hear the beautiful pink and black hoopoe bird of Kenya calling "hoop-hoop-hoop" in the garden outside. I can feel warm dry air wafting through my safari style hotel room with sweet scents of tropical blossoms, giving the aura of a luxury vacation. After Baidoa I returned to Mogadishu and gathered my belongings, said my good-byes and finished my contract with IMC. I'm now in the safe confines of Nairobi's famous Jacaranda Hotel, a comfortable refuge far away from the devastation of Somalia.

It's time to go, but *now* I don't want to leave Africa. I've fallen in love with the people, their unique way of living together and their rich culture. However, I know it's time to move forward. I also don't want to leave because IMC has become my surrogate family during the past thirteen months. I'm not sure how I will connect with the outside world with my new insights on humanity. I'm afraid my departure from Africa will seem like a divorce of sorts, leaving me feeling vulnerable and alone.

Many expats stay in Nairobi and find work with other organizations over and over again, but I will not let fear stand in my way. I will use adversity to move forward with compassion and bravery like my Somalis friends have taught me.

Salaam ah likum, peace, may you find it, may you cherish it, may you help promote it. Life is precious.

PEACE.

Where Are They Now?

I've lost track of some of the people I was with during my time in Somalia. However, some I remain in close contact, while others I've followed from afar. Here is what happened to several of my fellow colleagues:

DR. ABAAS

Dr. Abass still lives in Somalia. In 2001 I caught up with him in Baidoa, nearly ten years after our first meeting. His life has remained a continuous struggle to survive and to help his fellow Somalis. When we met the second time, he was still a dedicated physician and surgeon. He only charged $0.75 for every patient he tended, yet he told me that it cost him $1.50 to buy one chicken to feed his wife and two children. Abass kept his clinic open thanks largely to Brian's donations. I admire him a great deal and hope to someday have another chance to sit together and chat over a cup of chai.

AMINA

Amina remained behind at Digfer when I left Mogadishu. I do not know where she is now. It is possible that she was among the many unqualified Somali nurses who fled the country to attend nursing school in Nairobi, Kenya. I corresponded with some Somali refugees in Kenya. Amina was not among them.

AHMED

Ahmed was already married when he met Donna. He could have taken another wife, but it did not work out with Donna. I saw him several times over the years in two different countries since our work in Somalia. We ran into each other once on a dirt road in the Democratic Republic of Congo and many times in Nairobi, Kenya. Ahmed accepted a position with a major oil company, and moved his family to Pakistan. He travels extensively for work.

ANN

Ann married a handsome Australian and continues to be involved in humanitarian projects around the world. The last time I saw her in 2001 she and her husband were in northern Kenya volunteering with an NGO supplying South Sudanese projects.

ANDREW

Andrew is the Vice President of Program and Policy Planning for a non-governmental international humanitarian organization headquartered in the United States.

BRIAN

Brian disappeared for a number of years after leaving Somalia. One day in 2005 he called me out of the blue. He had finally attended medical school and became an Emergency Room physician. He donated a considerable amount of time and money to assist Dr. Abass's clinic in Baidoa, and was interested in finding another volunteer position abroad when we last spoke. I heard that he departed for a mission in Iraq shortly after our last phone conversation.

CARLOS

Carlos Mavroleon had not yet reached his 40th birthday when he was asked by "60 Minutes" to investigate the United State's bombing of Afghanistan in August 1998. One week after the American missile strikes on Afghanistan, Carlos was caught by Pakistani police as he tried to slip into terrorist training camps across the Afghan border. He was accused of being a spy but was released. Days later he was found dead in his hotel room in Peshawar, Pakistan. The authorities called it an overdose. Others, including myself, suspect foul play. Regardless of the circumstances surrounding his death, Carlos was a compassionate, dedicated journalist. He died doing what he loved, searching for truth to share with the world.

BOB (DAD)

Dad is still the benevolent he always was and is still always ready to help others. He continues to give away his few remaining worldly possessions to those who need more than he. Dad lived with me in Florida during the winters for several years. Now he lives with my sister helping her with the endless chores on her Ohio farm. Dad is still strong, healthy and one of my big heroes.

DAN ELDON

Dan lived and worked in Africa for years after I left Somalia. He dreamed of writing a book about the Somali people he so loved. One day in 1996 Dan, along with several other journalists arrived at the scene of a building bombed mistakenly by American troops. He was stoned to death along with most of his colleagues by an angry mob of Somalis. Since Dan was American they considered him and the other expats responsible for the loss of their loved ones. Dan's mother Kathy produced a beautiful documentary about his life entitled "Dying To Tell The Story."

DAVID

David continued his humanitarian work and remained in Africa for many years. He fell in love and married while in Kenya. He and his lovely wife decided a change of continents was in order and departed for the Americas. According to my last report, they were both doing NGO work in the jungles of South America.

DONNA

Donna is a composite of two different nurses. They both married men they met while on mission in Africa and have children. One I lost track of and the other lives with her husband and two children in France where she works as a hospital nurse.

LINDSEY

Lindsey married Mark to whom she was engaged during her time in Somalia. She now has two stepdaughters and six grandchildren. Although her husband has never traveled beyond the US borders, Lindsey continues to take adventurous trips to exotic locations around the world and has been known to venture far off the beaten path in her travels. She is currently nursing in a Los Angeles juvenile detention center and loves working with her "kids" in "juvie." We are still close friends and communicate regularly. Lindsey has never forgotten Leyla and in her memory has not eaten another apple since the day she passed away in 1992.

JOHN HOCKENBERRY

John is still wheelchair bound and continues to report the world news as a correspondent, journalist, commentator, and author.

MARC JOLIE

Marc returned to his lover, Florence, and resumed nursing in France after his mission in Somalia. We spoke on the phone once in 1993, while I was studying French in Paris. In June 2006, I received news that Marc was still alive and well. According to the report he now lives part-time with his new lover on their boat in Brittany when he isn't working in war zones with MSF.

MY MOTHER

My mother quit smoking, mellowed out a little and is currently remarried. Although her child-rearing methods were unusual, I must admit they contributed towards making me the person I am today and for that I'm thankful. Mom has a touch of emphysema and complains of old age, but she is otherwise healthy. We have become friends.

Glossary

Ahba: Somali word for "father."

Allah: Arabic word for "God."

Salaam ah likum: Arabic greeting meaning "peace."

Ah likum salaam: Peace, how one responds to the greeting of "salaam ah likum."

Base: A relatively safe, secure location where personnel working for organizations lived, slept, ate and managed their programs. This could also be known as "the compound," the "office" or "home." In safer areas the base and home were separated; in Somalia the base, office and home was all in one location.

Batik: Hand dyed fabric using wax. In Kenya these are often made into wall hangings.

Biyo: Somali word for "water."

Cali: Somali word for "come here."

Casualty: The British term used for Emergency Room.

Ça va: French for "how's it going?"

Celsius: Temperature is expressed in degrees as either Fahrenheit (F) or Celsius (C). An average temperature of 59° F is equal to 15°C. Freezing occurs at 0°C or 32°F.

Chai: Arabic word for "tea." In Somalia all tea was made with spices that sometimes included some or all of these ingredients: tea, sugar, cardamom, cloves, ginger, and cinnamon.

Clan: Group of related family members linked to a common ancestor.

CONCERN (also known as Irish Concern): An Irish non-governmental organization providing international relief.

Dirac: A dress worn by Somali women.

Expat: An abbreviated form of the word "expatriate." One who is a citizen of one country and then becomes a resident of another country. For example, I was an expat in Somalia during the time I lived there.

Gabsar: The cloth that is used to cover a woman's hair like a turban. (Also spelled garbasaar. Sometimes called a "massar.")

Gallo: Somali word meaning "stranger" or "infidel."

Gahleb Wahnoxin: Somali word for "good afternoon" and "good evening."

Ha: Somali word for "yes."

Haben wahnoxin: Somali word for "good night."

Hakuna matata: Swahili word meaning "no problems."

Hawker: A term meaning one who sells goods on the street.

Henna: A green powder derived from a natural plant which mixed with water can be used as a hair dye or to make temporary skin paintings. Arabic women often paint their hands, arms, feet ankles and legs, as well as other body parts, with this dye for special occasions.

Hijab: A piece of cotton cloth approximately two yards long which is worn over the head of a woman. One side hangs longer than the other, which is tossed over one shoulder. I used my "sarong" or "kitanga" as a hijab in Somalia.

Hilib: Somali for "meat."

ICRC: International Committee of the Red Cross, an international non-governmental humanitarian organization.

IMC: International Medical Corps, an American based non-governmental organization founded in 1984 to relieve pain and suffering around the world.

Inshallah: This word comes from Arabic meaning if "God is willing." It is often used in Muslim countries and is a good word to keep one from losing face if used in conjunction with a promise that might fall through.

Isbataalka: Somali for "hospital."

Je t'aime: French for "I love you," can also mean "I like you."

Keffiyeh: A plaid cloth fringed on two ends folded into a triangle and used by Somali men to cover their head. Can be placed loosely on top of the head, or one side can be twisted into a rope and wrapped around the head with the loose ends tucked up inside.

Khat: Also known as qat and mirrar. This substance comes from a plant grown in east Africa, which has a stimulant effect, similar to several cups of espresso, when chewed fresh. It was delivered daily in Somalia by private charter planes, even during times of heavy fighting. Side effects include nervousness, insomnia and impotence as well as irritability.

Kilogram: A unit of measuring weight equal to 1,000 grams; expressed as kg. One kilogram (1 kg) is equal to 2.2 pounds (2.2 lbs).

Kilometer (km): A metric unit of measure equal to 1,000 meters; 1.6 kilometer is equal to 1 mile. To convert km to miles just multiply the km distance x 0.625; For example, a 5 km race is 3 miles long (5 km x 0.625 = 3.12 miles).

Koofiyad: A cloth cap, the koofiyad can be embroidered, or designed with small holes in a pattern. Worn by some Somali men and elders. Also spelled "koofidaada."

Log/logistician: Someone who manages the procurement and storage of supplies, travel, local staffing and the general running of the compound or camp as well as a variety of other duties.

Macaawis: Tubular piece of cloth worn by Somali men, sometimes plaid or covered with exotic patterns. One could step into the tube, fold it twice over the abdomen, and then roll down to secure it in place. It covered men from the waist to the lower calf.

Ma chérie: French words meaning "my dear."

Mad Max: Also known as a technical. In Somalia, long barreled machine gun type anti-aircraft weapons were mounted into the back of Toyota pick-up trucks. Used by militias in battle, and almost every NGO could be seen with one in tow. They were used as part of their protection entourage.

Magacaa: Somali word pronounced Maa-gaa-ah, meaning, "What is your name?"

Mahahtsanet (also spelled Mahadsanid): Somali word pronounced Ma-haa-saa-nid, meaning "thank you." There is no Somali equivalent for "please."

Maya: Somali word for "no."

Mog: Shortened version of Mogadishu, the capital of Somalia.

MSF: Medecins Sans Frontieres also known as Doctors Without Borders in English speaking countries. MSF was originally a French based non-governmental organization founded in 1971 by several French doctors to provide advocacy and health care for victims of natural and unnatural disasters. Winner of the 1999 Nobel Peace prize, MSF is now present in more than eighty countries around the world.

Nahbaht or nabad: Somali for "hello."

NGO: Non-Governmental Organization usually providing humanitarian relief services. Examples of NGO's in this book include IMC, MSF, Oxfam, Concern, ICRC, CARE, PSF, AICF, Save The Children, and AAH.

Nin wayn: Somali for "old man."

OXFAM: Oxfam is a British non-governmental international relief organization, specializing in all forms of relief from agricultural to medical and veterinary.

P.A., Physicians Assistant: A P.A. is a professional qualified to diagnose and treat patients under the supervision of a physician.

Plus tard: French words meaning "later."

Safari: This word comes from Swahili meaning voyage, business meeting or trip, and does not necessarily mean that the excursion is for pleasure.

Samosa: A deep fried, delicious, triangular pastry filled with ground meat, and spices.

SCF, Save the Children Fund: A British, non-governmental international organization specializing in maternal/child health and feeding programs.

Somali language: In 1972 the Somali dictator, Said Barre, made Somali the official language of the country and introduced a Roman alphabet script. Prior to 1972 the official languages spoken in Somalia were Somali, Italian, Arabic and some English. Today Somali is pronounced and written phonetically. Therefore many words can have a variety of correct spellings. For example: Abass can also be spelled Cabass and Ahmed can also be spelled Axmed. The "C" is silent when placed before an "A" and the "X" can sound like "H."

Stoned: The action of throwing objects such as stones, rocks or other hard material at another person. Used as a form of punishment for an unacceptable social behavior. References to this activity can also be found in the Christian Bible. Being "stoned" might also indicate that one is under the influence of intoxicating substances.

Subah wahnoxin: Somali words meaning "good morning."

Taktar: Somali for "doctor."

Technical: In Somalia, Toyota, double and single cab, pickups were mounted with long barreled, heavy duty, anti-aircraft weapons, also known as a Mad Max's. These heavily armed trucks were used by militias in battle, and almost every NGO could be seen with one in tow. They were used as part of their protection entourage.

Theater: British term (spelled "theatre") for operating room.

Tribe: Group of related family members having similar cultural, traditional and social structures linked to a common ancestor and united under a single leader.

Tusker: African beer brewed and served throughout Eastern Africa in a large 16-ounce brown bottle with an elephant head on the label.

MARY LIGHTFINE

One day in 1992 Mary Lightfine, an ER nurse and self-professed adrenaline junkie, decided to pack up and move to Africa. This decision gave her a chance to feel what war, starvation and desperation was like from a completely different perspective. The experience changed her life forever. During the past twelve years she has lived and worked in more than a dozen countries, including some of the most hellish spots on Earth.

Mary is a seasoned veteran of International Medical Corps and the Nobel Prize winning organization Medecins Sans Frontieres /Doctors Without Borders. She is also founder and President of Volunteers Without Boundaries and Nurse Without Boundaries. Mary has been the subject of countless news articles, appeared on The History Channel, was written up in *LIFE* magazine, professional journals and books, and is a published author.

Today she has become a pilot and lives in Daytona Beach, Florida with her husband, Paul Rooy, and their two dogs. Mary travels extensively performing international charity work and sharing her experiences with organizations and colleges throughout the United States. Mary believes that one person can make a difference in one's own life and in the world around us. To learn more about Mary Lightfine visit her web site www.marylightfine.com

NOMINATED
FOR
COLLEGE LECTURER OF THE YEAR
By APCA & *Campus Activities Magazine*

Mary Lightfine, RN
Is available for
Speaking Engagements
Conferences
And
Professional Organizations

To book a lecture
Visit Mary's website
www.marylightfine.com

To order more copies of this book visit
www.nursesnomadsandwarlords.com